Asbury Theological Seminary Series in World Christian Revitalization Studies

It is a rare privilege for this project to break from the normal pattern of presenting specialized studies in aspects of Christian revitalization movements. But we do so on this occasion, and that is because of the nature of this title. In Professor Callen we have a seasoned scholar of the Wesleyan/Holiness tradition who draws from his commitment and knowledge of that legacy to frame a fresh account of the meaning and significance of the Christian tradition for our times. His "frank conversations" among great Christian thinkers brings to the table a diverse group of scholars from a range of theological options, disciplines, and genders to probe the deeper questions of the Christian tradition. Intended for both the seasoned scholar and beginning theological student, Callen writes with a sense of imagination that is a marvelous way of doing theology seriously. As he allows this diversity of voices to speak, he also sheds new light on the meaning of Christian revitalization for the early twenty-first century, framed as the "Heart of the Matter."

This volume is published in collaboration with the Center for the Study of World Christian Revitalization Movements, a cooperative initiative of the Asbury Theological Seminary faculty. Building on the work of the previous Wesleyan/Holiness Studies Center at the Seminary, the Center provides a focus for research in the Wesleyan/Holiness and other related Christian renewal movements, including Pietism and Pentecostal movements, which have had a world impact. The research seeks to develop analytical models of these movements, including their biblical and theological assessment. Using an interdisciplinary approach, the Center bridges relevant discourses in several areas in order to gain insights for effective Christian mission globally. It recognizes the need for conducting research that combines insights from the history of evangelical renewal and revival movements with anthropological and religious studies literature on revitalization movements.

It also networks with similar or related research and study centers around the world, in addition to sponsoring its own research projects. It is our privilege to locate Professor Callen's study within the Pietist and Wesleyan Studies sub-series of this publication project.

    J. Steven O'Malley
    Director, Center for the Study of World
        Christian Revitalization Movements
    General Editor, The Asbury Theological Seminary Series
        in Christian Revitalization Studies

Heart of the Matter

*Frank Conversations among
Great Christian Thinkers on the
Major Subjects of Christian Theology*

Barry L. Callen

*Asbury Theological Seminary Series:
The Study of World Christian Revitalization Movements in
Pietist/Wesleyan Studies*

EMETH PRESS
www.emethpress.com

Heart of the Matter: Frank Conversations among Great Christian Thinkers on the Major Subjects of Christian Theology, Revised

Copyright © 2016 Barry L. Callen
Printed in the United States of America on acid-free paper

All rights reserved. No part of this book may be reproduced, or stored in a retrieval system or transmitted in any form or by any means, electronic, mechanical, photocopying, recording, scanning or otherwise, except as permitted by the 1976 United States Copyright Act, or with the prior written permission of Emeth Press. Requests for permission should be addressed to: Emeth Press, P. O. Box 23961, Lexington, KY 40523-3961. http://www.emethpress.com.

Library of Congress Cataloging-in-Publication Data

Names: Callen, Barry L., author.
Title: Heart of the matter : frank conversations among great Christian thinkers on the major subjects of Christian theology / Barry L. Callen.
Description: Revised Edition. | Lexington : Emeth Press, 2016. | Series: Asbury Theological Seminary Series: the study of world Christian revitalization movements in Pietist/Wesleyan studies ; No. 6 | Includes bibliographical references.
Identifiers: LCCN 2016027616 | ISBN 9781609471040 (alk. paper)
Subjects: LCSH: Theology, Doctrinal--Popular works. | Imaginary conversations.
Classification: LCC BT77 .C215 2016 | DDC 230.092/2--dc23
LC record available at https://lccn.loc.gov/2016027616Library of Congress

Contents

Log of Conversation Voices Heard / vi
Preface / vii
Preface to the Revised Edition / xv

Conversation #1. Different Paths to Life in Christ
    Guest: Rosemary Radford Ruether / 1
Conversation #2. Exactly Who Is God?
    Guest: John B. Cobb, Jr / 23
Conversation #3. Depths of the Spiritual Life
    Guests: Lama Surya Das and Donald G. Bloesch /47
Conversation #4. Approaching Christian Theology
    Guests: Clark M. Williamson and Henri Nouwen / 69
Conversation #5. Faith's Solid Center
    Guest: Jürgen Moltmann / 87
Conversation #6. Having True Compassion
    Guest: Georgia Harkness / 105
Conversation #7. What About the Church?
    Guests: Harry Emerson Fosdick
        and Geoffrey Wainwright / 121
Conversation #8. Is It God *And* Country?
    Guests: Dietrich Bonhoeffer and James H. Cone / 139
Conversation #9. The Many Religions of the World
    Guest: John Hick / 157
Conversation #10. Are These the Last Days?
    Guests: Hal Lindsey and Stanley G. Grenz / 173
Conversation #11. Tramps for the Truth
    Guests: Malcolm Muggeridge and Roger E. Olson / 193

Bibliography of All Works Cited / 209

LOG OF CONVERSATION VOICES HEARD

Individuals are identified more fully in the chapters where appropriate for each. Many other persons are involved in the conversations but do not speak (see Works Cited).

Text IDs	Full Names	Conversations Speaking
Barry—	Barry L. Callen	All
Clark—	Clark H. Pinnock	All
Dietrich—	Dietrich Bonhoeffer	8
Don—	Donald G. Bloesch	3
Elton—	David Elton Trueblood	All
Geoffrey—	Geoffrey Wainwright	7
Georgia—	Georgia Harkness	6
Hal—	James H. Cone	8
Hal—	Hal Lindsey	10
Harry—	Harry Emerson Fosdick	7
Jack—	C. S. Lewis	All
Jeff—	Jeffery Miller, Lama Surya Das	3
John—	John B. Cobb	2
John—	John Hick	9
James—	James Earl Massey	All
Jürgen—	Jürgen Moltmann	5
Henri—	Henri Nouwen	4
Louis—	Thomas Merton	All
Malcolm—	Malcolm Muggeridge	11
Roger—	Roger E. Olson	11
Rosemary—	Rosemary Radford Reuther	1
Stan—	Stanley J. Grenz	10
Tom—	Thomas C. Oden	All
Will—	Clark M. Williamson	4

Preface

I hope to accomplish for new students of Christian theology what Steve Allen once tried to do for television viewers. In the 1970s there first aired his successful PBS-TV series called "Meeting of the Minds." It originated with the following perception of Allen: "I see the literary and philosophical tradition of our culture not so much as a storehouse of facts and ideas but rather as a hopefully endless Great Debate at which one may be not only a privileged listener but even a modest participant" (2).

Theology without Boredom

In these pages I want to do what Allen wanted. He tried to find "a method of imparting education without inducing boredom" (3). That's my goal exactly—*theological education through thoughtful conversation, and without boredom!*

Soon, the American public was watching the first episode of "Meeting of the Minds." It featured skilled actors engaged in a lively debate/discussion. They were playing President Theodore Roosevelt, Queen Cleopatra, Father Thomas Aquinas, and Thomas Paine, moderated by Steve Allen. The actors were in period costume and in one room at the same time, poised for vigorous conversation among themselves. It and the many episodes and "guests" to follow constituted colorful and lively occasions, unusually entertaining and very informing. It was something of a time-machine journey into wisdom.

As adapted here, prominent theologians will be our guests. They will skip the period costumes but won't avoid frankness and humor, and surely will serve up a wide range of Christian thought and mature wisdom as they seek *the heart of the matter*. Rather than different characters each episode, we'll keep the same ones and get really acquainted over time.

Middle, Not the Margins

Just as the church is a crucial necessity for an adequate living out of the Christian faith, so the "doing" of Christian theology is a corporate enterprise. Theology should be an ongoing conversation among believers about the roots, privileges, and responsibilities of being in Jesus Christ. Rather than featuring experiments, sidebars, incidentals, and personal eccentricities, it should be looking for the enduring and universal *heart of the matter*.

As put by one of the regular conversation partners in this book, "My intent is not to present the views of a particular branch of modern Christian teaching... but to listen single-mindedly for the voice of that deeper consensus that has been gratefully celebrated as received teaching by believers of vastly different cultural settings, whether African or Asian, Eastern or Western, sixth or sixteenth century" (Oden, 2009, Preface).

Twenty-Four of the Best

Here's an assumed presupposition for the doing of good Christian theology. Understanding and then living the truth in Christ lies less in isolation and more in the midst of serious sharing among thoughtful believers. This is especially true when those who share are well-informed people of wide experience who both speak with conviction, listen with care, and live with faith and courage.

These pages, filled with twenty-four such people, are a fertile learning place. They comprise another "meeting of the minds" arena, this time theological minds of the first order, women and men with different church affiliations, national origins, and theological emphases. These mature believers are shown in the act of faith sharing, honest listening, inspired truth telling, and intellectual and spiritual growing.

The subjects under consideration in the eleven sometimes intense exchanges include all the central aspects of the Christian faith. The conversations are frank and informed, sometimes disturbing, often inspiring, and always educational. Here's the good news. Prominent as the conversation partners are, you, even if you are a theological beginner, are invited to sit in on the whole thing. The doors are unlocked. The welcome sign is out.

Christian faith, ancient in its roots, is very much alive in today's world. Many of Christianity's deeply committed followers have freshly probed its beliefs and sought to explain and live out its implications in contemporary contexts. Seven of these believers participate in all eleven of the conversations recorded here. Each is widely published, with six having written personal autobiographies that document their individual journeys of faith and life. One of these autobiographies is by yours truly. I also authored a major biography of the seventh, and I function in these conversations, like Steve Allen earlier, as the convener and process facilitator.

What follows is articulate wisdom drawn from the lives and libraries of seven prominent Christians and the seventeen guests who join them—one or two per conversation. They combine to provide broad perspective on the entire field of Christian theology, ethics, biblical interpretation, and social policy, especially in the last century.

Four members of the core conversation group (C. S. Lewis, Thomas Merton, Clark H. Pinnock, and David Elton Trueblood) have now ended their earthly journeys, ceased their writing, and gone on to a better place. On their behalf and that of the others, I (Barry Callen) now have drawn them all into conversation with each other for the benefit of younger theologians. Both the living and the dead speak freely.

The seven of us who are always present in these conversations are in broad agreement regarding the heart of it all, and yet we are very different in some of our emphases, and certainly in the branches of the Christian faith tradition from which we come. We prove to be better together than any one of us is individually. That's the beauty and richness of the Christian community.

The seventeen conversation guests will be identified as each joins a particular conversation. Let me now introduce very briefly each of the seven "regulars." You will learn much more about them in conversation #1, and about their thinking as you hear them speak on various subjects in all the conversations to come.

C. S. Lewis was a Christian intellectual from Great Britain whose spiritual journey and numerous writings have had an impact rarely paralleled in any generation. **James Earl Massey** is the outstanding preacher, pastor-scholar, and only African-American theological educator in our group. For decades, when he has spoken on the radio or from the pulpit or lecture stand, people have realized that it is worth listening closely.

Clark H. Pinnock was a Canadian Baptist, prominent "evangelical," the fountainhead of the current "open theology" movement. He brought fresh air—some have thought a disturbing draft—into the conservative Christian community. Father Louis (**Thomas Merton**) was a Roman Catholic, a Trappist monk, the social conscience and spiritual mentor of so many, and one of the more widely read and loved Christians of all time.

D. Elton Trueblood was a thought leader among the Society of Friends, a Quaker philosopher/theologian and master teacher who was a specialist in combining the inward spiritual journey with serious intellectual pursuit. **Thomas C. Oden** is a United Methodist theologian who veered away from orthodox Christian faith and then came back in the 1970s to become a champion of "classical" Christianity. He has uncovered the substantial African roots of the shapers of earliest Christian thought.

I (**Barry L. Callen**) have focused on the history and thought of the "Radical" or Believers Church and Wesleyan/Holiness streams of Christianity, functioning as a dean in theological education and Editor of the *Wesleyan Theological Journal*, Anderson University Press, and Aldersgate Press. I have combined my academic pursuits with deep involvement in a ministry to AIDS orphans in several African nations through Horizon International.

The Range of the Regulars

We seven theologians who are the regulars are quite different from each other, and we've really been around. Typical of much of the theological history of Christianity, we all are men. I am apologetic for that exclusiveness and have sought to address this problem by including women among our conversation guests—in fact, we begin with a woman as our very first guest. Despite the limitations of geography and gender, the seven of us bring to today's conversational table much of the breadth and richness of Christian faith and its significant implications for life as it ought to be lived in this modern world.

Of course, C. S. (Jack), Clark, Elton, James, Louis, Tom, and I were never in the same room at the same time—not until the staging of these conversations. I assume they will forgive me for being so casual with their names. We want the young theologians joining us as welcomed listeners to be relaxed and not overwhelmed with titles and specialized words that make listening difficult.

We seven all are or were Christian searchers, teachers, and writers across our lifetimes. We have served in different institutions and represented different Christian traditions, although all of us were (are) deeply committed to the same faith. I view myself as the junior member of our group; the others are my honored seniors; we are friends and colleagues who will be relaxed and use our first names in these conversations (remember that "Jack" is C. S. Lewis). We are anxious to share with each other and our special guests—and with all others who choose to listen in.

Elton was my teacher in the 1960s at Earlham School of Religion in Richmond, Indiana. He inspired me to think deeply and write daringly, providing a gracious forward for one of my books (*Caught Between Truths*) and introducing me to the work of Jack (Lewis) that had been so important to him. A colleague of mine at Anderson University does dramatic monologues of Jack, keeping the range and power of his thinking before contemporary audiences, and my appreciative attention.

In the 1940s, Louis became a monk at the Trappist monastery of Gethsemani in central Kentucky, a place to which I have been drawn dozens of times over the decades for private spiritual growth. He and I never met, but I feel like I know him well. Clark was a treasured colleague and mentor of mine. We endorsed each other's books and we authored one together (*The Scripture Principle*, 2009). I was privileged to author his intellectual biography (*Journey Toward Renewal*, 2000).

James is a close personal friend and spiritual guide of mine. We have shared a deanship in seminary education—and much more. Tom wrote great books of systematic theology that I used for years in my seminary teaching. We share in the Wesleyan tradition, in African ministry, in advocacy of women's equality and rights in church life, and more.

Six of us have written about our individual journeys of life and faith that crisscross in multiple ways and cover virtually all of the theological landscape. Elton's is *While It Is Day* (1974); James' is *Aspects of My Pilgrimage* (2002); Louis' is *The Seven Storey Mountain* (1948); Jack's is *Surprised by Joy* (1955); Tom's is *A Change of Heart* (2014); mine is *A Pilgrim's Progress* (2008, rev. 2013).

The details, locations, and times of our ministries and scholarship differ widely. When it comes to the heart of the matter, however, there is not that much variance among us. We compliment each other generally, and critique each other on occasion, making available to you, the reader/listener, both a wide range of theological variation and a singular center of the faith. That would be Jesus, no less than God with us for our salvation.

Louis once said that he couldn't help but write. Clark had the same "disability," teaching, lecturing, and publishing all his adult life. Elton was an intellectual and literary giant rarely paralleled, except maybe by Jack who may never be paralleled. James has produced both volumes and sermons read and heard worldwide. My own published pages reflect the same preoccupation—thinking carefully, writing extensively, always hoping in increasingly wise ways to share the good news of God in Jesus Christ for today's world.

Person, Not Proposition

The seven of us regulars don't claim to have the last word on much of anything (see the last conversation especially). Part of our wisdom is that we have learned our limits. But we do have many words to share, words based on considerable life experience, spiritual journeying, and academic study, and at least we have one common conviction. Exactly what that is should become clear as our conversations proceed.

Here's a hint. The *heart of the matter* about which we will agree turns out to be more a *person* than a particular theological *proposition*. We invite you to join us as we find and converse about that center and suggest what it means for believing and living faithfully in these days. What you will not find here is any championing of new ideas that set aside the core teaching of the Bible or earliest exponents of the Christian faith. Actually, one or two of our guests might do that, but never the group of regulars.

We regulars have heard and explored—sometimes even tried out—most of the newest theological ideas over the decades, and certainly we will mention many of them along the way. Nonetheless, we all have tended to follow this direction of our regular Tom Oden: "My aim has not been to survey the bewildering varieties of *dissent*, but to identify and plausibly set forth the cohesive central tradition of general *consent* to apostolic teaching" (1992, vii).

Study Aids

Our group conversations, of course, are created artificially, although they are anything but fabricated. Many comments made are documented carefully in the text for the research convenience of the reader/listener. If at some rare point I have put into someone's mouth what they might not have chosen on their own, they will forgive me, I know. Every effort was made to avoid such unfairness.

A comprehensive bibliography of all works referenced in the conversations appears at the end of the book. Such an extensive list of prominent publications makes clear that this book is hardly a set of off-the-top-of-our-heads little chats! You can limit yourself to the conversations themselves or go to the sources for more depth.

In addition, questions are posed at the end of each conversation. Why? It's because we learn best in community, especially in a community comprised of people open to honest listening and sharing. With this book in hand, we encourage you to join a class in an academic setting or gather a group of people who want to grow theologically and spiritually. It's hoped that these twenty-four "specialist" voices will spawn and resource other conversations that include *you*.

All seven of us regular conversation partners have been committed to serious dialogue across our lives. This fact enriches what happens in these pages. We always have been reaching out, listening to others different from ourselves, willing to keep learning and growing. Why did we ask a special guest or two to join each of our conversations? It's because we seek greater wisdom in the broader dialogue. These guests bring to the table stimulating perspectives not necessarily shared by the seven of us—and thus they keep our conversations freshly spiced, alive, current, even controversial. So be it. We are always open to being corrected and learning.

Each of our seventeen guests is introduced at the beginning of the conversation that he or she joins. The first conversation allows you to meet more extensively the seven of us Christian leaders who are present and active in all conversations. We speak of our earliest life contexts and individual journeys to significant Christian faith. Maybe biographical introductions to Christian theology is the best approach for beginning students in the field. Actual lives carry a sense of realism that long narratives about theology rarely do. Our individual perspectives are not separable from the life paths we have walked.

Good, Not Last Words

Here are five reasons for choosing these particular conversation partners. First, each was or still is a pivotal thought leader in some sector of the Christian community. Second, each has produced a significant body of literature from which to draw elements of thought pertinent to these conversations. Third, we vary in our church affiliations, countries of origin, racial backgrounds, and particular specializations.

Fourth, each was or still is committed to the importance of serious dialogue as a way of clarifying and furthering the Christian cause. Fifth, apart from our many differences, we all sincerely believe that *God is Jesus Christ* is the heart of the matter, the bottom line of Christian believing and living.

The reader/listener will encounter here a wide range of mature thoughts offered for the sake of the health of the church of today and tomorrow. Before you begin reading/listening, however, be aware of this. What Steve Allen said of the guests who comprised his television experiment of the 1970s also applies here. No one should falsely assume that "the scant bits and pieces of information about the personages from history here introduced represent even an adequate scratching of their mountainous surfaces" (10).

That said, the twenty-four prominent Christian thinkers who are heard in these conversations/pages will say enough to launch you in provocative and transforming theological directions. If a beginning is not the total end, at least you will find here a very significant beginning!

Keep in mind that it's "the heart of the matter" that's ultimately important, not the passing spokespersons or their individual sidebars on this or that incidental subject. Our thoughts are fragmentary and our bodies mortal. As these pages were being written, for instance, death came to Clark Pinnock and Donald Bloesch, one of our regular conservation partners and one of our guests featured in conversation #3. They would both say the same thing to you. The witnesses come and go; it's the truth alone that remains!

Preface to the 2016 Revised Edition

Why a revised edition of this book after only five years? Certainly it's not because there's been any change in our view of the heart of the matter. The person of Jesus still takes precedence over all propositions about him and related to him, even the most "orthodox" ones. Nor have we lost focus on the young theologians who may be listening in on these eleven conversations—the technical language is still kept to a minimum, although not the significance of the topics addressed.

What we have done in these five years is listen to those who have greatly enjoyed the book but had a suggestion or two about how it might be strengthened. We also have taken advantage of some new resources that have appeared. including John Cobb's *Jesus' Abba*, Thomas Oden's *A Change of Heart*, Barry Callen's *Approaching Theology*, and other fresh publications by or about our conversation participants.

The flow of the dialogue has been smoothed throughout. More importantly, the breadth of theological representation in the dialogue has been enhanced. For instance, the perspectives of women have been given more attention, as have references to voices from Asia and Africa.

Particularly significant are the theologians who have been added to the group of conversation partners heard in the book. Thomas Oden newly appears as a regular in all conversations. James Cone is a new guest in conversation #8 and Roger Olson joins conversation #11. This gives fresh African-American and Evangelical perspectives, as well as a new emphasis on the consensual tradition of classic Christianity, including its significant African roots.

Although Thomas Merton is a regular and Henri Nouwen is a guest in conversation #4, the input from Roman Catholicism is now enforced by fresh perspectives from Pope Francis. In addition, the concluding sections of *Questions* has been enhanced for all conversations. We also have added a one-page *Log* of speakers heard and the conversations in which they speak. This is a ready reference for someone particularly interested in a given individual. For follow-up study, the *Works Cited* section has grown in length by nearly one-third.

Two overall beliefs have remained. First, the Christian faith, ancient in its roots, remains very much alive in today's world. Second, it's especially helpful to be introduced to the field of Christian theology by meeting and listening in on serious conversations among major thinkers with wide and differing experiences in the journey of faith that seeks to follow the Lord Jesus. Witnesses come and go; it's the truth alone that remains!

Conversation #1

DIFFERENT PATHS TO LIFE IN CHRIST

Biographical Backgrounds, Conversions, and Early Varieties of Christian Identity

In *The Voyage of the Dawn Treader*, C. S. Lewis pictures Eustace as a wayward boy now having the skin and heart of a dragon. Then comes Aslan, the great Lion and Lamb, the Son of the Emperor-beyond-the-Sea, the Christ figure of Narnia. The eventual un-dragoning of Eustace suggests the re-birthing possibility for us all, including for Lewis himself. Once reborn in Christ, we are truly different, even if still babes in the faith. We each come to the crisis of faith from different contexts, but the heart of the matter is the same. We all have sinned, put on dragon skin, and stand in need of divine grace that is universally available for the needed change.

People are said to see in distinctive ways. Their realities are influenced greatly by the contexts in which they live, by the stories that form the stories of their own lives (Callen, 2008-2013, 17). It may be that no theology is well understood apart from understanding the life story and times of the theologian who framed it.

Barry: Great to see the six of you who will be regulars with me in this series of conversations. You are all valued colleagues and treasured theological leaders in the modern Christian community. Being your convener is a personal privilege. Our goal is to hear each other well and all be the better for it. And we should always be aware that some young theologians will be listening in. We hope they also will be the better for hearing our coming conversations.

Our topic for this first of our planned eleven conversations is our early and individual Christian contexts and identities. We will ask of

Rosemary Radford Ruether (1936-) is a scholar, "ecofeminist," pioneer in Christian feminism. Her Texas childhood was ecumenical, humanistic, and free-thinking, influenced particularly by her Roman Catholic mother in a setting hardly to be characterized as "ghettoized" Catholicism. Her primary role models were sophisticated and self-confident women as she graduated with a B.A. in philosophy from Scripps College (1954-1958). Rosemary married Herman Ruether, a political scientist with whom she would have three children. She went on to earn an M.A. in Ancient History and a Ph.D. in Classics and Patristics from Claremont Graduate School in California (1965). For the first ten years of her career, she taught at Howard University School of Religion and was exposed there to the emerging literature of black liberation theology. Her subsequent and very distinguished academic career includes a long professorship at Garrett Evangelical Theological Seminary where was the Georgia Harkness Professor of Applied Theology. Her 1983 book *Sexism and God-Talk* has become a classic in the field of feminist theology, and her work in liberation theology has had particular relatedness to the Middle East and Latin America.

each other, "What have been our various paths to coming alive in Jesus Christ?" To use that excellent image you created, Jack, how has each of us "dragons" come to Aslan and begun the process of shedding our scales of sin in favor of new life in God? What are the differences and commonalities among us?

Jack: Don't be shy, Barry, about also noting your own thoughts that head this chapter. Maybe we will never really understand our several theologies apart from reviewing our several life journeys. I think that's what this first conversation is all about.

Barry: Right, Jack, and thanks. I really believe what I've said and that's why we are starting with ourselves. We'll first talk about who we are as we have found ourselves in God's world and, by God's grace, have found our way to meaningful relationships with the Divine. What have been our individual paths to spiritual renewal and theological identity?

How different and alike are these paths of ours? What is—and should be—the constants in the variety of our conversion experiences? In our different life contexts, what appears to be the heart of this matter of spiritual conversion?

Before the seven of us get started with our individual "testimonies," however, let me introduce our special guest for this day, Rosemary Radford Ruether. She will have her own significant conversion story to tell, the only woman among us so far. Note the brief vita of Rosemary on our screen over the fireplace.

Rosemary, we are delighted to have you with us as we each share something of our "conversion" stories and look together for the heart of this re-birthing matter.

Rosemary: It's my pleasure. A crowd of men is hardly intimidating. I'm used to it and you're a far better male group than many I've been in. Start us off, Barry, by saying something about yourself.

Barry: OK, gladly, but only quickly to start. I originally came to faith in Christ under the pastoral leadership of a strong and inspiring Christian woman, Rev. Lillie S. McCutcheon, in Newton Falls, Ohio. So, Rosemary, I'm most comfortable having your female wisdom in the room as we begin this set of significant conversations.

And we need to begin by asking for your patience, Rosemary. Since this is our first conversation, and the seven of us who will be regulars have never been together like this before, we are going to glance at a brief professional resume of each of us up on the screen. Then we'll get right to our serious conversation of today.

Yes, we regulars are all men—typical among theologians for most of Christian church history. At least we've seen fit to have you introduced first, Rosemary, and have you as our initial conversation partner. We are well aware that a woman's perspective is crucial and often missing in theological conversations.

Rosemary: Understood. I'll be patient while you men do your thing. Most women have had to be patient for centuries! And thanks for a little priority aimed—appropriately--my way. I know all of you at least by your writings and reputations, but hearing some detail will be helpful to me, and likely to some of our listeners who might not know any of you close up.

Barry: Thanks for that perspective. Here we go with the formal—but short—introductions of us seven regulars. Let's spend about a minute reading each of the seven slides that will start appearing on the screen just above the fireplace. First comes our respected friend whom we will be calling Jack, often known that way among his close friends back in England.

1. C. S. Lewis (1898-1963)—British Christian intellectual, novelist, apologist, and literary giant. He held academic positions at Oxford University (1925-54) and Cambridge University (1954-63). The second half of his life constitutes one of the more remarkable writing careers of the twentieth century.

Actually, Jack is arguably one of the more highly acclaimed and popular Christian writers of all time. His more than forty books include acknowledged classics in the diverse fields of Christian apologetics and meditation, science fiction, children's literature, and literary scholarship. Initially an articulate atheist, he came to Christ in 1931, affiliated with the Church of England, and quickly emerged as a brilliant translator and apologist for Christian doctrine in a skeptical age. His autobiographical work *Surprised by Joy* was released in 1955.

The popularity of the films *Shadowlands* and *The Chronicles of Narnia* attest eloquently to his influence with the public to the present time. Also extremely popular have been his books *Mere Christianity*, *Miracles*, and *The Problem of Pain*. J. I. Packer once wondered why Lewis, a non-evangelical Oxford don, has become a patron saint of evangelicals, calling him "the Aquinas, the Augustine, and the Aesop of contemporary evangelicalism." Packer's answer involves what he sees as "the combination within him [Lewis] of insight with vitality, wisdom with wit, and imaginative power with analytical precision" (1998, 60).

2. James Earl Massey (1930-)—prince of preachers, urban pastor, author/editor, and theological educator. Dr. Massey, a native of Detroit, Michigan, is Dean and Professor of Biblical Studies Emeritus of Anderson University School of Theology. For five years he served as Dean of the Chapel and University Professor of Religion and Society at

Tuskegee University. Earlier he had served for twenty-two years as senior pastor of the Metropolitan Church of God in Detroit and for five years as speaker on the "Christian Brotherhood Hour," the international radio broadcast of the Church of God (Anderson).

While preaching and lecturing on more than one hundred college, university, and seminary campuses and sitting on several editorial and seminary trustee boards, James managed to author several books, including *The Responsible Pulpit* and *The Burdensome Joy of Preaching*. In 2002 he wrote his autobiography, *Aspects of My Pilgrimage*, with Barry Callen as consultant/editor. On the back cover, Timothy George writes: "When James Earl Massey's career path turned from music to the ministry, the world lost a great performer but gained a magnificent preacher of the Gospel. Here, in his own words, is the story of his remarkable life as a pastor, scholar, teacher, evangelist, denominational statesman, and respected leader in the world Christian movement."

A friend of Martin Luther King, Jr., and himself an advocate for reconciliation, James was honored by the Wesleyan Theological Society in 1995 with its Lifetime Achievement Award for exceptional contributions to the Wesleyan/Holiness tradition of Christianity. From that particular tradition, he came to belong to the whole church.

3. Thomas Merton (Father Louis) (1915-1968)--Trappist monk, social visionary, and spiritual guide to countless modern people. In his more than fifty books and numerous poems, Merton explored contemplative prayer, nuclear war, the Black revolution in America, the existentialist quest for meaning in the face of absurdity, and the Christian dialogue with the religious traditions of the Far East.

This latter interest finally drew him from his monastery home in Kentucky to a conference in Thailand, where he died in an accident in 1968. Louis' classic 1948 autobiography, *The Seven Storey Mountain*, has exerted a profound influence on millions of readers. We will call our brother Louis instead of Tom to avoid confusion with Tom Oden, another of our regulars.

Despite his many professional activities that impacted the public, including essayist, social critic, ecumenical explorer, poet, photographer, artist, and correspondent, Louis was primarily a faithful monk. "He spent far more time at Mass, in prayer, and in meditation than in writing books and letters or doing anything else likely to bring him to public attention.... The ordinary substance of life is what is inevitably most neglected in biography; the stress is put on events rather than 'non-events.' But Merton was mainly interested in the latter" (Forest, xii).

4. Clark H. Pinnock (1937-2010)—theological educator, prolific author and lecturer, and leader of the "open theology" movement in contemporary evangelicalism. He was Professor Emeritus of Systematic Theology at McMaster Divinity College in Canada and wrote or edited many notable books, including *Flame of Love: A Theology of the Holy Spirit* (1996), *Most Moved Mover: A Theology of God's Openness* (2001), and, with Barry L. Callen, *The Scripture Principle: Reclaiming the Full Authority of the Bible* (3rd ed., 2009).

In the 1994 book *The Openness of God*, Clark and a group of colleagues set out a new evangelical vision of God, one centered in the openness, relationality, and responsive love of God for and with creation. This vision counters the more deterministic view of God so common in the evangelical community today. Beginning with the focus of his doctoral dissertation, Clark argued that theology is done best both on one's knees and walking in the Spirit.

As his good friend John Sanders has said, "in Pinnock's interaction with conservative Evangelicalism, Pentecostalism, Wesleyanism, Process thought, Eastern Orthodoxy, and Roman Catholicism, one sees the vision of an open and generous evangelical theology which still remains true to evangelical distinctives" (in Callen, 2000, back cover).

5. David Elton Trueblood (1900-1994)—philosopher, called the dean of American religious writers, master teacher, and visionary founder of the Yokefellow movement. At Haverford, Guilford, Harvard, Stanford, Mount Holyoke, and Earlham, this scholar-teacher and lifelong member of the Society of Friends informed and inspired thousands of students over half a century.

Elton's thirty-six books, clearly and simply written despite their often substantial subjects, captivated mass audiences rarely reached by academics. These books include: *Philosophy of Religion* (1957); *The Company of the Committed* (1961); *A Place To Stand* (1969);

The Validity of the Christian Mission (1972); and *While It Is Day: An Autobiography* (1974).

Combined in Elton were the tough-minded honesty of a true scholar, the life-changing piety of a true believer, the passion of a committed teacher, and focus on service to the neighbor. The most accurate theological term for describing him may be "rational evangelical." This label stays away from both old-fashioned liberalism and close-minded fundamentalism by emphasizing the twin necessities of a clear head and warm heart.

From an Iowa farm boy to a distinguished professor and writer of international renown, Elton was an advocate for the classic books of Christian faith and a leader in contemporary church renewal.

6. **Thomas C. Oden** (1931-   )—a United Methodist minister, theologian, seminary teacher, prolific writer, editor, and publisher. He has authored prominent books widely used for promoting "classical Christianity" as a guide for understanding Christian "consensual" theology, biblical interpretation, pastoral care, and even African

church theology and history. This early-church focus insists that the wisdom of the ancient church is more reliable for today than much modern theology often tainted by faddish political agendas.

Coming from modest beginnings in Oklahoma, Tom was educated and taught in several seminaries (Perkins, Yale, Phillips, Drew) and encountered and was mentored personally by many of the pace-setting theologians and philosophers of the twentieth century. Eventually he challenged several of the popular illusions of "modernism" that he had once embraced.

In the 1970s Tom underwent a remarkable transformation in perspective. A "liberal" at age forty, he became a champion of "classical" Christianity. Some of his book titles reflect this change: *After Modernity...What?*; *Agenda for Theology* (1990); *The Rebirth of Orthodoxy* (2003); *How Africa Shaped the Christian Mind* (2007); *Classical Christianity: A Systematic Theology* (2009); and *A Change of Heart: A Personal and Theological Memoir* (2014).

Following the loss of his wife and his retirement from Drew University, he has pursued the depths of the Christian spiritual life, following an ancient pattern, the Benedictine "hours" explained in his book *In Search of Solitude* (2010).

7. Barry L. Callen (1941-)— minister, theological educator, seminary and university dean, prolific author, academic journal editor, editor of Christian presses, and servant to AIDS orphans in Africa.

According to a biographical dictionary, Callen is "a truly 'catholic' theologian who unites traditional Church of God (Anderson) ecclesiastical concerns and an Anabaptist emphasis on discipleship with a Wesleyan soteriology" (Kostlevy, 40). This breadth of concern and ministry roots in part from Barry having earned four academic degrees from prestigious institutions representing four different wings of Christianity, and one other granted by a state institution largely unsympathetic with Christianity in general.

Barry has served ecumenically in many capacities. The fifty books he has authored or edited range in subject from Christian history, theology, ethics, and biography to secular history and fiction. His systematic theology is *God As Loving Grace*, his methodology is seen in *Approaching Theology* and *Caught Between Truths*, and his autobiography is *A Pilgrim's Progress*.

A professor, dean, and university press editor at Anderson University, Barry is a founding officer of Horizon International, a ministry to AIDS orphans in Africa. For his decades of functioning as editor of the *Wesleyan Theological Journal*, he was honored by the Wesleyan Theological Society with its 2009 Lifetime Achievement Award. His leadership in the Wesleyan/Holiness tradition of Christianity continued with his being Secretary of the Wesleyan-Holiness Connection and Editor of the Connection's publishing arm, Aldersgate Press.

Barry: Alright, enough of the brief introductions, and probably more than enough about me. We've delayed our guest and first conversation long enough—although knowing each other and our "conversion" stories is the substance of this first time together. So now, back to Rosemary. Allow me to note a few things that appear to connect the seven of us to her.

Rosemary, your professorship at Garrett carries the name of one of our future conversation guests, Georgia Harkness. Your free-thinking roots in the Texas area resonate with Tom's in Oklahoma. Your vigorous opposition to anti-Semitism echoes one of my own deep concerns. For many years, I taught a course at Anderson University titled "Hebrew Roots of Christian Faith." I was concerned that Christian young people be aware and appreciative of the Jewish world so basic to their faith. And more, Rosemary, as a Roman Catholic, your activities in the civil rights and peace movements form a special kinship with Louis, another of our regulars. So, for these and other reasons, we are truly delighted that you have joined us.

Louis: Hello, Rosemary, it's good to see you and have you as a guest. Your Roman Catholic identity helps me not feel so alone in these conversations, at least not until Henri Nouwen joins us later. I'm teasing, of course. We're all fellow travelers on this difficult journey of becoming children and then agents of our Christ on behalf of righteousness and justice in this troubled world.

We're all "catholic" in one sense, and that's the heart of the matter! And, by the way, I share Barry's sensitivity to our regular group being all men. We insisted on that exclusiveness in our monastery until recently, and the Roman church still does with the priesthood. Despite all that, we're hoping you won't feel like a token woman, Rosemary. Your reputation assures us that you'll hold your own with no problem.

Having said that, I want to observe with appreciation that you've often critiqued the male preference that has been the case for much of Christian church history. We Catholics catch our share of criticism for this. You certainly have worked hard against the tradition of hierarchy and patriarchy, including in our Roman church. Be assured that this particular group of men is not the male-domination kind. We understand ourselves to be open to many differences, gender included.

Tom: True, but let me admit, Rosemary, that from my Methodist tradition I've been involved with this gender issue from two directions. First, while reading materials of the early Christian centuries, I discovered "the profound influences of women on the earliest and richest traditions of spiritual formation" (2014, 138). Then some years ago I was addressing a group of Russian female intellectuals on the subject of Western feminism. I explained to them that, if feminism is defined as defending equal economic, political, and social rights for women, I've been a sincere feminist since 1964 when I first read Betty Friedan.

But, secondly, I returned home from Russia to our chapel services at Drew University and encountered a twisting of the traditional Christian liturgy by a political tirade with "a fixation on the advocacy of the goddess Sophia as an object of adoration" (2014, 229, 259). To me that was more than an insistence on the equality of gender rights. It was an intolerable affront to classic Christianity.

Rosemary: Thanks, Louis and Tom, for your honestly and your support of the equal rights for women, although, Tom, I struggle with how much "classic" Christianity has failed miserably on the gender front. I do sense that I'm at home here, so I feel no need to turn up my defenses and turn on my attack mode to ward off narrow-minded males.

The fact is that my life experience, and that of so many women in church life, has been negative. The more one becomes a feminist, the more difficult it is to go to church. My early years of teaching at Howard University saw me as a white woman having a very difficult time raising needed questions of gender discrimination. Even the black women there had little voice with the mainly-male faculty. I managed to begin developing my feminist theology while briefly at Yale, and especially while on a sabbatical at Harvard.

Tom: I too developed much of my theological thinking while a doctoral student at Yale. I chose that school largely because of H. Richard Niebuhr. Soon Kierkegaard, Heidegger, and Bultmann became the prevailing sources for all that I sought to do, although already I was beginning to wonder whether what I was absorbing from Bultmann's demythology project was really what the biblical writers had meant to say (2014, 69). So, Rosemary, Yale has been a spawning ground for much change in Christian theology.

Clark: Let me take us back to a focus on the emerging Christian identity of our guest today. How easy it is, Tom, to wade right into heavy academic theology. So, Rosemary, what theological vision had begun to emerge early for you, a vision that spawned your feminist theology?

Rosemary: Well, Clark, I repeat what was said of me in the brief introduction earlier. My Texas childhood was ecumenical, humanistic, and free-thinking, and it certainly was influenced particularly by my Roman Catholic mother in a setting hardly characterized as parochial or "ghettoized" Catholicism. My primary role models were sophisticated and self-confident women, which helped me later to set about the tough task of establishing an alternative to what I found typical in church life.

I once called that alternative "women-church." Many of us women met countless times in homes where we told each other our painful stories of being the victims of male domination. We naturally avoided praying to "God, our Father," preferring more gender-neutral language. Obviously, heavy criticism came our way when some of us used language like "Mother Goddess." I feel a touch of that now coming from you, Tom.

Addressing injustice can be an experimental and risky business, especially when it comes to the use of language and the challenge of public relations in the church. As I said, realizing and more freely expressing one's true identity under God can make it difficult to go to church at all, and certainly to be fully appreciated by all the members.

Tom: Sorry for what you felt was a little barb from another defensive male. I grant you the difficulty of being a prophetic voice on a controversial subject like language for God. For me, using feminine references for God is no problem as long as we continue to worship the God who was and is the "Father" of Jesus—although I clearly understand the difficulty of some women using "Father" language at all.

Elton: For your information, Rosemary, your experience is a good example of a central point I'm sure we'll all agree on in our next conversation--which will be about the true nature of God. Our view of the person and work of God in Jesus Christ colors dramatically how we perceive all else in our faith lives, and even the theological language we prefer to use. So, if God is viewed as a patriarchal tyrant, then praying to *him* obviously would be difficult for any woman, especially those sensitive about gender discrimination because they have been abused by men in other ways.

It would be helpful if you would tell us, Rosemary, a little of your personal path to faith in Jesus Christ. How could this Jesus, God among us as a man, be for you something other than just another symbol of gender discrimination?

Rosemary: First, even though I love life, in fact maybe because I so love life, I soon learned to hate injustice, especially when carried on in the name of religion. I've been known to be anything but gentle in some of my comments. There's no question that many followers of Jesus have deliberately oppressed women by use of their faith assumptions. So I want to remind you men that classical Christology mirrors the establishment of Christianity as the imperial religion of the Roman Empire. In other words, the church came to conceive of the Christ in imperial terms.

That historical fact might well have kept me far from Jesus. Instead, I was pleased to discover something very important. Once the patriarchal layers are stripped off Christology and one has returned to the Jesus of the Synoptic Gospels, the *real* Jesus turns out to be remarkably compatible with the concerns of feminism. In fact, Jesus disrupted the patriarchal structures of society—and I've done what little I could to carry on his ministry! He loves me, and I love and serve him,

God with us, yes in the *man* Jesus.

James: We all want to know the real Jesus, of course, and know ourselves properly in light of him. Rosemary, I identify strongly with your experience of growing up with a healthy sense of who you were. You and I both have deep pride in our particular identities. For you, it was strong, independent, and intellectual women. You became self-confident as a woman, even as I grew up in Detroit as a proud African-American man in a largely racist society.

My conversion experience came when I was only six years old. I walked to a kneeling rail at the invitation of a guest evangelist from Selma, Alabama, and found my harmony with God. I once put it like this: "I knew sin as a teenager because that early consciousness of God's claim upon my life was not honored without interruption as I grew older. But God graciously renewed my joy and dismissed all felt judgment when I prayerfully returned to him, chastened by that divine love that would not let me go" (2002, 30).

Christian ministry was not my intent; I was a musician and was going to be a classical pianist. But, for reasons known only to God, my future would be ministry.

Barry, when you graciously gathered and edited the materials for the volume about Christian preaching designed to honor me and my ministry, you were wise to title it *Sharing Heaven's Music*. The gospel of Jesus Christ had become for me the music I have played and proclaimed all of my adult life. Its lovely notes and rhythms tend to dissolve things like racism and sexism.

Barry: How did the big shift of professional focus happen, James, your moving from keyboard to pulpit?

James: It all began with a divine call that was nurtured in the midst of a strong community of believers in Detroit, especially by the mentoring of Raymond S. Jackson. My "sitting under" him helped me gain an understanding of "what a solid preaching and pastoral ministry means, involves, and makes possible for people" (2002, 58).

Then, when I was nineteen, I first heard Howard Thurman speak. "I was moved by his preaching, very deeply moved.... I thanked him for his ministry to my life that day. As I left the sanctuary, I knew that I had found a preacher whose insights spoke to the depths of my own spirit and yearning after God.... His message and manner made me sense again that wholeness of being which since a child I had come to believe belongs to the experience of hearing the word of God!" (2002, 65-66).

Louis: That's quite a testimony, James. Your childhood and early coming to Christ were like Rosemary's in some ways, and so very different from mine! For me, a major path to life in Jesus Christ has been my life as a monk in Gethsemani, the Trappist monastery hidden away in the hills of Kentucky. It's in an area known mostly for its sour-mash whiskey and purebred race horses. While that setting doesn't sound promising for spiritual nourishment, it has worked for me.

Before the monastery years, I wish I could report a healthy and stable period of growing up to be a confident young man living a constructive life—like you did, James. I can't, but no matter now. God's grace got me through it.

My first day at Gethsemani was in December, 1941, when you were only six months old, Barry. While you were being born in Pennsylvania, I was being re-born in another place and way. I arrived at the monastery with a troubled young life already on the books.

In the 1930s I had struggled with the idea of accepting Catholicism, was deeply depressed by the looming war in Europe, and assumed that I'd be drafted and then "get a piece of metal with my number on it . . . so as to help out the circulation of red-tape that would necessarily follow the disposal of my remains" (1948, 214).

Barry: One thing is for sure, Louis. I'm glad that one of those chunks of metal never got you! So, as it turns out, while I was a new infant you were expecting little in life except death. What moved you from such dark thoughts to a vibrant Christian faith?

Louis: One thing was reading a biography of the English poet and Jesuit priest Gerard Manley Hopkins. One day in my room on West 114th Street in New York, with rain outside and a big hunger inside me, I read the chapter on Hopkins' 1866 conversion to Catholicism. Something stirred in me.

Why did I keep waiting? I knew what I should do. I lit a cigarette, looked out the window at the rain, tried not to act, and finally put on my raincoat and went down the stairs and out into the street. "And then everything inside me began to sing" (1948, 215-216).

That was it, friends. The big change inside me had begun. I soon was baptized. What contrasts I was living! Not long before this I had driven a friend to Philadelphia. We had stopped at some roadhouse, argued about mysticism, smoked cigarettes, and gradually got drunk. While it took days to recover from that hangover, I am pleased to report that I have never gotten over what became my new life with Jesus Christ, thanks partly to Hopkins.

Barry: An extensive report of your dramatic journey to faith, Louis, soon appeared in a celebrated book you wrote. However, I hear that you have mixed feelings about ever having released it to the public. Am I right? Why would that be?

Louis: That's right. My writer-self followed me into the monastery and my superiors recognized it as a gift of God and allowed me to use it. It was in 1948 that my spiritual autobiography, *The Seven Storey Mountain*, came out. Soon people were saying that it was one of the more compelling conversion stories of all time. It sold so many copies that the fame that followed worried me, as did some of the narrow attitudes I had let slip into the big manuscript.

While we Christians have an obligation to witness to our faith journeys, the process can be hazardous. Ego can invade our best of intentions, and a celebrity-oriented society can drag our witness into places we would prefer that it not go.

Jack: I have known some of that very problem, Louis. And since you mentioned an English poet, I'll take that as my cue as a good Englishman to report on my own path to Christian conversion. I have recounted it in detail in my book *Surprised by Joy*.

The long journey began at age fifteen when I said bluntly to a friend that I believed in no religion or God, and that, if I did, it wouldn't be Christianity. But in 1929 I gave in, admitted that God is God, and actually knelt and prayed, becoming "the most dejected and reluctant convert in all England" (Downing, 137).

That was quite the reversal, I admit. When I first went to Oxford, my materialism and spiritualism already had begun to recede and I was exploring metaphysical worldviews seriously. I walked out of the railway station carrying my luggage and headed down the street the wrong way. It was only when I reached the edge of the city that I realized that the fabled spires and towers of the great university were somewhere back of me.

In fact, that walk in the wrong direction has become an allegory of my whole life. I did get turned around and finally found my destination, even my destiny! I had always wanted to call my soul my own, and without outside interference, but finally I realized that the real call was *to surrender*. My quest had led me to an overwhelming sense that it was time to relinquish control and find my way through being guided by another, God.

Barry: Yours is quite a story, Jack. We'll gladly take the time for you to tell us a little more.

Jack: Thanks, I will. I went through stages, an amazing journey as I now look back. As a Materialist, at first I tried to deny the reality of any immaterial realm. Then, as a Dualist, I came to view the human spirit as at war with the material world. Then, as an Idealist (did I try everything?) I began to ponder the possibility of a Universal Spirit who is immanent in nature.

Finally, as a Christian I learned that God is the supreme Spirit, not merely in nature or clearly against it, but above it as its Creator. We humans should not spurn nature as evil, or worship it as divine, but treasure it as part of God's creation. I had finally found my way home.

And there's still more. At first I didn't think it possible to encounter God for myself, any more than Hamlet could have met Shakespeare, a play character meeting the play writer. The startling thing I came to realize was that the Hamlet-Shakespeare analogy can work—that is, if Shakespeare would write himself into the play script!

And that's exactly what I came to believe happened in our world. It was the *Incarnation*, God in Jesus *with us*, the Son written into the play script of human history, making real spiritual encounters with God very possible through the continuing presence of God the Spirit. The Incarnation, God in Jesus with us, is the heart of this whole matter of Christian life and theology.

James: You certainly came out at a good place, Jack. Beyond your philosophic advance, I hear from various sources that you have become one of those rare souls who combine *goodness* and *greatness*. Let me explain.

Prominence too often is polluting. Someone, however, has said that you are "the most thoroughly converted man I ever met." For many of us, Jack, quite beyond the rational arguments for Christianity that you put forth so ably, it's the quality of your life that really communicates the credibility of your faith. I sense in you both intellectual brilliance and a refreshing authenticity. How good that you're my brother!

Jack: I humbly accept that gracious compliment, James, even if it's only partly deserved. And I concur with your point. Any man—or woman, like you, Rosemary--must walk humbly with Jesus, not just talk about him in impressive ways. The public will recognize the walk even when not appreciating the talk.

As for myself, I don't want to claim too much for the thoroughness of my own conversion. Our journeys continue in this life. Even so, I surely have been changed by God's grace, "surprised by joy" as I have been pleased to put it. It happened in one way for me; it doesn't have to be the same journey for everyone.

And what about you, Clark? You've not spoken about yourself yet, and I hear that you also have an English connection like me. How did you come to faith?

Clark: You're right, Jack. While I was born in Canada, my paternal grandparents were from the British Midlands. I soon found my way back to England to pursue a Ph.D. under my treasured mentor, F. F. Bruce.

Jack: OK, coming back to England is surely a good thing, but what turned you to Jesus Christ and propelled you into such doctoral studies and then to the heights of theological influence?

Clark: Barry has sketched this conversion story of mine (2000, 15-39). I was reared in a "liberal" Baptist church, but my blessed grandmother Madora and a faithful Sunday school teacher witnessed to me. I accepted the Lord and soon was nurtured by conservative radio preachers, an association with some para-church groups (especially Youth for Christ and Inter-Varsity Christian Fellowship), and extensive reading of fundamentalist writers who shaped early "evangelicalism."

One great writer I encountered—one not fitting neatly into any mold--was you, Jack. Barry rightly reports that I found you to have an "imagination that mixed evangelical apologetics with 'a liberal twinge' that made you a free thinker 'who didn't worry about saying things that no one else was even thinking'" (2000, 23). That helped to set me free to journey in my spiritual development, not fearing new thoughts or even changing my mind when fresh insights called for it.

Jack: Good for me. I'm glad to have set you free from a fundamentalist trap where new thoughts are treated as dangerous things. Now, Clark, I have a question for you. You've certainly been a theological traveler ever since, changing your mind and even direction on occasion. What has held you steady? What has been your anchor in the storm of intellectual conflicts?

Clark: That's easy to answer, Jack. It's what we plan to talk about in detail in our fifth conversation when Jürgen Moltmann will be our guest. Let me just note it quickly here. Our Christian faith, in my judgment, is centered in Jesus Christ. Getting dependably to him is essential, and that happens necessarily through divine self-revelation. The big question often tends to be put in a false either-or fashion.

As we seek and encounter the divine revelation as our primary path to Christ, is it—to put the options in their extreme—content-less religious experience (liberalism) or timeless and virtually context-less propositions (conservatism). I say that these are false options.

My view is that "revelation is not primarily existential impact or infallible truths, but divine self-revelation that both impacts and instructs. The mode of revelation, I have come to believe, is self-disclosure and interpersonal communication. As such, it is pregnant with significance and possible development" (1996, 226). Divine revelation is our introduction to a *Person*. Meeting Jesus is seeing the Father (Jn. 14:9).

At its most basic, then, here is the heart of the whole matter as I see it. "Being a Christian is knowing Father and Son and walking along the pathway of cross and resurrection through the power of the Spirit" (1996, 47). I'm so glad that such knowing came to me. And, Rosemary, the God we see in Jesus is no divine discriminator on the basis of culture or gender!

Rosemary: So true, Clark. As I said before, if we can get back to the Jesus of the Gospels, many of our concerns will fall away and the grace of God can shine through again. We need to meet the real Jesus stripped of the various perversions added on across church history.

Barry: Absolutely. And we also still need to meet the real Elton Trueblood. Let's bring you into the conversation this way. Clark says that true Christian faith is not content-less religious experience (liberalism). In that regard, Elton, the Society of Friends or Quakers, your home Christian community of faith, is sometimes thought of as a body of liturgy-less and even word-less believers, quiet people who focus on the inner experience of faith, maybe sometimes to a fault. Please tell us of your early faith journey in a context like this.

Elton: I may say something later about that jaded view of Quakers that many people have. But, as for my own beginnings, they were in a strong Quaker community of farmers in Iowa. "A few miles to the south there were German Catholics, while a few miles to the east were Lutherans, but all of our close neighbors were Quakers" (1974, 11).

When I was eight, my parents sold their farm at a great sacrifice so that we could move to a farm near Indianola, Iowa, where the educational opportunity for us kids was much better. I am so thankful to my parents for that! I was attracted increasingly to the academic life, beginning as a student at little Penn College in Iowa. Soon I would be able to be in some of the best educational centers in the western world.

Religious life at home was strong, as it was in the new high school in Indianola. I heard early and believed deeply an aphorism of the early Greeks--nothing comes from nothing. So, I concluded, the emergence of self-conscious beings in our universe is something that came from something, a compelling reason for belief in God. The biggest influence on me was the Christian Endeavor Society in the local Friends Church.

I was very active in church, including engaging in the practice of daily Bible reading and prayer. For the first time I learned "something of the power released by the voluntary acceptance of discipline. Years later, when I began to dream of a new redemptive society, to be called

Yokefellows, my experience when I was fifteen and sixteen was influential" (1974, 15).

Enough about me for now. Barry, you became my student in the 1960s and soon I was encouraging you to keep writing—you have a good head and heart and a special skill with words. Tell us something of your own religious beginnings.

Barry: I'll never forget being in your classroom, Elton. It was filled with the books of Quakers, ancient Greeks, and you in particular. Frankly, it was intimidating for me at first. I came from a small village in Ohio and a Christian religious tradition that didn't put much stress on the value of the intellectual life.

My context of origin was the American Midwest and holiness revivalism. It featured camp meetings and frequent calls for "getting saved," often through emotional times of repentance of sin and then witness to immediate new life in Christ.

I knew well the campgrounds of the Free Methodist Church in East Liverpool, Ohio. I spent at least one week each summer in the cottage of my grandparents and would hear the visiting evangelists at least twice a day. The cottage had no plumbing, radios were not allowed, and there were several beds separated only by curtains hung on a network of overhead wires.

It was in the tabernacle on those grounds that I finally accepted Christ at thirteen (2013, 68). There also was lots of talk about "sanctification." That meant the deeper spiritual life that usually comes later when shame for sin is not the central issue, but rather the question of maturity of faith and the willingness to "go all the way" with Christ in giving oneself to his service. I became associated with the same Church of God movement that you, James, have known and loved all your life.

By the way, this Church of God tradition is a reform movement rooted heavily in Methodism, as are you Tom. We need to hear something of your beginnings.

Tom: We were an Oklahoma Methodist family whose days began with *Upper Room* devotional readings with our parents before breakfast. At the end of the day we would gather with Grandmother Oden to hear the Scripture read and get on our knees to pray. The house was also full of music.

James, you spoke of "sharing heaven's music" and your own musical beginnings. Well, in 1945 I saw the epic film *A Song to Remember* about the life of Chopin and the romantic idealism and social conscience of this great musician. I identified strongly with him. He was my first intellectual passion (2014, 31).

Once off to the University of Oklahoma in 1949, "I was peculiarly drawn to the agnostics and atheists, partly to let them test my belief system, which they did" (2014, 42). Soon my social radicalism was on the loose and my intellectual trajectory was to the political left. I was a pacifist after the atomic bombs in Japan and a romantic idealist in general.

The liberal elements of Methodism at the time gave me encouragement and outlets. I was challenged to enter the Christian ministry, not the traditional Word and Sacrament kind, but a social revolution with questionable links to New Testament revelation. It was exciting even if driven in part by unrecognized ego and self-serving. I entered ministry "to use the church to elicit political change according to a soft Marxist vision of wealth distribution and proletarian empowerment" (2014, 50). It wasn't exactly your revivalistic campgrounds, Barry.

Barry: Except, Tom, that we shouldn't forget an important fact. The founder of Free Methodism, and that of Methodism itself originally, were prophetic men with a great social conscience. It is no easy task to balance our inner lives and our outer social settings, our family biases and our educational visions.

More on that later, my friends. Our time is running out for this first conversation. Next time we will turn our attention to our thinking about the existence and nature of that supreme being we call "God," that Something or Someone, Elton, presupposed because of the emergence of the self-conscious something that is us. As we now end, let's invite our guest to have the last word.

Rosemary: Thanks, Barry. Gentlemen, and you seven men are indeed more gentle and wise than so many I've known, talking with you and listening to you have been a pleasure. And learning more about your biographical and educational backgrounds certainly sheds helpful light on who each of you has become as theologians.

Do know that I'm pleased that one of your later conversations will have Georgia Harkness as the special guest. I was honored for so many years to fulfill the professorship at Garrett that carries her name. Georgia's journey has impacted mine significantly, and now so have all of yours in different ways. Thanks for the spiritual enrichment and just good conversation—and say "Hi!" to Georgia when she gets here.

Let me say one more thing. Georgia's style was usually more gentle than mine. I once heard that one of my students said my lectures were as dry as two-day-old toast. At least the student admitted that occasionally an aside of mine would bring the house down with laughter—

and that sometimes I would dissect a good-old-boy male network with a surgical strike more devastating that a stealth bomber.

Today you men haven't brought out that more strident side of me, but many things in theological history have. There's a place in the doing of Christian theology for honest directness, and there's a crucial place for women, as you men have readily admitted.

Barry: A forthright honesty is not be avoided in our conversations, Rosemary, else we wouldn't have invited you and have risked a surgical strike! Thanks for your presence and wisdom, and be aware that our next conversation is about the true identity of God. Who knows. Maybe "He" will turn out to be "She"! We'll leave that for next time and our special guest, John Cobb.

Questions Related to Conversation #1

1. In order to really understand our individual journeys to faith in Jesus Christ, how important is it to know the details of our differing life contexts--place, time, surrounding people, etc.? How important are biographical introductions to Christian theology?

2. In the midst of the different life settings of these seven conversation partners and their first guest, can you identity two or three *common factors* in the coming of each to faith in Jesus Christ?

3. The Bible emerged out of a culture that was male dominated. Do you agree with Rosemary's strong negative reaction to this, and to her judgment that much of Christian theology has been based wrongly on gender discrimination? Don't we all do our theological thinking in our home cultural contexts? How should we compensate for them?

4. Do you find it helpful to know a person before you begin evaluating that person's belief witness? Do we, then, have a significant problem when affirming classic Christian creeds with little or no understanding of the conflicted contexts out of which they originally arose?

5. Having read brief accounts of how these conversation partners found their way to Jesus Christ, does one of them mirror your own early journey more than the others? Who is it and why? Can looking back and evaluating your own journey to faith help you in some way as you travel on?

Conversation #2

EXACTLY WHO IS GOD?

Classical, Reformed, Open, and Process Theologies; God, Power, and Human Freedom

> This hiddenness of God must not be forgotten as we stand in wonder before the divine self-disclosure. Only as we remember the depth of the mystery will we with sufficient awe and gratitude receive the revelation. Only thus will we be possessed by that "fear" of the Lord that is the beginning of wisdom. The one God, when truly encountered, remains the *mysterium* and *tremendum*, never fully comprehensible or comfortably familiar (DeWolf, in Callen, 2004, 5).

> A loving God is necessarily a related God.... Far from the remote, all-powerful deity of classical thought, a God accessible to modern Christian piety would be always incarnate in the world, accepting the risk of that involvement, bearing the world's sorrows and sharing its joys (Brown, in Pinnock/Brown, 1990, 86).

Barry: Great to see you again, all such good and wise friends, as different as we are. Our topic for this second of our eleven conversations is the nature of God and, given that nature, how God relates to this world of ours. We'll likely stray into some related issues, but that's just how free-flowing conversations often go. It's good to begin with the lead quotations on our screen today—they both warm the heart

John B. Cobb, Jr. (1925-) has been called the dean of process theologians. Son of Methodist missionaries, John joined the U. S. Army in 1944, met intellectuals from other religious perspectives, developed belief questions that were new and unsettling to him, and decided to attend the University of Chicago to prepare intellectually for meeting the objections to Christianity. He first experienced disillusionment there and then was helped by Charles Hartshorne who taught him about the philosophy and metaphysics of Alfred North Whitehead. This gave John a renewed confidence in theistic belief and led eventually to his teaching at Claremont School of Theology from 1958 until his retirement in 1990. Over these many years he sought to construct a fresh vision of Christian beliefs by applying aspects of Whitehead's cosmology to traditional Christian teachings—theism particularly, but not exclusively.

An ordained minister of the United Methodist Church, John's 1995 book *Grace and Responsibility: A Wesleyan Theology for Today* is an extended attempt to show the relevance of his theological work for his particular Christian affiliation. He has remained convinced across his long and distinguished career that the "process" view of reality is foundational for living responsibly and transformingly in our modern world.

with awareness of God and humble our intellectual quests. At our best, we will know only in part, at least in this life. And being able to know even in part is only because God comes, relates, reveals, and enables.

Tom: I like these reminders, Barry, and I have one of my own that shows up in one of your books: "The healthier the study of God, the more candid it remains about its own finitude, the stubborn limits of its own knowing, its own charades, Band-Aids, closets, masks, and broken windows. That is why the study of God is best understood from within a caring community that laughs a little at its own sober efforts" (2004, 14).

One more thing as we begin. We will have to talk sometime today about Delwin Brown's critique of "classical thought." I don't read such thought as negatively as his quote sounds, unless by "classical" he means the later deterioration of the original apostolic tradition. We'll sort that out as we go along.

Barry: Thanks, Tom. I'm sure we'll get that clarified.

When the study of Christian theology is approached, surely nothing can be more foundational than theism, today's topic area. Fortunately, among us regular conversation partners there resides quite a pool of wisdom on the subject, cautious and humble as it should be. In addition, our special guest is someone with much to say that should further enrich our conversation. Let me introduce John B. Cobb, Jr. Please view a brief vita now on our screen over the fireplace.

Welcome, John! Although everyone in the room understands basically what process philosophy and theology is, and has varying degrees of appreciation for its relevance to today's work of Christian theology, none is as thoroughly committed to it as you are. So, your presence is important.

John: Good to be here, gentlemen. You're quite a prominent group to actually have in one room. It should be a good conversation, a healthy *process*—something I'm all about. By the way, since your information about me was prepared, I've published my most mature thought on God in the book *Jesus' Abba* (2015). More from that source as we go along. And Barry, as you promised Tom, there also will be more said about Delwin Brown's lead quotation—he was a prominent "process" theologian, a valued colleague of mine, and a personal friend of you and Clark.

Barry: You're right, John, this should be interesting and enlightening. To begin, let me recall for us the late 1960s in the United States. I was in Chicago with a wife and baby pursuing a doctorate at Chicago Theological Seminary, just across the street from the Divinity School of the University of Chicago where you, John, had earned your doctorate some years earlier. I had come to Chicago deeply ingrained in orthodox Christianity and was ministerial career building. By contrast, you were in the process of theological rebuilding after difficult ministerial experiences, as were many of my student colleagues. Am I right that your years in Chicago involved considerable personal turmoil and faith reconstruction?

John: Yes, Barry, I went through a very difficult personal experience, a crisis of faith, which for me was something like the death of God. As I look back now, you could say that in Chicago I launched a quest for personal recovery and theological reconstruction. It was not only for myself, but hopefully for the faith of the whole church now living in a modern context and needing a viable, relevant, rationally defensible, and truly satisfying Christian faith. I concluded that it had to be somewhat different from the one I'd inherited.

Jack: Your manner of eventual theological reconstruction, John, has become quite the story in recent years. As I understand it, by 1952 you had in hand your Chicago Ph.D. and had found the basic intellectual tools for your life-long theological task, especially the philosophy of a fellow Englishman of mine, Alfred North Whitehead. Tell us about these tools and how you had come to view the basic task of Christian theology today.

John: You're right about that fellow Englishman, Jack. It was Charles Hartshorne who directed my studies in Chicago. Through him I was introduced to the process philosophy of Whitehead. From 1958 until I retired in 1990, I taught and wrote from my academic base at Claremont School of Theology and Graduate School in California. For the first years, I tried to show how Whitehead's thought addressed the concerns left by Karl Barth and his neo-orthodox colleagues. Then came something of a transition in my focus.

In 1969, just as you were leaving Chicago, Barry, it hit me that the destructive structures and policies of the modern world were bringing into serious question the very survival of humanity. Therefore, I shifted the application of my process theological work away from theism. From then on, my work went more in political and ecological directions, as is clear in my book *Process Theology as Political Theology*. Even so, the theological goal I have pursued all along has centered on one consistent task, to demonstrate the relevance of Christian faith to a modern culture increasingly imbued with the sense of *becoming* rather than stuck in the older and more static metaphysical concept of *being*.

In short, gentlemen, here's my working assumption. I think Whitehead provides a constructive alternative to now-antiquated Christian concepts of God, particularly God viewed as the unchanging and passionless Absolute who controls all things and sanctions the social and religious status quo. God is very much *not* what my former and esteemed colleague Delwin Brown wisely criticized.

Delwin and I, armed by Whitehead, have opposed the view of God as "all-knowing and all-powerful ruler and judge," the "monarchial" and "repressive" God. That's the faulty view that "has infected so much of Christianity" (Brown, 2008, 44). By sharp contrast, Brown and I and many others think that it is more philosophically sound and biblical to follow Whitehead's general trajectory. So, there's the task and these have been my essential tools.

James: What about that newest book of yours?

John: *Jesus' Abba* follows the Whitehead trajectory back to the Bible and rings true there. I think that serious attention to what the Bible actually teaches would release biblicists from their least attractive teachings, like it has you Clark. Didn't you begin "as a fundamentalist, but were led by your belief in the divine authority of the writings to study them carefully. The results are to be found in 'open theology,' which I consider a particularly promising evangelical movement" (2015, xvi).

Clark: Thanks for the compliment, John. It surely has been quite a journey for me as well. And Barry, your latest book, *Bible Stories for Strong Stomachs*, has a provocative section of seven Bible stories showing God to be very surprising and truly wonderful in the face of so many distortions of the Bible's teaching about God. You show God to be "open" as I also have tried to do in some ways that John can appreciate, if not fully agree with.

But back to your new book, John. What have you tried to do in calling God "Abba"?

John: Simply this, Clark. I'm a liberal who has tried to free Christian theology from unbiblical views of God that have dominated Western church history—God as omnipotent, morally judgmental, exclusivist, the God who supposedly created all from nothing and demands sacrifice as the price of forgiveness. I am trying to reintroduce Abba, the God of Jesus. My argument is that "when we free ourselves from the atheism inherent in modern metaphysics, Abba appears in our experience, quite normally, whenever we feel called to serve our neighbors or open ourselves to new ideas" (2015, 60).

Elton: While Tom and I would be inclined to see more in the Bible's teaching about God that you as a liberal are ready to affirm, John, you certainly are correct about the waywardness of many streams of historic and modern theology. And I do see in Whitehead an answer to some of modern atheism. For instance, William Temple moved wisely from Whitehead to this conclusion: "When we turn from the World as apprehended by Mind to Mind which apprehends the World, we find among its functions a principle which is self-explanatory—the principle of Purpose or of Intelligent Choice" (1964, 131). In other words, God is, has purposed, and can be apprehended in our world (mind perceiving Mind), and especially so in Jesus Christ.

Tom: Yes, Elton, right on. And I must admit that I'm most uncomfortable with some things that you, John, deny, things that I think the Bible does teach about God—and certainly that the classic tradition of the church teaches. It is so easy to perceive and try to use God for our own agendas or feel free to redefine God as dictated by our latest philosophic orientation.

I admit that I strayed in my early years. In fact, I now know clearly that "God is more than a means to an end for social change." I wanted to adjust God to modernity and finally learned that God had come to us humans in more than some "symbolic sense acceptable to modern assumptions." The big truth is that classic Christianity has "survived the death throes of thousands of supposed modernities" (2014, 147, 149).

One of these contemporary modernities, if I may be forthright, is "the reifying of the idea of *sophia* into a goddess acceptable to neo-pagan feminists who want to remain vaguely within the Christian community, but only on terms unacceptable to the apostolic tradition" (1995, 150). God is who God is, not who we want God to be for our own ends.

Jack: The fact is that some would see Whitehead himself as a modernist of sorts, representing significant if sometimes subtle divergence from biblical teaching. The problem is the fear of pantheism, which asserts that God "animates the universe as you animate your body; that the universe almost *is* God, so that if it didn't exist He wouldn't exist either…. The Christian idea is quite different. They think God *made* the universe—like a man making a picture or composing a tune. A painter isn't a picture, and he doesn't die if the picture is destroyed" (1989, 33).

James: As a preacher, I care deeply about the relevance of the Christian gospel to the actual lives that people are now experiencing. So, John, this tension between "classic" and "modern" is an important one. We want both roots and relevance. Where do you see the Whitehead trajectory, as you call it, sending us? How do you see it enabling a better connection with "modern" people? Beyond philosophical abstractions, what will preach effectively to common folks in the pews and communicate to the masses who never come to church?

John: Well, James, I appreciate your skillful pulpit communication. Good preaching tends to connect with people of any time—if they'll come to listen in the first place. Regarding the theological work that should lay behind preaching today, Whitehead shoots us in the direction of seeing God playing a crucial but nonetheless limited role in the process of this world's ongoing becoming.

This trajectory argues that God provides the initial aim to every occasion of experience and is the final "repository" of each such occasion once it passes from human view. God lovingly lures all in the best direction of becoming—that should preach, James! People are not left alone in their struggles, although they do retain their dignity and freedom and final responsibility.

God is with us, wonderfully with us in the process of our faith journeys. In fact, God is also in the process of becoming by retaining all that is or has been in one comprehensive experience, thus guiding the becoming world toward the goal of a wonderful unity. God is the One who calls us forward; God is *Creative Responsive Love*. That's my view of who God really is. I know that many "classic" Christian thinkers disagree, fearing the suggestion that God is, in any sense, also becoming, and thus in process of becoming with us. They remain caught in a static mode of thought that doesn't translate well with most modern people.

Tom: I'm tracking with you, John, although hardly agreeing at key points. Like your intellectual struggles with the traditional Christianity you inherited, I also veered away from my early religious training. After World War II I became a pacifist, joined the Student Christian Movement, and headed rather far left on most subjects. Marx, Nietzsche, and Freud filled my imagination, and before the U.S. got into the Vietnam war I thought of Ho Chi Minh as an agrarian patriot. "For me, the *theo* in theology had become little more than a question mark" (2014, 77).

But things changed for me, although differently than for you, John. I was an observer at the Vatican II Council of Roman Catholicism, got my first taste of ancient Christianity, and slowly abandoned my view that all the answers lay somewhere in the interface of theology and psychotherapy. Of all things, a Jewish scholar, Will Herberg, helped me turn, not to Whitehead, but to the great minds of the early church. That led to my writing extensively, and with great conviction, a trilogy of books on God framed by the classic core doctrine of the Trinity.

Clark: I certainly have come to agree, as you well know, John and Tom, that there are significant problems with the "classical" view of God—and I don't mean by classical the many positive meanings that you have drawn from the ancient writers, Tom. When theology highlights the supposed negative characteristics of God--monarchial, repressive, unchanging, passionless, etc.—I agree that something is very wrong.

A static view of the all-controlling and ever-judging God is so common among conservative Christians today, and it has many implications that indeed are unbiblical in my view. While I join you, Tom, in not buying into Whitehead as an adequate philosophic alternative, as you have, John, I have gladly joined both of you in challenging the status quo of the faulty theism of evangelical orthodoxy—and I've gotten a lot of criticism for it!

Elton: So, what's your alternative, Clark?

Clark: Rather than God being that motionless, all-controlling, passionless Absolute, I have titled a whole book of mine *Most Moved Mover*. As I understand the biblical perspective, on the one hand God is full of passion and empathy, risking and suffering because of our wayward human ways. God also is always *separate from* and *other than* us humans and our world, even while always redemptively engaged with us (in the "process" as you would have it, John).

Viewed biblically, God is indeed much like your "Creative Responsive Love" designation, John, although also truly *transcendent*, responsible for, involved in, and yet not part of or trapped by the creation. God changes, yes, but in strategy toward the changing creation, never in the divine nature or will.

John: I do appreciate you good men and your agreeing and disagreeing with me. To you, Clark, I would say one thing. We certainly do need to go back to the true biblical perspective of God by finding again the "Abba" of Jesus, the universal and ever-loving God. We should shed the unbiblical idea of divine "omnipotence," God as the big and all-controlling Judge. In fact, the idea that the mission of Jesus "was to die to appease the wrath of Abba was as remote from Jesus as devil worship" (2014, 3, 23). Modern atheism could have been avoided for the most part if over the centuries such false views of God had not come over the centuries to be dominant in the Christian community.

Barry: Thanks, John, Tom, and Clark. That gets us started with variations of the current attempts to reconceive God's nature in our modern setting. Now, before discussing further the nature of God and God's relationships with this creation, maybe we should speak directly of God's very existence—something often questioned in our day. John, you say modern atheism is an understandable reaction to unbiblical views of God. Jack, let's bring you in here. Your intellectual journey is quite dramatic in this regard. Please tell us about it.

Jack: Sure, Barry. John, you, Tom, and Clark have gotten us off on the right foot. Believing in God today has much to do with how God is conceived and whether or not we can square such belief with the best of our intellectual pursuits in general. My personal journey into theism certainly has been quite eventful.

Like others of us, I lost my Christian faith as a young man and started calling myself an atheist. I got "trapped between imagination that gloried in nature, myth, and romance and an intellect that dismissed it all as a tale told by an idiot, signifying nothing" (in Downing, 156). But here's the good news, friends. I made it back! Eventually, I became a "reluctant convert" to the Christian faith. I managed to come home to Christ. As I said last time, I have told about the big change for me in my book *Surprised by Joy*.

Having said that, let me throw out a warning. Overly cocky modern intellectuals who pride themselves in being atheists need to be careful. They must be aware that an atheist is in danger when reading people like G. K. Chesterton. "God is, if I may say it, very unscrupulous"

(1955, chap. 12). God's very presence lurks everywhere, searching for the non-believer, ready to bring him home to himself. The God of Creative Responsive Love whom you speak of, John, finally caught up to me—and I'm so glad! I've been loved into faith and newness of life.

Elton: I so appreciate what you're saying, Jack. Let me report that I'm honored to be in this conversation with you, and with you too, John. Now that I've cared for the pleasantries, here comes my little soapbox that you two have inspired me to get on.

We moderns need to put God back on life's center stage. I think pastors could make a tremendous difference today if they did less of operating clubs for human enjoyment and general community betterment and started becoming "arousers of conviction." And by conviction I don't mean insisting on marginal matters like the best manner of baptizing or details of God's future intent in judging this world. The situation today is not only confused at the periphery but bankrupt at the center. We must locate and champion the heart of the matter. Theism is indeed *the* issue. "Why bother to trim the branches if the root is dead? God *is* or *is not*. What is the evidence?" (1970, 112-114).

Louis: I for one want to hear your evidence, Elton.

Elton: OK. As a philosopher, I have come to believe that the single most important fact which we humans know about our universe is that "it is the home of *persons*.... It is obvious to me that self-consciousness cannot be the product of unconsciousness! Nothing comes from nothing" (1974, 35, 37). Let me quote William Temple whose thought I value highly: "To suppose that a physiological organism becomes conscious only because its own evolution has brought it to a certain stage of complexity would be like supposing that the mechanical robot at a street corner will automatically turn into a policeman if the traffic is sufficiently congested" (Temple, 199).

You emphasized, John, that *becoming* as opposed to *being* is now widely recognized as the fundamental fact of reality. Let me use a slightly different rubric. Here's my central point as it relates to God's existence. The dramatic fact of the presence of self-consciousness in this world of ours should be approached with wonder and seen as a revelation of the basic nature of reality. From the existence of the *divine Person*, we *human persons* have come to be.

In my book *Philosophy of Religion* I discuss at length the "theistic hypothesis." I explore the streams of evidence for God's existence that come from scientific, moral, aesthetic, historical, and religious sources. All of these sources point in the same direction, the probability of God's existence. No one of them is close to being intellectually conclusive, admittedly, but their cumulative effect is truly compelling.

Faith is still required, but not faith that lacks a substantial rational foundation.

Barry: Thanks, Elton. If we assume God's existence, and that God is at least "personal" and both ultimate (transcendent) and yet involved with us in the process of human history and destiny (immanent), what follows? What about the really big question of *how* God chooses to relate to this creation? Surely it's the case that how we understand such a fundamental matter determines how all else in Christian faith will be viewed.

Tom: Bring up the "TULIP" rubric, Barry. It's a common way of approaching this fundamental matter.

Barry: Certainly. By the eighteenth century, much "Reformed" theology rooted in the thought of John Calvin "had solidified into dogmatic assertions about the being of a sovereign God and God's relations to the fallen creation. Formalized at the Synod of Dort (1618-1619), this 'TULIP' solidification had become firmly scholasticized Calvinistic dogma.

Hardly a fragrant flower lacking rigid and defensive thorns, this particular TULIP consists of the five affirmed articles of Dort . . . (1) **T**otal depravity; (2) **U**nconditional election; (3) **L**imited atonement; (4) **I**rresistible grace; and (5) **P**erserverance of the saints. These five petals of the theological TULIP became tightly interconnected in a logical chain that now is standard theological thinking for much of conservative 'evangelicalism' in the twentieth century" (2009, 11).

Each petal of this theological flower is identified in a way that leads necessarily to the next. In brief, we sinful humans are understood to be helpless to right our sad sin situation (total depravity). God must intervene in this humanly hopeless circumstance, choosing to save some, but not all people (limited atonement). When God chooses, the divine gift of saving grace will be accepted (irresistible). What God chooses cannot fail to be completed as God predetermines (perseverance), or God would not be God.

John: That, Barry, is precisely the view of God that we process thinkers, and also Clark and other "openness" thinkers, have been resisting vigorously. Thanks for the flowery lesson in theological history.

Barry: No problem. I acknowledge that you, Clark, have been my personal mentor here. Your pivotal 2001 book on the theology of "God's openness" was gladly received by me. Here are a few of my endorsing words that appear on the back cover: "The church and her mission cannot be more dynamic than her doctrine of God. Here is a . . . compelling call for an amicable conversation among evangelicals about the truly transcendent God who is said to choose significant involvement in the life of creation." My hat's off to you, Clark, for this clearly written, anti-TULIP work.

Clark: Well, the appreciation goes both ways, Barry. Your writing of my intellectual biography in 2000 was done with insight and fairness, unlike much that has been written about my thought—evangelicals are strongly committed to their TULIP view of God and resist vigorously any suggested modifications, seemingly biblical or not. So I was pleased in turn to endorse your *Discerning the Divine* book with this: "Barry Callen offers the vision of a God who relates dynamically with us in our history. He then places his numerous biblically informed insights concerning God's nature in the context of the modern discussion, guiding us through the material and always keeping his careful eye steadily on the ball."

By the way, Barry, since you've reviewed the TULIP pattern for us, go ahead and tell us what you created as a more acceptable, more dynamic alternative, one that "openness" people like me can relate to readily—and maybe even "process" people like you, John.

Barry: I'm more than glad to finish my thought. Another "flower" that many of us perceive as more biblically authentic and pastorally satisfying is the *ROSE*. God is **R**elational, **O**pen, **S**uffering, and **E**verywhere-active. God willingly, and out of love, chooses to relate to the creation, being open to its freely-made decisions, suffering when the wrong ones are made. God always remains redemptively engaged with all people on behalf of their reconciliation and fulfillment.

This new floral rubric reflects well your work, Clark, and that of John Wesley much earlier. I judge it a source of hope for contemporary Christian theism (2009, 12). It is not exactly your process approach, John, but it leans in the same dynamic direction, driven that way less by a modern philosophy like Whitehead's and more by a "relational" understanding of God's nature drawn directly from biblical revelation.

Elton: I've never heard of this *ROSE* analysis before today, but I resonate with it. I like the stress on human freedom and its relationship to who God is and how God relates. The possibility of evil, unfortunately, is the necessary price of this freedom that God gives us. God chose to create *persons*, not *pawns*, and "it is intrinsic to personhood that people make choices, and it is inevitable that, if people are free to choose, they are free to make wrong choices…. The determined world would have no meaning at all" (1996, 10-11).

The God who chose to create an "open" world filled with persons must have a divine nature that is at least no less than "person" itself. In your ROSE rubric, Barry, God created the circumstance that makes possible the emergence of evil, and did so by loving choice, even at the risk of the divine intent being frustrated. This "open" approach of love in no way compromises divine sovereignty, but rather reflects the very character of God and the nature of divine sovereignty. In my judgment, this is the proper balancing of the various threads of the biblically revealed divine reality.

Jack: I like your *person* versus *pawn* play on words, Elton. You have a little of the British literary DNA in you! I also affirm that sin was made possible by God giving us free will, "thus surrendering a portion of His omnipotence (a death-like or descending movement) because He saw that from a world of free creatures, even though they fell, He could work out (the re-ascent) a deeper happiness and a fuller splendour than any world of automata would admit" (1947, 126). As you said, John, it's an ongoing process of freedom exercised, wrong choices often made, and loving redemption pulling us forward.

Barry: This issue sharpened for me when a large earthquake struck the poor country of Haiti in January, 2010. One family on mission there is very close to me personally. They survived and served frantically as they could. Tens of thousands were suddenly dead. Soon a prominent Christian leader, one with a highly "classical" view of God, made a dramatic comment on his television program. He suggested that the earthquake may have been God's judgment since, generations ago, so a legend has it, Haitians sold their souls to the devil for his help in their achieving independence from France.

So, a natural disaster, mass death and misery, and an articulate fundamentalist Christian suggest that God controls the quakes and passes out horrible judgment on today's people for yesterday's evil choice made by others. Personally, I don't think so. That's not the God who is the Father of Jesus, surely not the Abba of Jesus whom you affirm, John.

John: Wow! That fundamentalist sure isn't me. The Haiti example is sad and sobering. My process approach to things helps get around an awful conclusion like that of this television preacher. I agree instead with one of the opening statements made today concerning the overarching importance of what a believer holds about God's nature and ways of working. After all, "Christian spirituality is the formation of life in response to the divine Spirit as that is known in Jesus Christ. The divine Spirit is God. Hence, what we believe about God determines our spirituality" (1991, 152). Our TV preacher friend is seeing a God I don't know—and don't want to know!

James: We must be so careful when speaking in public to avoid the temptation of saying what people want to hear or hearing a headline and moving quickly to put words in God's mouth. God's ways are not always our ways, and certainly not always in line with our preferences. John, do you see in the Bible examples of humans projecting themselves onto God?

John: Yes, James, and they get scolded severely for doing it. In fact, Clark, you and I have touched on this in our dialogues together over the years. We have found agreements and disagreements between us on the subject of Christian theism—and we put some of them in our jointly edited book *Searching for an Adequate God*. Our agreements are several, including a common willingness to rethink theism in a time very different from the biblical thought world, and our willingness to affirm God's "self-limitation" in relation to a free creation.

But here's a key difference I see between us—and it addresses your question, James. "Open" theists like Clark and Barry tend to draw a line that we process theologians think is unfortunate and inadequate. You stay very close to the biblical presentation of God as you understand it, seeing it freshly through your relational themes (which I appreciate) as you try to correct "classical" Christian theism (an attempt I also appreciate). But sometimes I think you stay too close to what is truly outdated.

As it appears to me, you two still affirm the biblical tendencies to anthropomorphism (making God in our human image) and fail to address the rational coherence of a theistic doctrine that could satisfy our contemporary world of post-modern thought. We process people, on the other hand, "suppose that theology can be convincing today only if it makes contact with contemporary scientific and historical knowledge" (2000, xiii). I would add from my own experience that a serious encounter with Buddhism can reinforce an interest in the philosophy of Alfred North Whitehead and its potential for adequate thinking about God (1991, 31-34). I know, Louis, that you've done just that.

Louis: Yes, John, I have, and I'll talk about that in our next conversation. But for now I want to hear Clark's response to what you just said.

Clark: Thanks. It's true, John. You and I both criticize "classical" theism in similar ways. We both want to resist the subjectivists who present God as merely "a symbol of our human values, as little more than a poetic expression of our own ideals.... I, too, want to replace a static view of God with a dynamic view, although it cannot be just any dynamic view but must be the dynamic theism of the scriptural witness" (1990, 95-96). I know Barry agrees with this "must be" of mine. We've not gotten involved in the Buddhist encounter, and have our hesitations about Whitehead. Even so, we know, John, that you agree with our criticism of "classic" evangelicals who dismiss as mere anthropomorphism the relational aspects of God that are actual biblical revelation about God.

For example, when God is reported in the Bible to have changed his mind or been impacted by our prayers or suffers over human sin, Barry and I assume that this reflects aspects of God's actual nature—they are not merely gestures to our limited understanding that are not to be taken seriously when it comes to who God actually is. At these points, we think we are more biblical than the evangelicals who cannot accept such assertions as factual.

And why can't they? Because these biblical assertions are contrary to their basic theological stance that God does not change in any way in response to human actions. What is predetermined is predetermined. By contrast, we say that God never changes in nature or intent, but does in strategy and action in loving and flexible response to us humans.

Elton: John, I'm sympathetic with Clark's view that the nature of some evangelical judgments about what is biblical are not acceptable. Your mentioning of Buddhism certainly adds a new dimension to this conversation. Having high respect for certain great thinkers of the past, and not having been caught up in today's openness-process dialogue myself, or dialogue with Buddhists, I'd like you to explain something to me.

Why is a philosophy of today like Whitehead's particularly satisfying intellectually to post-moderns, and why do you think it's better beyond just being in vogue at the moment? Philosophies do slip in and out of fashion, you know. I'm certainly all for "rational coherence." Still, it's not clear to me that moving to Whitehead necessarily gets us there in a way that's more biblical than the wrong reasoning of the classical theists we all seem to be critiquing.

John: Well, Elton, I want to be sure that one point is clear. Process people like me are very open to thinking in ways continuous with the Bible—we are not at war with the ancient as though there is no lingering wisdom there. In fact, just as Clark and Barry see relational categories prominent in the Bible, I see process categories and themes to be quite biblical. But I also am keenly aware of our dramatically changed times, so I think it best to express our biblical continuity by use of a new cosmology that makes it possible to recover Christian truths for many thoughtful people today. This new cosmology just happens to derive largely from the work of Alfred North Whitehead.

One distinction is helpful, I think. It's significant to note that we process thinkers often tend to come from and primarily are addressing different Christian communities than others of you. Open theists hope to free conservative evangelical traditions from the rigidities that impede their creative development and current relevance. Their biblical relationalism works well in addressing that overly conservative crowd—although that crowd is not easy to move from its rigidities. Process theists like myself are more often members of mainline denominations. In these settings, we are seeking "to give content and assurance to the wandering beliefs of their members" (2000, xiv). We're all trying to be effective intellectual missionaries wherever we find ourselves.

Elton: That's an interesting perspective, John. I surely agree with your call to serious thinking in the modern context. I have insisted across my career that "the vocation of Christians in every generation is to outthink all opposition" (1970, 126). Now, in relation to your own current thinking, your point about the differing constituencies being addressed could use a good illustration for our clarity. Give us one example of how you see Whitehead making an important difference in how some mainline Christians can think more seriously and relevantly about God in our changed times.

John: Sure. Several examples come to mind. I identified in one book a few contributions Whitehead has made to things like the fragmentation of contemporary thought, the ecological crisis, and the concerns of feminism (1991, 23-31). Another contribution of importance is the way Whitehead has understood God and God's relation to the creation. His thought, in my view, provides a more viable way of affirming God's goodness in a world of continuing evil, a way that lacks the paralyzing paradoxes and distortions required by other ways—including that preacher blaming the Haitian earthquake on God.

A central issue in Christian theism is one's understanding of *power*. Typical thought about power focuses on the ability to *force* others in some required direction. Whitehead worked with a different model of power. It was the ability and will to *persuade*. Persuasion, lovingly but intentionally exercised, is how God typically works. I think that's biblical as well as Whiteheadian.

Barry: On the question of divine power, John, the relational tendencies of open theists certainly have sympathy with your emphasis on divine persuading, as opposed to unilateral forcing. Where we differ some with you is our "classic" assumption that, by definition, God possesses all power, both to persuade *and* to force. Because of God's loving nature, a gentle and redemptive persuasion is what God typically expresses—but the force alternative is always there and occasionally used.

My friend Randy Maddox has said that John Wesley's teaching should be thought of "fundamentally in terms of *empowerment* rather than control or *overpowerment*. This is not to weaken God's power, but to determine its character!" (1994, 55). That's the thinking I follow, and I certainly think it's biblical (where we see God usually acting persuasively but also forcefully on occasion).

Elton, John is insisting that the church think freshly and seriously in order that thoughtful people today can see the credibility and relevance of Christian faith. I know that you have had much to say on the subject of careful thought in the service of faith. Please share a little from your viewpoint.

Elton: Yes, indeed. In my student days I encountered Rendel Harris at Johns Hopkins University. He had that ideal combination of the *warm heart* and the *clear head*. He was a meticulous scholar with an unabashed piety, "the Doctor" as we all called him, the great teacher who could "drop to his knees and pray vocally with the simplicity of a little child" (1974, 25). My mentor at that university was Professor Arthur O. Lovejoy, a man who cared deeply about his students, including not tolerating any ambiguity in their thinking and writing. I have sought to be a Lovejoy ever since.

Barry: May I remind you of something personal, Elton? When I was your student in 1964 at Earlham School of Religion, I felt your own deep caring for me—and, frankly, I also was intimidated at first by your announcement to the class that you "hated fog," especially when it was in the heads of your students! You invited our class participation for the coming term, but only after we had thought carefully and the fog in our heads had cleared. Your students that day—me included--tended to fear saying anything. Theology has its lingering fog, thus the continuing need for faith and ongoing theological work.

Elton: Sorry about the intimidating, Barry. That was a little of my Harvard background and rational bent. Sometimes I led with a demand for the clear head and followed up only later by showing my warm heart. Faith does remain a necessity. Reason cannot answer all questions. Nonetheless, our heads should never be allowed to drift in neutral gear. I'm glad that apparently I did scare some serious scholarship into you!

Now, back to our topic and to you, John. Too many personal diversions can create fog. I hear you saying that Whitehead is one of those great minds that can help Christians think well today. Lovejoy was one such mind for me. He helped me make logic central. "If Christianity is not true, it is an evil. It is not enough for a conviction to be comforting or to satisfy some psychological need" (1974, 33).

Our faith must stand the test of the best of modern reasoning. The church has the duty to think carefully about its faith, and help others do the same. To be effective in our confused world, the Christian must love God with all the mind. "When Christianity is demoted to the dispensing of soft drinks and the organization of recreation, the salt has already lost its savor" (1974, 96).

Tom: OK, friends, so much for that. Now, Clark, I want to hear you give us a quick sample of your thought on God. John said that process and open theists have been in dialogue, and we've heard his justifications for highlighting Whitehead. What have you been bringing to that dialogue table that might help us now?

Clark: It's been a fruitful dialogue, Tom, and both parties have brought much to the table. Barry's book *God As Loving Grace* and my own *Flame of Love* came out the same year (1996). We both highlighted relational themes and the importance of the classic doctrine of the Trinity in the Christian's understanding of God. So, here's a quick sample of my thought, using the Trinity as the central theme.

"If the Father points to ultimate reality, and the Son supplies the clue to the divine mystery, Spirit epitomizes the nearness of the power and presence of God" (1996, 9). This mysterious and marvelous divine reality leads Christians to believe that God is a community of love and mutuality. The inner life of God will always be beyond human comprehension; even so, there is a three-ness in it which was disclosed biblically when God saved humanity through incarnation (the Son) and remains graciously with us (the Spirit).

From this Trinity "we learn that the Creator is not static or standoffish, but a loving relationality and sheer liveliness" (1996, 23). As biblically revealed, the very essence of God's nature is relational—and the truly sovereign God wants to relate lovingly to us, even though we are sinners and there is divine risk involved. It's the nature of God's love and the wonder of God's grace that we're granted the freedom to defy even the will of a sovereign God.

So, Tom, that's the thinking I've brought to the table. I think my view of God is rooted deeply in biblical revelation and represents well the best of the "classical" tradition, and without perpetuating the static features that process theologians like you, John, and we "open" people find so objectionable—and unbiblical. While not growing out of Whitehead's philosophy, John, I think my thought communicates well with lonely and community-hungry post-moderns.

Tom: Agreed, with one key caution. While critiquing what has become "classical" for many current evangelicals, we dare not lose the consensual tradition of the faith that goes right to the heart of the Bible and the apostolic age and its foundational teaching. There we find that the Triune understanding of God gives us the best way to view the meaning of God's coming into the whole of human history and into our human hearts. You and the openness people, Clark, appear to be keeping and championing the classic Trinity doctrine.

As I explained in my *Classic Christianity*: "The simple act of baptism teaches, rehearses, and embraces the entire story of salvation. It attests to the church's attempt to view history synoptically, to grasp a unified picture of God in acts of creation, redemption, and consummation. Classical Christianity views the history of salvation as an inclusive threefold movement from beginning to end....

Universal history is therefore a history of the activity of the triune God: (1) Given all by the Father of all, the fall of humanity from its original uprightness is (2) redeemed through God's justifying activity in the Son, and (3) our faithful response is elicited through the power of the Spirit.... God meets us in history as Father, Son, and Spirit. This triune history of salvation brings together all the basic issues of Christian theology in a single wide-angle frame: creation, redemption, and consummation" (2009, 106, digital ed.).

James: Comprehensive and biblical, Tom, excellent. And here's another key issue that lingers among conservative Christians. It can be summarized by the confusingly similar words "pantheism" and "panentheism." John, you and other process thinkers have been accused of being at least semi-pantheists, people who virtually *equate* the world and the world process with God. You, of course, have denied this, and I think rightly so. As to the second word, your teacher, Charles Hartshorne, affirmed it. The reason was that panentheism suggests that, while God has a distinctive identity, the creation, and especially humans, have been freed to act as co-creators along with God. In the process, they contribute to God's life and are taken up into God's consequent nature, which is itself in the process of becoming. God is understood, then, as the one in whom all reality is gathering, so much so that, for process thinkers, it becomes difficult to conceive of God apart from God's relationship with the world.

I hope I'm putting no foreign words in your mouth, John. There is a clear contrast here, I think. Open theists like Clark and Barry separate from process thought at this point since process theology appears to eliminate an important aspect of the biblically revealed God. God is presented biblically as the *sole* creator of all that originally was, although now God is very much engaged jointly with us and the rest of creation. God can and should be conceived as both *prior to* and *separate from* us, although now actively engaged *with us* in the ongoing historical and creating process.

Many of us still insist that the God who prefers loving persuasion over brute force should also be known as the God who is not lacking in potency to create from nothing and finally achieve the divine will despite human sin and defiance. Persuasion is prominent, as Randy Maddox has shown was John Wesley's view, but power—understood as the potential of sheer force--also emerges on occasion as God relates to this free and fallen creation and eventually will judge it. The truly loving God persuades without having lost the capacity to bring about the divine will in the face of human sin. I have preached many sermons that took this for granted. I've heard nothing yet that encourages me to change my approach.

Clark: Let me emphasize this point of yours, James, and it's an important one. I argue this contrast as a key difference between open evangelicals and process theologians. The former affirm without qualification that God exists sovereignly apart from and in advance of this creation. We also gladly affirm that this loving God voluntarily self-limits in order to have meaningful relationship with the creation, especially with humans to whom the freedom of choice has been granted.

Again, we think of God as existing *apart from the creation* as well as now deeply involved with us *in it*. What we don't do, as process people generally do, is reduce theism to a "panentheism" where God and the world are *necessarily* interdependent and somehow overlapping, even in some sense shared realities.

Barry: Maybe a little theological history would be helpful. Two of our later conversation guests, Stanley Grenz and Roger Olson, joined in writing the significant book *20th-Century Theology: God and the World in a Transitional Age*. They reviewed recent theological history and found cycles of emphasis, first on divine transcendence and then on divine immanence, and then back and forth again. I am aware, Clark, of your concern that modern God concepts, including "process" ones like John's, seem to go too far to the immanence side, reducing God to a dimension of the world itself, thus doing an injustice to God's transcendence.

I'm also aware of the important caution issued by our mutual friend Delwin Brown. Reductionism is everybody's problem, he insists. "Conservatives" sometimes reduce God to the boxes of their own creeds and spiritual experiences. "Liberals" sometimes reduce God to a symbol of their best values or a poetic expression of their own social ideals. None of us should create God in our own image! So, here's advice I would offer. We all must be on guard, staying open, keeping theological matters in balance.

The fact is that we all perceive within our own range of knowledge, experience, and cultural influences. Even so, and as the biblical Christian tradition insists, God has become incarnate, joined our stream of human experience, and thereby chosen to be self-revealed, especially in Jesus. Therefore, we can proceed in our theological work, cautiously to be sure, but with a meaningful starting-point. That point, in an important sense, is the heart of the whole matter of Christian belief. Later we will have an entire conversation on Jesus Christ as the center of all Christian belief.

Clark: Brown is right, Barry. Quite apart from the problems of the "liberal" approach, I do see considerable reductionism among contemporary evangelicals on the conservative side. Theism for them is developed too much by use of ancient Greek categories, resulting in a wholly unchanging deity, absolute in power, unaffected by life in this world. All of us naturally tend to use available philosophic categories in our theologies, but such categories should be viewed tentatively and never absolutized—and that includes Whitehead, as I'm sure you'd agree, John.

I'd like to mention Delwin Brown's name again. He and I used to debate in public on these matters—we even formalized our discussions in the book *Theological Crossfire*. Delwin drew on the process philosophy of Whitehead, insisting that the Christian concept of God must cohere with the rest of modern knowledge, but he also added another piece of wisdom: "To say this, however, is not to absolutize modern knowledge" (83).

While some of Brown's conclusions seem to me to give too little weight to the theism developed within Scripture, I surely agree with him that "the life of faith as it manifests itself in the biblical tradition is in considerable tension with the technical structures that evolved in later traditions of reflective Christian thought" (89). My own theistic thought is detailed in my book *Most Moved Mover*. It seeks to identify the solid biblical foundation and then separate it from the later overlay of "technical structures."

Jack: We've heard John and now a series of cautions and balances to the process approach to Christian theology—and likely we'll hear more of the process approach when Clark Williamson joins us as a guest in a later conversation. But now I think it's time to yield the floor back to you, John.

John: Thanks, Jack. Many of us are aware that we do not live in the same thought world as the one in which the Bible was written. Thus, at least we process theologians are willing to adapt to a revised cosmology that makes it possible to recover Christian truths for so many thoughtful people today. Admittedly, we differ in an important way or two with our "open" colleagues. We have dialogued with each other in good faith and have been criticized sharply for doing so. The "liberals" accuse us process people of supposedly yielding to "fundamentalists." The "evangelicals" accuse Clark and Barry of scheming to smuggle radical process ideas into the conservative camp. Thanks, Clark, for once announcing this: "Together we say to the critics—we will not allow ourselves to be led by such fears" (Cobb, 2000, xii).

James: Let's do a little biblical reflecting. We humans obviously struggle with language and philosophy, and how best to speak of God in changing times. My instinct is to return to Scripture. Let me direct our attention to Psalm 19 where we learn some clear truths *about* God, even as we are inspired to respond in depth *to* God.

The psalmist reports in celebrative awe about how nature speaks a "thought-enlarging word of witness about the God who fashioned it all in our interest. But nature is not our only or our best witness to God. The Scriptures are a word *from* God." The psalmist understood this divine word as one of "testimony" (*edah*) and of "law" (*torah*), granting wisdom to the simple and direction for life. God's gracious Word is filled with "heart-inspiring, hope-instilling, life-sustaining promises, all given by the God who is worthy of our worship because he made us, and in love he meets our need for guidance, salvation, and a meaningful life in this world" (2000, 48). Again, what is God's supreme self-witness? It's none other than Jesus who came that we might have life and have it abundantly (John 10:10b). What a wonderful and mighty God we serve! That's the heart of the matter.

Barry: Thank you, James. Your wisdom is always so rich and warm, only one step short of being pulpit ready. And John, our thanks to you for being with us today.

Now, one final thing. I notice, Louis, that you've been rather quiet today. I know that there are signs at Gethsemani, your famous monastic home, that say "Silence Is Spoken Here." Be reminded that you can talk here and we'll never tell!

Louis: Don't worry about me, guys. I once referred to my early years as living like "a stray dog"—some promiscuous habits when I went sinfully beyond talking when I shouldn't. I came to practice and appreciate silence, but I also have done my share of talking, and certainly writing. Here's something I once wrote that I think brings a little application and closure to this conversation about God.

One of my jobs at the monastery was that of a forester. I became very sensitive to nature and have contemplated it's relationship to divine revelation. I once argued that a tree gives glory to God mainly by being a tree. For in being what God means it to be, it is obeying Him. It is expressing an idea which is in God and which is not distinct from the essence of God. In my view, the creation is reflective of God's nature and intentions.

We understand only in part, of course, but there are gracious avenues available for our greater understanding. We must honor God by being what God intended us to be—reflections of the essence of the divine nature that we see most clearly in Jesus Christ. There lies the true heart of the matter.

Jack: Good, Louis! When speaking of God, the fact is that our standard language fails us. Since God is bigger than our ideas and words, they should be more dynamic than static, somewhat like your *process*, John, and they should be love oriented and biblically faithful, somewhat like your *relational*, Clark, and your *apostolic* focus, Tom.

Let me further wrap up this conversation by a little of my allegory. This is a specialized language combining *allos* and *agora*, "something else of a similar kind" and "marketplace." Thus, allegory presents something similar to the subject needing clarification, but presents itself in a different marketplace of discourse. Changing the contexts of our language can be profitable in shedding new light. I did this in an early piece I called *The Pilgrim's Regress*. I included a reference to metaphor.

The fact is that God is so much bigger than our concepts and words about him. We have spoken of "classical," "feminist," "process," "openness," "TULIP," "ROSE," and other languages about God, and we've done so helpfully. And yet, as I once wrote, "Take not, oh Lord, our literal sense, but in thy great, unbroken speech our halting metaphor translate."

The great joy is that, despite our own halting speech, God accepts us, receives us to himself, and graciously translates our humble thoughts and words into what is appropriate and adequate. Praise to our wonderful God!

Barry: Amen! And thanks to you, John, for being our guest for the day.

QUESTIONS RELATED TO CONVERSATION #2

1. John Cobb speaks of a "modern context" requiring the whole church to launch a quest of theological reconstruction. What was that context in the 1960s? Did he judge properly? Does such a context, or another new one, still require reconstruction of Christian believing? How dependent is or should theology be on the prevailing cultural context?

2. What is said to be wrong with the "classical" view of God? Do the alternatives offered appear to be an important step forward?

3. Can you distinguish between the "classical" affirmed by Tom and the "classical" critiqued by John, Clark, and Barry?

4. Look again at the Grenz-Olson reading of theological history. Do you sense today too much emphasis on divine "immanence" at the expense of God's "transcendence"?

5. Did you get the significant difference between the proposed TULIP and ROSE models of God and their related theological stances? Which do you prefer—and why? John sees one big difference between them being how we understand "power" and how God uses it. What's the difference?

6. Do you agree with Elton that many churches today are not particularly God-centered, but are more clubs for human fellowship and general social betterment? If they are, is that enough? What could be done to change this?

7. Think about the final thoughts of Jack. Do they bring an appropriate humility to all of our theological reflections?

Conversation #3

DEPTHS OF THE SPIRITUAL LIFE

Biblical Authority, Mysticism,
the Holy Spirit, Pentecostalism,
Buddhism, Life in Christ

> In the perspective of biblical faith, life is a demonstration and manifestation of the holiness that the Spirit works within us. For the mystic, life is the cultivation of personal holiness—an all-consuming passion to make oneself holy. For the modern person, life is an exercise in human remolding or in social engineering (Bloesch, 2007, 131-132).

> Natural meditation means fully inhabiting the present moment. Meditation is finding yourself in that natural state of wakeful pure presence or lucid contemplation where you discover your authentic condition.... We call it the fourth time, the transcendent, timeless moment of nowness, the atemporal eternal instant—the essence of beingness (Das, 2009, 11).

> Authentic Christian spirituality . . . is personal life lived in union with Christ—a relationship with the incarnate and risen Lord through the power of the Holy Spirit, where his death is my death, his resurrection my resurrection.... Spirituality in the New Testament sense is not a moral program, not a set of rules, not a level of ethical achievement, not a philosophy, not a rhetoric, not an idea, not a strategy, not a theory of meditation, but simply *life lived in Christ* (Oden, 1995, 109).

Barry: Great to see all of you conversation regulars again. You are good and wise friends. Previously we have given attention to our individual paths to Christian conversion and the distinctive nature of the God toward whom we have turned in faith. Now we focus on the dis-

Donald G. Bloesch (1928-2010) for a long time has been a "middle man" in the contemporary evangelical community of Christian theology. An Indiana pastor's son, he received the best of formal education, including degrees from Chicago Theological Seminary, the University of Chicago (Ph.D.), and post-doctoral work in famous European institutions—Oxford, Tübingen, and Basel. From 1957 until his retirement in 1992, he was a professor of theology at the University of Dubuque Theological Seminary in Iowa. His productive professional career was capped by the publication of his 2005-2006 seven-volume systematic theology titled *Christian Foundations*.

Calling himself a "progressive evangelical," Don has sought middle ground between neo-orthodoxy and a "right-wing" evangelicalism, writing often about Christian spirituality in our time. His has been a prominent and respected voice in contemporary Christian theology.

tinctive nature of the lives we are to lead in light of knowing this God of the Bible through Jesus Christ.

Tom: Let me repeat what John Cobb, our guest in the last conversation, said well: "Christian spirituality is the formation of life in response to the divine Spirit as that is known in Jesus Christ. The divine Spirit is God. Hence, what we believe about God determines our spirituality" (1991, 152). That should get us started today.

What are the various goals and dimensions of the Christian's spiritual life? As we pursue the mission of faithfully incorporating into our very existence Christ's continuing presence and transforming agenda, we naturally raise questions about how we are to understand, value, and sustain our interior life with God.

Barry: Let me introduce our special guests. This is the first time for us to have two for one conversation, but the topic at hand is complex and our guests are so different from each other that, in this case, it seems wise.

The first is Donald G. Bloesch, an articulate "evangelical" Christian who has had a deep burden for our topic over many decades. In fact, so have all of us regulars in these conversations.

The second guest is Lama Surya Das, earlier in his life known as Jeffrey Miller. Jeff is not a Christian, the only non-Christian to be in any of our conversations, but he is knowledgeable of the Christian tradition and specializes in the spiritual life. His views should stimulate some interesting discussion among us.

Note the three quotations above. The first and third clearly reflect the biblical faith, while the other is much more the mystic model of spirituality. All hope to be highly relevant to modern persons. Addressing them together is surely a provocative way to launch our conversation. But first, please give attention to the two slides on our screen above the fireplace that identify our two guests.

Welcome, friends, to our conversation number three. It's wonderful to have both of you with us as special guests. Would any of the conversation regulars like to pose an opening comment or question?

Clark: I would. Don, you have spent years criticizing both the abandonment by liberals of traditional Christian beliefs and the sometimes ugly attitudes and habits of reactionary Christian conservatives. I can identify with that difficult double task. Is such an assessment a fair way of viewing your theological work in general?

Don: Well, Clark, it's fair. At times, the fallout from my criticisms has come very close to home. I've had to criticize my own de-

Lama Surya Das (Jeffrey Miller, 1950-) was born an American Jew in the state of New York. After the tragic 1970 deaths of student war protestors at Kent State University in Ohio, he went on a spiritual journey to find a more peaceful way to bring about needed social change. The journey soon took him to Tibet where he since has twice completed the traditional three-year Vajrayana meditational retreat. Now living back in the United States, Jeff is a leading spokesperson for Western Buddhism.

A poet, translator, and full-time spiritual teacher, Jeff's new name means "Servant of the Sun." He lectures, publishes, leads meditation retreats worldwide, and during the 1990s organized international Western Buddhist Teachers Conferences with the Dalai Lama. In 1991 he established the Dzogchen Foundation and Centers to further the spread of Tibetan Buddhism in the West. He is active in inter-faith dialogue and has considerable acquaintance with the Judeo-Christian tradition and its approach to God and spirituality.

nomination, the United Church of Christ, for some of its more liberal theological and ethical trends. On the other hand, for years I have carried a concern that much of American Protestantism has entrenched itself in a narrowly intellectual definition of doctrine, an entrapment that tends to exclude the mystical dimension of the faith—which is the intended governing element of the ministry of the Holy Spirit in all of life. I've been on an important and sometimes difficult theological and political journey.

James: As a former seminary dean myself, I assume, Don, that your sensitivity to particular theological trends somehow roots in your own seminary experience as a younger man. Tell us about that.

Don: Yes, it certainly does, James. I chose Chicago Theological Seminary for my initial graduate degree because of my church affiliation. I found there some upsetting things. There was an excessive amount of quite liberal theology. Several of the professors were calling themselves "neo-naturalists." They seemed more enamored with the philosophy of Alfred North Whitehead than committed to biblical revelation.

James: Remember that the guest in our last group conversation was John Cobb. We heard the name Whitehead often that day.

Don: Yes, I heard that and understand why a conversation about Christian theism would want to consider carefully Cobb's use of Whitehead. But it was a shock to me as a young seminarian. Anyway, while at CTS, my own church's seminary, I discovered another group, the "neo-orthodox" writers like Karl Barth. I was greatly influenced by their negative reactions to the local liberalism.

I soon determined that a crucial paradox must be honored in Christian theology. On the one hand, we must not sacrifice the conceptual truth of divine revelation in order to honor emotive or existential truth. On the other hand, we must recognize "the critical role of the *experience* of faith" (1992, 14). This is basically why, in my later years, I came to refer to my own thought as a theology of "Word *and* Spirit," in some conscious contrast to Karl Barth's "theology of the Word of God." My point has been that we must not overstress the *objective* pole of revelation in our reaction to the *subjectivism* of liberal Protestantism. Revelation is not grounded in mere feeling, to be sure, but the life of the Spirit is nonetheless central to all aspects of Christian faith.

Barry: I'm identifying with you strongly, Don, as apparently Clark and James are. I chose the same Chicago Theological Seminary for a doctoral program, but in my case only after my basic theological education had been done elsewhere (Anderson and Asbury seminaries). I too was struck by the liberalism at CTS, but struggled to be open to what it might have to teach me. What I found was a modest commitment to objective revelation and a high distrust of "spiritual experience."

It was the late 1960s that I was there and the CTS focus was heavily on the social relevance of the faith—Chicago and other cities were in chaos as the society was shifting its values and standards quite dramatically. Like you, Don, I had a conservative background that I wanted to defend in the face of "modern" theology and social ethics that seemed to carry with them only a thin layer of orthodox Christianity. I was being stretched, but was determined not to be stretched too far away from real biblical authority and life-changing spiritual experience.

Don: Sounds familiar. I eventually learned to unite the objective and subjective aspects of the faith, insisting on the reality of divine revelation, especially the Bible, while also highlighting the central role of the ongoing ministry of the Holy Spirit. In relation to the Bible, I concluded that "when the Reformers spoke of *sola Scriptura*, they meant the Bible illuminated by the Spirit in the matrix of the church. *Sola Scriptura* is not *nuda Scriptura* (the bare Scripture). It means rather that the Bible is our primary authority, but not our only authority" (1992, 193). The Spirit's illumination is a crucial factor, as is the steadying wisdom of church tradition.

Louis: Don, being a Roman monk, I suppose I'm the one to ask this. Are you supporting or critiquing the mystic spiritual tradition of Christianity?

Don: I'm doing both, Louis, although I'm not resisting much that you have stood for. I do want to highlight spirituality, certainly, but not much of what is associated with classic mysticism. In my view, the mystical way, quite reflective of our other guest today, leads a serious believer away from this world. Christian spirituality, based on the prophetic tradition of biblical faith, does not do that. "Those who adhere to the biblical worldview will seek not to forget or disparage created things but will bring all creation into submission to the high and holy God. Their attention is directed to the highway of holiness rather than the mountain of purgation or the stairway to a wholly transcendent perfection. God does not call us into the desert in order to escape the follies of the world. Instead, he creates a highway in the wilderness to lead us to a new city that will arise out of the ashes of the old. By means of this highway, the holiness and truth of God will find access to all areas of human life" (2000, 319).

James: It's obvious that "mysticism" is a word that must be defined very carefully. I know, Don, that you're not claiming that mysticism is completely wrong, or that the many sincere Christians who have sought the mystical depths of faith should not be respected highly.

An admirable example is John Wesley. He sought so sincerely for "perfect love" and was influenced by the mystical tradition of Christianity. But, as Robert Tuttle has shown (1989), Wesley initially accepted much of mysticism and then, Don, like you, saw its serious downsides and backed off some distance. Finally—and cautiously—he came back to some of its abiding values once the necessary theological foundations had been established.

Don: That's an excellent analysis, James. It's yes and no on mysticism, depending on exactly what's meant by it, and whether or not it's well-grounded theologically.

Tom: Let me inject here what I mean by authentic Christian spirituality, one that is biblical, theologically responsible, and deeply impacting on the inwardness of life, a "postmodern evangelical spirituality" if you will. It's a mysticism with ancient theological roots and transformative power. It's personal life "lived in union with Christ—a relationship with the incarnate and risen Lord through the power of the Holy Spirit, where his death is my death, his resurrection my resurrection.... Spirituality in the New Testament sense is not a moral program, not a set of rules, not a level of ethical achievement, not a philosophy, not a rhetoric, not an idea, not a strategy, not a theory of meditation, but simply *life lived in Christ*" (1995, 109).

So I agree with Don and James, and John Wesley, fountainhead of my own Methodist church tradition. It's yes and no to mysticism, depending on how you define the word and what substance lies at the heart of its goals.

James: These carefully chosen words I'm hearing call to mind Colossians 3:1-2. We are instructed there to be serious about living the resurrected life in Christ, being alert to what's around us, and seeing it from Christ's perspective. Christian spirituality is just this—because Christ lives, so do we in the power of his Spirit! Galatians 2:20 is the heart of Christian spirituality. It is no longer my fallen ego that lives, but Christ who lives in and through me. Can you tell, friends, that I feel a sermon coming on!

Barry: Well, Don, Tom, and James, you men speak eloquently of central biblical truth that does include a certain "mysticism." And sorry, James, that we haven't time for a sermon just now. We had better shift our conversation to our other guest, a meditation specialist who's likely to have a different slant on some of our thoughts on mysticism so far.

Jeff, I judge it fair to refer to you as a modern mystic. Bringing geography to your biography, one question is obvious. I thought Tibet was some magical land of ancient wisdom where foreigners are rarely allowed to travel. Am I wrong? And how and why did you get there, especially since you were reared in a middle-class Jewish family in New York? I didn't know that Buddhism in Tibet was all the rage in American Judaism!

Jeff: It's not, Barry, and the questions are obvious. It's a long way from New York to Tibet, and there's a considerable distance between Don, Tom, James and me, even though we are all deeply committed to spirituality. And yes, it was quite a trip from where I started to when my mother teasingly called me "The *Deli* Lama."

I grew up in the turbulent 1960s, was deeply affected by the student killings in 1970 on the campus of Kent State University, and found out that one of the students killed was a Jeffrey Miller—exactly my name. I attended a Zen retreat in Rochester, New York, hoping to find a non-violent way to contribute to a more harmonious and sane world. That eventually led me, not to Jerusalem, but to Tibet. I boarded a Kathmandu public bus in 1971. It was packed with people and chickens and headed out of town to meet my first Tibetan lama. I had begun seeking a meaningful and relevant mysticism because I hoped to address this troubled world and not run away from it.

Don: This is an interesting story, Jeff, so different from my own. Although I understand that you now go by the name Lama Surya Das, I assume you don't mind us calling you Jeff. You still seem to have that New York flavor and classic Jewish humor.

Jeff: Calling me Jeff is fine, Don, and I suppose I'm still flavored by my upbringing—we all are. When I was young, the North American public was just beginning to become acquainted with Buddhism, including silly stuff starting to make the rounds. Here's one. Did you hear what the Dalai Lama said to the New York hot dog vendor? It was, "Make me *one* with everything!" (1997, 26).

Tom: That's really funny, Jeff, but we all know that you take the spiritual life seriously, as do I. You really are hoping to "become one" with everything in some profound sense, as mystics typically do. Could you tell us your perspective in brief? I know we differ at crucial theological points, but I'm anxious to clarify how we nonetheless affirm some of the same things that lie at the heart of spirituality.

Jeff: I'd love to, Tom. First, let me be clear that one doesn't have to be a card-carrying Buddhist to long for spiritual insight and guidance—just look at the people in this room right now! None of us has a corner on truth. My Buddhist mentor encouraged me "to serve and apprentice myself to all sages, seekers, and saints, no matter what their denomination or belief system, for it is *the heart of the matter* that counts—the living spirit, not just the letter of the law" (1997, 42).

So, I consider myself in this conversation with some honored spiritual sages, like you, Louis, with your fine book *New Seeds of Contemplation*, and you, Tom, with your wonderful book *In Search of Solitude*. And we shouldn't take ourselves too seriously. "To be torchbearers in a benighted and violent world, we need to collaborate harmoniously, effectively, and with a spirit of mutual respect, genuine understanding, and openness" (1997, 381).

Don: I'm with you so far, Jeff. I'm missing the component of objective divine revelation in your general view of things—which I expected, but I also want to be respectful and open to hear you on your own terms, so please go on.

Jeff: You'll probably keep missing exactly what you hope for on the revelation front, Don, but thanks for listening respectfully. What I've already learned on my spiritual journey is this. "Knowing truth is Buddha; expressing truth is Dharma; embodying truth and living truly is Sangha.... The Buddha once said, 'There is nirvanic peace in things left just as they are.' That is the innermost secret refuge, the ultimate practice of letting go, the art of allowing things to be as they are. That is coming home in a spiritual sense.... Whatever we are looking for, it is always right here. *We are usually elsewhere*. That's the problem" (1997, 69-70).

Without reference to any god, I picture the human dilemma and its solution. Here's the true secret of spiritual living. "*You are*. It is your authentic life which can save you, would you only find and genuinely live it" (2009, 2). We are all looking for authenticity, satisfaction, fulfillment, well-being. Likely, everyone in this conversation today has and will see the defects and limitations of life lived on the terms of this outer world with its selfish materialism. The sole purpose of Buddhism is spiritual enlightenment or full self-realization. The path toward this is the one we humbly travel. The goal does not include "a dogma or belief system that we need to accept" (2009, 28).

Don: Sorry, all you conversation regulars. I assume it's OK for your two guests to dialogue with each other. I hear you, Jeff, and I admire your call for mutual respect as fellow torchbearers of spirituality in this troubled world with its many materialistic distractions. Even so, as an evangelical Christian, I need to draw a clear line between mysticism, your approach to the spiritual life, and what I call *biblical per-*

sonalism. My belief is that no attempts at achieving an authentic life can save us. That's God's doing.

I stand in the tradition of the biblical prophets and the Protestant Reformation, seeing prayer as "dialogue between a living God and the one who has been touched by his grace. God is reaching out to humanity and calling for a response of obedience, not humanity rising to God in order to become one with him (the mystical ideal)" (1988, vii). In my tradition, "biblical spirituality focuses not on the human quest for God but on God's search for humanity. The Bible teaches that the natural person does not even seek for God because sin has irrevocably bent the human will" (2007, 79).

So, Jeff, I rejoice in your deep sensitivity to the spiritual. Even so, I must be plain. For me, "so much mysticism begins in mist and ends in heresy.... Mystical awareness needs to be united with a fervent belief in the biblical message.... For many people today, tantalized by the new fashions in theology and religion, prayer is an experience of self-awareness by which one enters into the inner sanctum of the soul....

Evangelicalism, by contrast, signifies a type of religion where the knowledge of God is mediated through a particular historical witness to divine revelation and where the accent is placed on the service of God's glory rather than elevation into glory.... Mystical religion is ahistorical in that it deemphasizes or obscures the historical particularity of the biblical revelation.... The object of our hope is not escaping from time into eternity but the transformation of time by eternity" (1988, viii, 1-2, 105). Again, Jeff, I don't wish to sound arrogant, only plain about my view.

Jeff: OK, Don, you're certainly plain, and I don't hear you as arrogant and attacking. You make your case based on the assumptions of God's existence, humanity's fundamental sin problem, and God's coming to us humans, seeking us out lovingly for redemption. I don't share these assumptions. I've found them to be unnecessary for experiencing a rich spiritual life. I know well the Jewish belief tradition and that I've departed far from it. I sense no loss.

Don, I do have one question. May I take your assumptions to mean that, in your view, the Spirit of God is at work throughout humanity and among all the religions, potentially bringing a saving legitimacy to the sincere seeking faith of believers other than Jews and Christians? Is your loving God seeking everyone or just select "evangelical" Christians?

Don: I do think that there is a "hidden Christ," Jeff. Christ's Spirit is ministering everywhere. Even so, my insistence is that God's ultimate self-revelation is in Jesus Christ and stands in judgment over all religions, including, by the way, the institutionalized forms of Christianity. True religion exists only where and when it is purified by the holy grace of God revealed in Jesus Christ and administered through Christ's Spirit. Therefore, Christianity, rather than bragging about its own superiority over other faith communities, should be submitting its own ambiguities and inadequacies to the judgment of Jesus Christ.

Barry: It should be clear now why our conversation about God preceded this one on spirituality. Now allow me to push this conversation further by pointing to a key concept. A central word honored by both of our guests is "awakening." Don, your emphasis is that we can be awakened to true faith only after God in Jesus Christ has addressed us sinners and graced us with awakening faith (2007, 79)—John Wesley called it "prevenient" grace. To you, I know that this view is basic to your understanding of the biblical perspective and that of the Protestant Reformation. However, it appears to be very different for you, Jeff. Please explain how you champion the goal of "awakening" in your different context.

Jeff: Well, Barry, for Don and me some of the results of being truly awakened are similar, like self-insight, humility, love, joy, etc. But the assumptions surrounding getting to spiritual wakefulness are indeed different. I have no "god" assumption, with an enabling grace coming to me from outside myself. Humans tend to reify things and ideas, including belief in a god who supposedly is a being separate from our personal selves. In fact, as I see it, the real human goal is to meditate in order to become more sensitized to the immediacy of the moment. Once adequately sensitized, the spiritual mind within us begins to know itself and discover that "we *are* what we experience." The Buddhist "Dharma" is the way of "developing transcendental wisdom and loving compassion within oneself and eventually overflowing to others" (2009, 28-29). That overflowing, Don, makes it concretely relevant to this world.

Don: That's very clearly put, Jeff, showing the sharp differences between us. So many secular moderns go your way, often dropping even the Buddhist context, seeking only the spiritual "high" of the immediacy of the moment. They find themselves spiritually hungry in their secular worlds, so it's easy for them to gravitate toward a belief-less self-development program such as you describe. I grant that such a program is noble, can have significant psychological and even physical benefits for some, and can, as you say, eventually overflow in some betterment of social relationships. That's all fine, it's just so limited, rootless, self-centered, missing of the larger spiritual context of our little selves and planet and the big God who underlies and surrounds it all.

Jeff, you are like some Christian theologians who work with extreme versions of John Cobb's "process" philosophy/theology. For them, God is and maybe is no more than "the power of creative transformation." The focus easily shifts from God's prior and separate existence, transcendence, and grace-full incarnation in Jesus to our sense of human need for wholeness, creativity, and liberation, God or no God in the traditional sense. Being a committed Christian in an "orthodox" tradition, I gladly risk the possible sin of "reifying," as you would have it, Jeff.

Just one more thing. I'm pleased to affirm with enthusiasm Barry's book *Authentic Spirituality*. In a distinctly Christian context, being deeply spiritual is indeed a fundamental goal even though it may have various streams and emphases. For spirituality to be "authentic" in a Christian sense, it must have a theological framework that is biblically defined. Therefore, our chief human concern as Christians is to seek first the reign of God and his righteousness, "not by striving for our own security and happiness but by clinging to the promises of God as our only hope and recourse in life and in death. We are animated by the hope that we will find true happiness when we seek to give glory to God through self-sacrificing service to our neighbor" (2007, 150).

Tom: I also want to be most respectful, Jeff, as Don has been. Even so, I must say something about my own journey here and its outcome that is so different from yours. I took a trip into the world of pop psychologies early in my career and tried to blend them into understandings of Christian ministry. I finally concluded that a bridge would never get built between them "by an acquiescence of classic Christianity to the reductionist assumptions of psychology. Only when I learned to trust the classic Christian consensus on the care of souls did I see the way ahead" (2014, 150). And, Jeff, that consensus certainly stands on the assumption of God's existence and ministry among us through Christ in the power of his Spirit. That's my journey and firm conclusion.

Jeff: Understood and appreciated, just not agreed.

Elton: We were right, friends. Having both Don and Jeff as our guests today would certainly broaden the conversation! Let me add a little from my own past.

I was Acting Dean of the Chapel of Harvard University in the 1930s when I wrote my little book *The Essence of Spiritual Religion*. When it was republished forty years later, my judgment had not changed: "The supreme paradox of our time is that of the combination of obvious spiritual need with the failure to provide reasonable answers. It is part of our contemporary tragedy that, just when the world is becoming more aware of its need, the church is becoming less sure of its mission" (1936, 1975, x). I agree, Don and Tom, that to lose the God assumption of the Bible is to lose our identity and message as Christians.

James: You speak of "spiritual religion," Elton. What do you mean by that?

Elton: I mean that which is alive and not dominated by the formal, literal, legal, ceremonial, hierarchical, creedal, material, external, and traditional. The truly spiritual is actual fellowship with "a Power which sustains us in our finest efforts and aids us in our allegiance to ideal ends" (1936, 1975, 9). Religion is akin to poetry. "The poet goes beyond facts to meanings; he sees the world, not as something to be measured or even analyzed, but as something to which his whole being must respond.... Man cannot live by bread alone, and he cannot live by prose alone" (1936, 1975, 17).

True religion "is like falling in love; theology is like a treatise on courtship." Both are necessary, the relationship and the rational analysis. Theology has no substance, no life, no real meaning without the corresponding spiritual life. "We need great believers who are loving, and great lovers of mankind who really believe" (1936, 1975, 27-28).

Don: Quite a proper and powerful paradox you highlight, Elton. It's basically what I mean to say. We need the reality of the spiritual life, but not separated from the belief that gives it a reasoned framework in reality well beyond ourselves. Christian faith is far more than mere creeds; but, if creedless, as Jeff advocates, I say that it is only a subjective mysticism, that "mere mist" that I spoke of earlier. Christian spirituality, to be truly Christian, needs reasoned substance (theology based on divine revelation), and it also needs to be truly alive—a lived spirituality that builds on but rises above reasoned response to revelation.

Elton: That's well put, Don. I'm always advocating both *head* and *heart*. In the tangled world of religion, "our task is to look beneath this accumulated mass and discover, if we can, the genuine religion of the spirit which has existed in all generations" (1936, 1975, 1).

Louis: Jeff, I'm a committed Christian in the Roman Catholic tradition as much as Elton is among the Quakers, although our monasteries look a little different! You spoke of the 1960s as key in your own development. I also acted boldly in those turbulent times. Despite my monastic residence at Gethsemani, I managed permission for a wonderful tour in Asia. It was a spiritual pilgrimage of a lifetime. Let me testify to one powerful spiritual experience I had then. It's one I think all will appreciate, especially you, Jeff.

One of the significant moments of my life was my visit to Polonnaruwa in Sri Lanka. I was stunned by the colossal figures of the Buddha carved out of stone. I was "jerked clean out of the habitual, half-tied vision of things, and an inner cleanness, clarity, as if exploding from the rocks themselves, became evident, obvious" (in Forest, 209).

I once wrote a prose poem called *Hagia Sophia*. It begins, "There is in all visible things an invisible fecundity, a dimmed light, a meek namelessness, a hidden wholeness. This mysterious Unity and Integrity is Wisdom.... There is in all things an inexhaustible sweetness and purity, a silence that is a fount of action and joy. It rises up in wordless gentleness and flows out to me from the unseen roots of all created being, welcoming me tenderly" (1961, 61).

Jeff: There's a delicate beauty in your experience and words, Louis. I teach Buddhist meditation all the time, usually to Westerners, most of whom have never even heard of Polonnaruwa. But I've never put better than you just did the sheer wonder of rich spiritual insight. Obviously, you have found open windows into the spiritual world. I am so pleased for you. I gladly affirm and join you, apart from your Catholicism, of course.

Louis: Thanks, Jeff. It's all by grace, you know, *God's* grace as I would put it in my Christian setting. I know that we can learn from each other, regardless of our differing traditions. This spiritual journey of mine really began back in 1933 when I toured Italy and became fascinated with Byzantine mosaics. Through them I sensed Christ's gaze. My Christ became the Christ of the icons. He is reached not so much through scientific study, but through direct faith and the mediation of liturgy, art, worship, and prayer, and much of this is bound up with the Russian and Greek tradition that I was learning to appreciate. But icons or not, I had trouble making spiritual progress. Let me report just a little of the trouble.

I had an aversion to Catholicism and a problem with alcohol. Once I was a barker for a strip-tease show, and even fathered a child out of wedlock. When I left Europe for the last time in 1934, I was an unpleasant person—vain, self-centered, undisciplined, sensual, and proud. My spiritual journey grew in intensity during the early 1950s, my first years living at Gethsemani. My Abbot graciously gave me more access to the solitude I longed for by creating the job of forester. Access to the woods brought me a sense of relief and liberation that is hard to explain. My spirit flourished with the nurturing of God's revelation to me in nature.

Jack: I affirm what I've heard from several of us. Really *being* is crucial for true religious faith. So is really being aware of inward *brokenness*. Let me illustrate. You all know my bent to allegory. The other day the allegorical sense of the famous act of Mary Magdalene dawned on me. "The precious alabaster box which one must *break* over the Holy Feet is one's *heart*. Easier said than done. And the contents become perfume only when it is broken. While they are safe inside, they are more like sewage" (unpublished letter, November 1, 1954).

That's us—original sin tells us that something terrible has gone wrong with the species called humankind. No solution is possible without sorrow and repentance. It is necessarily the case that God is the one to whom one repents, the God outside ourselves to whom we are accountable. At this point, I'm much more with you, Don, than with you Jeff.

Clark: Louis and Jack, what both of you are saying is moving and powerful. While not all Christian believers are able to be monks, or necessarily have a strong "mystical" side to their personalities, like Jack, all do have to become broken. Like you, Don, I have thought and written much about the central place of the Holy Spirit in a Christian's life. Let me share a personal testimony.

I wrote this in the Foreword to one of your books, Barry: "I have valued doctrinal formulation but have been less sure-footed when it comes to issues of the soul. Fortunately, I was touched by God in many contexts of renewal, and the Lord has drawn me higher up and deeper into his trinitarian love, which embraces us all. I have been enabled to go beyond mere thinking and to become an intimate with Christ himself" (in Callen, 2006, 7). My brokenness has been transformed by grace into a wholeness that God intended for me. And I'm so grateful!

James: Wonder and intimacy with Jesus Christ are surely critical, but they are hardly attained easily, as I'm sure we all know. That's why I wrote about the discipline of meditation-prayer. I wanted to center attention on the work of faith, encouraging believers to think of meditation "as a way of enlightenment, as an openness to God in the depths of the consciousness, a process in which the wonder and engagement that we experience in life become doors into the presence of God" (1985, 37). In my view, meditation and prayer are natural partners. "Meditation keeps prayer thoughtful, while prayer sanctifies the meditation, claiming it for God" (1985, 38).

Your pivotal visit to Polonnaruwa, Louis, is an excellent example of what I mean. There are times in the higher reaches of prayer when the analytical functions of the mind become suspended. The experience itself is "so compelling that analysis fails, interrogation seems a sacrilege, and the only reasonable action is that of yielding oneself to the experience" (1985, 46). Occasionally, it's just a fact that one can encounter God in a way that transcends the need for words and speech, creeds and religious institutions.

Jeff: I track well with you there, James. The difference between us appears to be that one big issue, the prior assumption of a singular, transcendent being typically called God. I have in view the fulfillment of the self rather than the glorifying of any god—the assumption of which too often works to the destruction of the disciple.

Clark: Jeff, I hear you, appreciate your spiritual depth, and understand the caution you make. Even so, and without apology, I and James, and I think the rest of us, do indeed begin with that God assumption. I also sorrow over religious communities that trade on honest faith in God to the injury of sensitive and seeking believers—making God in their own image so that they can satisfy their own perverse desires, even at the expense of others. Nonetheless, I rejoice in my belief that God is, is beautiful, and is the source of my highest good and greatest joy.

As you can see, friends, this subject is very close to me. I wrote my Ph.D. dissertation on the Holy Spirit in the writings of St. Paul, and I have found myself working very closely over the years with scholars in the contemporary Pentecostal movement. However much we choose to critique some admitted spiritual excesses of that tradition, I'm with them all the way when their hearts cry out for the fullness and immediacy of God in their lives.

Louis: Let me make a typical Trappist suggestion. Maybe we should observe a moment of silence together. Clark, the weight of your comments deserves the chance to sink deeply into our beings. I'm impressed by the necessary journey that most of us have had to take. The depths of authentic spiritual life do not always come to us on short or easy paths. The word "pilgrimage" is in the title of your autobiography, James. And Barry, the title of your own autobiography speaks of the progress of a pilgrim, and your biography of Clark is called *Journey Toward Renewal*. The universal need for renewal of life and thought and the long paths involved in reaching it are our common experiences.

In my own case, my year as a student at Cambridge, with all of my moral depravity, yielded my autobiography's title. I took Professor

Bullough's class on Dante's *Divine Comedy*. I read my way to the frozen core of hell and ascended through purgatory toward the eventual warmth of heaven. It was my personal identification with the *Purgatorio's* seven-storey mountain of painful ascent that gave me my autobiography's title, *The Seven Storey Mountain*. The fact is that how we respond to contradictions, dilemmas, and paradoxes is pivotal to progress in our spiritual lives. Sometimes we just have to enter into the mystery of God and rest, even rejoice in the mystery.

Barry: I agree, Louis. My book *Authentic Spirituality* explores the Christian traditions, languages, and practices that try to describe and enable growth in the Christian spiritual life. Progress is not automatic or uniform or without pain, although there can be rejoicing in the mystery of God and in the challenges of the spiritual journey. Given these challenges, I'd like to comment briefly on the ministry of the Holy Spirit as understood in the Wesleyan tradition that Tom has represented so well.

Recent years have featured an emphasis on the Wesleyan "quadrilateral" (Scripture, tradition, reason, and experience). This quad has been misunderstood as meaning four relatively equal sources of Christian insight and authority. A better reading of it is that Scripture functions as the primary source, with the other three being necessary tools of proper biblical interpretation. I suggest improving this better reading even more by emphasizing that the Spirit of God surrounds and informs the whole process, inspiring Scripture originally and now illuminating its current meaning and applications through the right (grace-enabled) use of our reason, tradition, and experience.

Clark: You're very right, Barry. John Wesley was wise and balanced here—even though the actual language of "quadrilateral" is not his. Religious experience is crucial, but notoriously erratic if not grounded in good theology. "The heart does not supply us with new information, but leads us to a deeper acquaintance with the divine mysteries and a finer sensitivity to their timeliness" (1996, 13). Experiencing life in God is enabled by the flame of God that cleanses and brightens. Joining this enlivening and enlightening fire should be God's revealed Word which brings objective grounding and concrete wisdom to our experience of the flaming and pulsating life of faith.

Louis: Agreed, and that deeper acquaintance with God yields some demands on our spiritual lives that at times are difficult. For instance, my early thinking about a possible ordination to the priesthood caused me to struggle with the requirement of celibacy, a word that both fascinated and gave me cold sweats. Given the unfortunate character of my early life, I doubted that anyone would ever consider me fit material for the priesthood. I tried to be celibate, but failed. I repented and still journey on, committed, yes, but also conflicted. Our humanity is always with us on the journey.

I readily confess that I was so aware of my humanness, even in my later years at Gethsemani. I realized that we must learn to live without self-defeating concerns that can't face death. We monks are embracing death all the time, at least death to this world. We seek a freedom to which all monks, indeed all Christians, should be dedicated. The goal of the Christian life, and of mature spirituality, is self-abandonment that leaves us free enough from self-seeking to truly love God. We must not be troubled by the fears and regrets that a sinful self-absorption always brings. In some ways this, I think, is part of what Jeff is trying to say to us.

Tom: Likely so, Louis. Let me say this to you, Jeff. I see you as a noble and especially sophisticated example of the spiritual self-help movement of our day. "There is a hole in the standard shelf of books on self-help. That hole is waiting to be filled by classical Christian reasoning on grace. The spiritual formation popularizers have offered us centering without a center, meditating without a divine Thou, individual fulfillment without a history. . .strategies for personal growth controlled by ideas of human planning and convenience, but lacking plausible empowerment" (1993, 15). Forgiving and healing grace is essential, and it presumes a generous and loving grantor of the grace, God.

Elton: Granted, Tom, and I need to add something from my own Quaker tradition. Divine grace comes to us in many ways. The quadrilateral Barry speaks of seeks to be inclusive of all authority sources for the Christian life. While I readily accept the *heart* (Christian experience), and Tom speaks eloquently of the essential past (tradition), I have stressed that the *head* (reason) too often is missing in conservative Christianity. Beyond these, I now want to add the *incarnational*.

I first heard of the concept of the "sacramental universe" in my reading of William Temple's masterful Gifford Lectures presented at the University of Glasgow, Scotland, in 1932-1934 and then published as *Nature, Man and God*. I judge this work to be one of the premier intellectual achievements of the twentieth century, and I find great theological meaning in Temple's presentation of the sacramental universe. Let me explain briefly.

Recognizing that the center of Christian faith is the earthly appearance of Jesus, the incarnation, Temple affirms that ours is "the most avowedly materialist of all the great religions.... Christianity is committed to a belief in the ultimate significance of the historical process and in the reality of matter and its place in the divine scheme" (478). There is a critical conveyance of spiritual meaning through the material. Says Temple, God "renders Himself in a particular degree accessible to those who seek Him through such media" (485). This world is expressive of God by God's sovereign choice. The God who is spirit chooses to create a material world, and through its matter and historical process God intends to foster our awareness of and union with Himself.

Many Christians, much like Roman Catholicism, Louis, insist that particular material elements are the primary and necessary vehicles of the divine presence and grace (e.g., the Eucharist); others of us can honor that amazing presence without being limited by its exclusivity of location. Rather than select icons over in Italy that grabbed your attention in the 1930s, Louis, I think *the whole universe is sacramental*. "The gist of the matter is that a full acceptance of spiritual religion entails *the abolition of the secular*. There is no part of life that is necessarily secular, and our task is to see to it that no part is thus removed from the area of the sacred" (1936, 1975, 90). Now, for me, that's the heart of the matter of Christian spirituality!

Jack: Don, I think a little known aspect of your life illustrates well what Elton is saying. I'm told by one of your former students that sometimes you would host them in your home. You would pass out lyrics you had just written. They weren't to be words in a new church hymnal, just playful lines in country music style (I'm not really sure what that is). You then would proceed to play as they sang. The fellowship was rich and the words would lead to smiles and then serious conversation. Sacredness would infiltrate even a fun song of your origination.

Don: I haven't thought of that for some time, but I did do that and it was rich. God can arrive in any place or on any occasion if our hearts and minds are open enough.

Jeff: That's great perspective, Elton, Louis, and Don, so affirming of life. I know that you men worry that my spiritual emphases lack the necessary theological framework to support them, and you fret over my mysticism drawing me away from this world more than it should. Let me say at least this from my current understanding of spirituality.

"The second principle of enlightened living is *sila paramita*. Externally, it implies ethics, morality, doing what is wholesome and helpful rather than harmful.... Ethical discipline upholds purity and simplicity as a fulfilling standard of living, accomplishes good karma, and protects, inspires, and benefits others" (2009, 151). Going back to some of your words, Elton, I find this both universally sacramental and deeply incarnational, just not very theological.

James: Let me speak specifically in a Christian context again, this time about the practice of fasting. This spiritual discipline is a reaching out for the spiritual by a temporary suspension of the material. I view this in a "sacramental" way that is much more than giving up food. Despite the fear of many people that fasting is only a private sacrifice, a voluntary isolation from the normal stream of life, I disagree. I insist that it's a positive discipline that actually opens a person more widely and can be vital preparation for deeper living and broader public service for God.

At its best, fasting is more than abstinence. It's "an affirmative act; it's a way of waiting on God that tends to induce within us an awareness of the spiritual dimension of life. Fasting is not a renunciation of life; it is a means by which new life is released within us" (1985, 66).

Louis: Yes, James, I fully agree about the essential value of discipline in our lives of faith. Fasting and other spiritual disciplines help us die to ourselves and transcend the person trapped in self-centeredness and conventional social living. We must rise to the Christ-life that is animated by the Holy Spirit. And maybe even more should be said about how spiritual disciplines can and should impact our world.

We must affirm the spirituality of a Christian involvement in politics—I know we plan to talk much more about that in a later conversation. We who believe in the God of peace must work for an end to the madness of war. To be politically passive or yield to fatalism is to cooperate with the forces that lead to war. On the other hand, to rely solely on political activity to solve the world's problems is a mistake.

"Prayer and sacrifice must be used as the most effective spiritual weapons in the war against war.... This implies that we are also willing to sacrifice and restrain our own instinct for violence and aggressiveness in our relations with other people. We may never succeed in this campaign but, whether we succeed or not, the duty is evident" (in *The Catholic Worker*, October, 1961).

James: Absolutely, Louis. Engaging constructively in politics can be one effective way to exhibit the incarnational principle you mentioned, Elton. Let me restate my comment about fasting being an affirmative act by recalling comments that one of our future guests, Dietrich Bohnoeffer, wrote from prison to his friend Bethge immediately after Dietrich learned of the failed attempt on Hitler's life. It had been a plot in which he had been involved and for which he would soon be executed.

Dietrich argued that the essence of chastity, much more than the suppression of bodily lust, is the total orientation of one's life toward a goal. Being a Christian, his great goal, should be incarnational, less about avoiding sin and much more about courageously and actively doing God's will in this world. We might well think of a serious engagement in Christian spirituality as the full focus of our lives toward the goal of God's own life being alive in us and lived out through us.

Barry: I recall that the great Swiss theologian Karl Barth resisted an emphasis on religious "experience," fearing that it was a threat to the more objective substance of divine revelation in Jesus Christ. But even he, at least late in life, felt the need for a more adequate theology of the Spirit. Another prominent theologian who soon will be our conversation guest, Jürgen Moltmann, has distanced himself from Barth's early polemic against religious experience, just as Barth might have done had he lived longer. I think he would have liked Moltmann's book *The Spirit of Life*.

It now may be time for the church of the West to heed the long complaint of the church of the East, namely that the Spirit should not be confined to the church's margins and subordinated to the Son. The Father known to us in the Son is richly with us now as the Spirit. This is our source of life!

Jack: I agree with this emphasis on the Spirit. But, as I think we all know, it's a matter of balance. The protagonist of my *The Pilgrim's Regress* is John, a young man on a pilgrim quest. He encountered mountains to the north, Reason, and swamps to the south, Romanticism. We must find the appropriate concord between the two, avoiding a rigid legalism and a shallow sentimentalism.

John Wesley, a good Englishman I might add, worked hard at such balance, as is reflected in the title of his biography authored by Henry D. Rack, *Reasonable Enthusiast*. Faith's vitality and spontaneity range beyond mere reason, although, if true to themselves as God intends, they certainly are not unreasonable.

Another one of our future guests, the Englishman Geoffrey Wainwright, has written an excellent work of theology titled *Doxology*. He makes plain that serious theological work goes on best in the context of joyous worship of God. Spirituality and theology are each impoverished without the other.

Barry: Breadth and balance, head and heart, a quadrilateral, the mountains and the swamps, work and worship, all are crucial, and all are a problem if separated from the larger whole. Thanks, Jack and the other regulars, for this wisdom, and we all thank you, Don and Jeff, for joining us today and greatly enriching our conversation.

We'll talk much next time about how best to approach and do Christian theology. Allow me to close this great conversation with a little prayer that you, Clark, once used to begin a book of yours:

> Welcome, Holy Spirit, come and set us free! Let each one catch the living flame and be ravished by your love! Let our souls glow with your fire (1996, 9).

Questions Related to Conversation #3

1. Is there a meaningful and workable distinction between theology as reasoned substance and spirituality as the experienced life of faith? Are both necessary? Do they compliment or work against each other?

2. Jeffrey Miller uses the word *dharma*. Try doing a little word study. How does Jeff's word relate to *Torah* in the Old Testament or *Logos* used of Jesus in the New Testament? What about Louis' reference to *Sophia*?

3. Note the exchange among James, Jeff, and Clark about the Christian spiritual life and the necessity or lack of necessity of a transcendent God as the working assumption of the spiritual life. If a rich spiritual life is essential for a mature Christian, does the heart of this matter root necessarily in the existence and present ministry of a transcendent God known through biblical revelation?

4. Is Christian spirituality at its best a release from this life, a plunging more deeply into it, or what? Do "mysticism" and "sacramental universe" go in different directions? Is fasting a renouncing of the material or a greater opening to it?

5. Explain how this sentence of Donald Bloesch highlights clearly the major difference between the views of the two guests: "The object of our hope is not escaping from time into eternity but the transformation of time by eternity." Dare we as Christians become so open to the material—incarnational--as to engage actively in politics? See more about this in conversation eight.

6. Are we all on a spiritual journey, alternating between the mountains and the swamps, as Jack puts it in his allegory? Is the heart of the matter our managing to stay on course, valuing both mountains and swamps without getting lost in either?

7. Try to put in your own words what Elton means by saying that true religion is like falling in love, while Christian theology is "like a treatise on courtship."

Conversation #4

APPROACHING CHRISTIAN THEOLOGY

The Roles of Paradox, Philosophy, Spirituality, and Divine Revelation

> What we have in the biblical text is a *human* document, a product of daring, evocative human imagination. But serious readers of this text of human imagination regularly are recruited, in the process of being addressed, to the conviction that what is surely daring artistic human imagination is, at the same time, as act of *divine revelation* (Brueggemann, 2009, 16).
>
> There have been monstrous wars fought over small points of theology and waves of emotion about a doctrine's exact wording. When you are sure that you are exactly right, and theologians sometimes think they are, even one inch of variance by a competitor can be judged intolerable and bodies could start falling.... The church can be a wonderful and a dangerous place for the simple and sincere soul, especially one with an independent mind (Callen, 2015, 34).

Barry: Great to see you all again, good friends. Our topic today is the best way(s) to approach the large task and extensive field of Christian theology. Once we have a perception of who God is (conversation #2) and who we can come to be in relation to God (conversation #3), it's natural now to ask about how we should go about thinking God's thoughts after him. Put as questions: What is the task of Christian theology? What are the organizing principles of good theology? What is its authority base? How should we perceive and approach the theological task?

Clark M. Williamson (1935-) is a native of Tennessee and a 1957 graduate of Transylvania University. His graduate work took place at the University of Chicago, culminating with the Ph.D. in 1969. This educational experience included his being a teaching assistant of Paul Tillich's and editor of the third volume of Tillich's *Systematic Theology* in 1963. Ordained by the Christian Church (Disciples of Christ) in 1961, Clark pastored and in 1966 was appointed Assistant Professor of Systematic Theology at Christian Theological Seminary in Indianapolis. He became dean and vice-president of CTS in 1998. Referring to himself as a "conversational theologian," he has authored numerous books and articles, lectured on many college and seminary campuses, and was editor of the journal *Encounter* from 1968 to 1998.

Doing theology seriously will quickly get us into the world of paradox. Note the quotes above. The Bible is said to be a human text that nonetheless draws the conviction of being divine revelation. We who believe both sides of this paradox seek to derive doctrines from the Bible's text, sometimes hurting each other in the process. Let's not do that here today!

Allow me introduce our special guests, Clark M. Williamson and Henri Nouwen. A little about each is now up on our screen over the fireplace.

Barry: Welcome, gentlemen. Since we use first names in our conversations, yours works well, Henri. But Clark, yours presents a problem. Since we already have a Clark among us regulars, may we call you Will?

Will: Of course, Will it is. I've been called much worse and I'm glad that Clark Pinnock is among us. Clark, you're one evangelical I can resonate with in various helpful ways. And let me say something about the design of this whole process you're conducting as a group.

Your line-up of guests is impressive. I'm honored to be included, and I so appreciate the conversational approach you have chosen to take in probing the many dimensions of Christian theology. On occasion, I have called myself a "conversational theologian."

Barry: Wonderful. As we launch into a conversation concerning how best to approach the hard work of Christian theology, let's be reminded of something important. Many of our Christian brothers and sisters don't judge theology of significance for their Christian identity and life.

"Increasingly, the membership roles of the Churches are filled with people not particularly 'brand' conscious....Some of the most prominent religious leaders today are *therapists* more than *theologians*.... When new congregations are planted, often by sophisticated marketing techniques aimed at selected target groups, those who comprise the new congregations tend to be attracted by things quite other than a particular theological tradition, and maybe not by theological concerns at all" (1996, 52).

Clark: Will, I appreciate your kind words about me. We do work in real settings that must be taken into consideration. So, how do you see us best conceiving the task of doing Christian theology, particularly when many of our fellow believers aren't really that interested in the subject?

Will: I've thought about this very question all of my professional life, and I agree that the church people we hope to address must be understood and communicated with effectively—sometimes on their own terms. In short,

Henri Nouwen (1932-1996) is a Dutch-born Roman Catholic priest who became a prolific author on matters of Christian faith, ministry, and spiritual life. Ordained to the priesthood in 1957, he began immersing himself in the study of psychology, focusing on the relationships between psychology and religion, contemplation and action. Harvard psychologist Gordon Allport guided him to the program on religion and psychiatry at the Menninger Foundation Clinic in Topeka, Kansas. Then came decades of teaching at Menninger, Notre Dame, Yale, and Harvard. He became a pastor to pastors, partly with popular books like his 1972 *The Wounded Healer*. During his Yale years he published ten books and enjoyed four sabbaticals, the first in 1974 he spent in the Abbey of Genesee, a Trappist monastery in upstate New York. In 1981 he left Yale and lived in the slums of Lima, Peru, immersing himself in the "liberation theology" of his new friend Gustavo Gutierrez. A major turn in his life and ministry came in 1986 when he moved to the L'Arche community of Daybreak in Toronto, Canada. There he shared his life with severely handicapped people, no longer relying on books, lectures, and reputation for his self-identity.

as I see it, "theology is an ongoing conversation with ourselves, with others (for example, with Jews who also follow Abraham and Sarah in the way of faith), with our contemporary context, and with our tradition.

Theology is not the absolute Truth (capital "T") worked out in solitude from the point of view of someone perched on a mountaintop looking down on all the human beings struggling through the valley below. It is generated on the way by a community committed to walk the way of life and blessing faithfully through the terrors of history" (1999, 23).

My own theological work has been aimed more at the church than the academy as such. Unfortunately, "some theologians write as though they would be offended should anyone understand them!" (1999, 2). Please let me add that Henri, my fellow conversation guest today, is quite the exception to my criticism of overly-abstract theologians.

Henri, you have been so vulnerable personally, so transparent in your writing and speaking. I think that you are both a disturbing and a particularly hopeful mirror into the inner selves of struggling spiritual beings today.

Henri: Thank you, Will. If you're right, only God is to be praised.

James: I appreciate so much how both Will and Henri have carried on their lives and ministries with an intentional focus on clear and effective communication with the church—something dear to us preacher/scholar types. Will, please elaborate further on how you conceive of Christian theology and its main task in church life today.

Will: Gladly, James. By the way, I love to hear you preach! Now to your question. I think that the best theology strikes up a serious conversation "between the Christian scriptures and tradition, on the one hand, and the context in which we live on the other.... Conversation becomes the controlling metaphor, the way of approach to all other matters" (1999, 3).

Naturally, then, I'm very affirming of what's being attempted in this set of conversations that you seven are staging. And what a range of conversation partners you're inviting to join you over these eleven weeks. Already here have been Rosemary Radford Ruether, John B. Cobb, Jr., Donald G. Bloesch, and Lama Surya Das. A diverse and daring group like that says much about your openness to lively conversation and serious searching. I should point out that John represents a group of process thinkers with whom I've been conversing appreciatively for a long time—as have you, I think, Clark.

The church must finally learn something important in order to build bridges and advance the truth in dramatically changing times and a rapidly shrinking world. Fellow believers, whether of other Christian traditions or outside faith communities, are not "objects" for us to talk *about*—and often we do such objectifying and depersonalizing. Our sisters and brothers are live "subjects" *with whom* we should have profitable relationships. That clearly should include the "post-Shoah" community.

I've had many enriching conversations, and with one principle always relevant. We should not come to idolize our own ideas or absolutize our individual spiritual experiences and traditions. We should come to speak honestly, listen carefully, and learn gladly. That's exactly how I have come here today to continue doing my theology with you good brothers.

Jack: Will, maybe I've spent too much time locked away in the English academy or spinning tales way off in Narnia somewhere. I admit to not being acquainted with the term "post-Shoah" as a type of Christian theology. Help me here.

Will: Sure, Jack—and I would say with great appreciation that you, a real academic in my view, have not been guilty of the "ivory tower" problem. You have been a great example of encountering a wide world of people and ideas and generating creative communication with diverse publics in our time. Now to your question.

Post-Shoah means much the same thing as "post-Holocaust." It's an attempt to be in conversation with the tragedies of the contemporary Jewish community as we seek to develop our own Christian theologies. In 1993 I wrote *A Guest in the House of Israel* to challenge churches and theologians to become aware of the inherited ideology of anti-Judaism that has distorted the whole Christian community. I think we can hardly proceed in doing our theology without dealing head-on with this corrosive inheritance of ours.

Clark: The truth is, Will, that Jack wasn't the only one here who didn't know what "post-Shoah" was. Now that we both know, please go on explaining how you approach Christian theology.

Will: Happily. Since Paul Tillich isn't one of your scheduled conversation guests, I'll let him speak a minute. It was from him that I first learned that theological statements are answers to critical life questions about how we understand ourselves in relation to God, Christ, the kingdom of God, and so forth. Theological statements can't be separated from who and where we are as humans. If they are, they will have no meaning.

And the questions we humans ask change over time. Tillich identified the deepest questions being asked and answered by the early church (death, sin, and idolatry, each answered by Christ as the life, light, and redeemer of the world). Martin Luther's cry, "How can I find a gracious God?" focused on questions about guilt and condemnation, and it brought forth the answer of the sixteenth-century Reformers-- justification by grace through faith.

In our time, other issues have pushed themselves to the forefront of our theological conversations. Tillich saw these newer "religious" questions as emerging from anxiety over our modern feelings of emptiness, meaninglessness, despair, and estrangement. Therefore, conversations between our deepest questions and the answers available in the Christian tradition lie at the heart of the theological enterprise.

Elton: Conservatives are always quite nervous when theological work does not begin with the assumed certainty of divine revelation, but rather within our life experiences, concerns, and questions. Their assumption is that our having fallen into sin has thoroughly perverted our question-asking and answer-hearing ability. The difficult issue, then, it seems to me, is not so much focusing on life questions, but on how we go about being sure they're the right ones. Maybe more difficult still is determining how we can come up with the right answers, the clearly "Christian" answers.

Will, your famous mentor seems to represent both of the main options at the same time. First, Tillich sounds like he's going to follow one path and then actually follows the other. His stated intent is to apply the content of the Christian faith as answers to the questions people are asking today, linking revelation and relevance—always the twin tasks of theological work. Tillich's method of *correlation* sounds for all the world like an imaginative conservative theologian. But this is hardly how he really did his theology.

What I see Tillich actually doing is finding the needed answers in the arenas of modern existentialist and idealist philosophy, relying only marginally on biblical categories. The result easily becomes moderns asking and answering themselves on their own terms, with biblical revelation only a thin covering that supplies a little of the historical context and language.

Tom: I admit my own guilt here, Elton. Before the mid-70's my covering of biblical revelation was thin indeed. I was doing theology "on the hidden premise of four key value assumptions of modern consciousness: hedonic self-actualization, autonomous individualism, reductive naturalism, and moral relativism.... Now I preach less about my own sentiments and opinions and more from testimony canonically received and grasped by the believing community of all times and places, trusting seed will bear fruit in its own time and that the word will address these hearers without too much static from me.... Once hesitant to trust anyone over 30, now I hesitate to trust anyone under 300" (*Christian Century*, Dec. 12/'90).

Jack: OK, it sounds like Elton and Tillich are two heavyweights ready to slug it out, with Tom clearly in the conservative corner. I want to know where you are, Clark. Given your major concern about his kind of theological work, tell us how you see the methodological options in theology.

Clark: My ideal approach can be understood only if first the two competing options are seen clearly. Let me explain them. They are what I call the "Progressives" and the "Conservatives."

> **Progressives** ("liberals" if you prefer, Paul Tillich included). Their central intent is to respond with integrity and as much innovation as necessary to the fresh challenges to the faith being presented by the present time. They are ready to "update" theological categories and language, even introducing far-reaching changes to some of the faith's classic substance as judged appropriate in light of modern knowledge and circumstances. Theology is "from below," emerging upward from the cultural contexts of the theologian's time and experiences. The danger, of course, is the loss of a distinctively Christian identity in an all-out pursuit of relevance.
>
> Looking at our line-up of conversation guests, I would name two progressives. For Rosemary Radford Ruether who's already been here, theology is rooted in human experience. Given her identity and experience as a woman, she judges that theology should draw heavily on the insights, concerns, and reform agendas of feminism.
>
> For John Hick, to be with us later, the contemporary context which guides his work is religious pluralism. The progressive assumption of Hick is that "theology must learn to center itself on God, rather than on Christ, and learn to regard the other faiths as honest responses to the one God of us all.... God is the reality behind all religions" (1990, 20). This approach seems particularly relevant today, although it may forfeit much of essential Christianity in the process by devaluing the finality of Jesus Christ.
>
> **Conservatives** (particularly "fundamentalists" like Hal Lindsey who will be with us later). Here is a sharply contrasting method, theologians with the central intent of protecting and maintaining the heaven-given deposit of God's Word as revealed in the inspired Bible and captured in the great creeds and sometimes the classic authority structures of the historic church. Established authority is highlighted, be it

the Bible held up by many Protestants as the last word or the church and infallible pope of Roman Catholicism.

All conservatives insist that God's grace is with us to ensure the preservation of God's truth and its global proclamation. Theological giants like Karl Barth, or more recently Carl F. H. Henry, different as their emphases and settings may be, are both clear conservatives featuring deductive and exegetical methods, drawing from and unpacking the meaning of an established authority source believed to yield unchanging truth relevant for all times. Whatever our current religious questions, the eternal answers are unchanging.

Jack: Your two types are clear enough, Clark, and we've planned well in having both types represented among our guests. But where are you? Likely you're not either method exclusively. Maybe few ever are.

Clark: One book of mine titled *Tracking the Maze* was meant to help with this. There seem to be two main impulses in Christian theology, one *apologetic* and one *dogmatic*, and you're correct that they are not mutually exclusive. We all hope to hold substantial beliefs with deep roots (the dogmatic) and engage our world convincingly on their behalf (the apologetic).

Unfortunately, these impulses tend to pull away from each other, especially in times of major social change. When they do, there are always "moderates" who hope to establish a meaningful middle ground. I suppose I'm one of them, a theologian claiming that "the achievements of the past can be respected while the ongoing work of reformation can proceed" (1990, 72).

A good example of a moderate is Donald Bloesch who was with us last time. He rightly criticizes theologians who view the work of theology as little more than a useful reflection on human experience without managing to provide conceptual or rational content to the object of faith (1992, 11). On the other hand, he also is unsatisfied with the theological right (fundamentalism) that identifies quite directly the text of the Bible with propositional revelation. Moderates always seem to have these opposing extremes to deal with.

Will: Yes, Clark, the rightness surely is in a careful combination of the two impulses. I personally think that Tillich was being your "moderate" with his method of "correlation." I judge that "we are to carry the scriptures with us as we walk; and, with their help and the inspiration of the Holy Spirit, we are to wrestle with them in relation to the contexts, promises, and difficulties of our times" (1999, 97). I guess, Clark, that approach also makes me a moderate along with you.

Barry: Thanks, Will and Clark, for lots of good input. Now we had better move on with our second guest of the day. Henri, let me suggest that your approach to Christian theology is different from the usual.

We typically encounter theologians who begin their work by establishing the sovereignty of God, or a particular philosophic principle, or even a personal or political agenda that then dominates all that follows. In your case, would it be fair to say that you begin with the complexity, even the delicacy and richness of *paradox*? Are you also a moderate, but of a different sort?

Henri: Yes, Barry, it would be fair to say that I begin with paradox. As to the "moderate" business, that's not a category I'm used to, so let's allow the group to answer that later.

Barry: That's fine, Henri. We don't want to force you into someone else's box. Go ahead on your own terms.

Henri: Thanks. First, let me say that, in Clark's terms and as a loyal Roman Catholic myself, I appear to belong to the relatively conservative side of things. Still, as I expect you'd agree, Louis, as a fellow Roman Catholic, that you and I both have been on active "reformist" journeys. Maybe that makes us something like "moderates," hopefully not "protestants"! I'm assuming, gentlemen, that a little humor never hurt the theological world.

Now allow me to report on the paradox focus. I wrote the introduction to the 1980 edition of Parker Palmer's book *The Promise of Paradox*. He had given up a large salary and moved away from a successful career to find true community, accepting paradox with humility. I wrote about Palmer with great appreciation: "He has challenged me by his own decisions to keep moving to unknown fields without apprehension or fear. He has taught me to live boldly and freely" (xii).

Our lives get filled with contradictions, dilemmas, and paradoxes that frustrate, irritate, and often discourage us. I sometimes think that I've experienced more than my share. We then come to matters of theology from the matrix of this malaise.

Have you ever been at home and felt homeless, or maybe were popular and still felt lonely and unfulfilled, or were a believer who just couldn't shake the doubts? Such things can paralyze us or, and this is a paradox, they can "bring us into touch with a deeper longing for the fulfillment of a desire that lives beneath all desires and that only God can satisfy" (1997, April 20). If we choose the positive path, then our very interruptions can become our opportunities.

James: Are you saying, Henri, that a wise approach to Christian theology includes a careful analysis of our own spiritual journeys that have faced dilemmas and life's paradoxes? Is our theology tied closely to our spiritual experiences?

Henri: Yes, James, I am and they are. Let me explain a little about my own often-troubled experience. I eventually managed to see my personal interruptions as invitations to previously unexplored arenas of spiritual experience. I saw the dying seed rushing into new life and soon to be a new plant full of fruit growing just for me.

I joined Palmer in embracing the promise of paradox, the mysterious but fruitful cohering of opposites in our lives. This, I admit, is an unusual kind of theological method, but one rich with potential. If you really want to know God, you should study the lives of the saints, not merely your own. Get in close touch with those who have fallen in love with God. Having said that, there is an obvious caution. When we hope to hear God speak, we risk our own wounded selves speaking to us instead, parading as God's voice. So we must be careful here.

Tom: It probably would help us to really understand your point, Henri, if you would give an example from your own life. For instance, how about your life at the L'Arche community of Daybreak in Toronto, Canada? Didn't you discover there the paradox of a divine light when others were seeing only clouds of darkness?

Henri: Absolutely. I decided to give myself to caring for others, especially those virtually helpless. This brought me back to paradox and how best to think about life, faith, and approaching Christian theology. "The cross is the main symbol of our faith, and it invites us to find hope where we see pain and to reaffirm the resurrection where we see death.... We should trust that every moment of our life can be claimed as the way of the cross that leads us to new life" (1992, 40).

Louis: Let a lowly monk join you, Henri. I say that we shouldn't live our fragile little lives trying to earn credits in the divine treasury. All is by God's grace. But I'll take a bit of credit here anyway. I'm pleased, Henri, that Parker Palmer so helpfully instructed your life. At an earlier time, my own experience and thought had impacted him. I was a monk committed to solitude, and yet I wrote some sixty books and, say some, became a patron saint of political activists resisting racism and militarism.

How about that? I was a monk behind walls leading activists outside the walls! In the midst of my many personal contradictions, I found the grace of God at work. "I have had to accept the fact that my life is almost totally paradoxical.... It is in the paradox itself, the paradox which was and is still a source of insecurity, that I have come to find the greatest security" (1974, 138).

Here's an example from my life. I once published a journal of my early years as a monk, influenced by the Jonah sign that Jesus promised. My life has been particularly sealed with this sign because, like Jonah himself, "I find myself traveling toward my destiny in the belly of a paradox" (1953, 11). And yet, by God's grace, I travel on in the midst of it all, even propelled forward by it.

Henri: Well, Louis, except for today you and I have met only one time, but I'm profoundly in debt to you anyway. You Trappists have been so kind to me. For instance, you may know that I spent the last half of 1974 at the Abbey of Genesee, your order's monastery in upstate New York. It was there that I confronted directly my conflicted inner life. I told about my struggle and healing in *The Genesee Diary*. I too was in the belly of a paradox, but God sustained and nurtured me even there. Maybe good theology comes only from within the belly.

Jack: Let me testify here, and I'll do it before Elton has a chance to gloat over another Quaker being so influential—I assume you all know that Palmer is a Quaker, and before Henri and Louis go too far with their mutual admiration and belly metaphor. I once heard you say, Elton, "You don't count Quakers, you weigh them!" Well, I admit that you and Palmer and several others have been pretty heavy! Now on to our guest.

Henri, when you speak of lives filled with contradictions and paradoxes, you need to know that I came to faith out of the matrix of such a malaise. I had the problem of developing a worldview that would finally satisfy both sides of my divided personality. When young, I seemed to have two hemispheres of my mind, intellect and imagination.

I was trapped between an imagination that gloried in nature and myth and an intellect that at first discounted everything as a meaningless tale told by an idiot. Later, after a better sorting out of things, I decided that imagination generates metaphors and myths to convey our understandings of the world, and intellect analyzes the products of imagination to determine how well they correspond to otherwise known reality. The good thing is that imagination and intellect turn out not to be hurtfully competitive, just like you point out about paradox and Christian theology, Henri. They can be graciously complimentary.

Let me say just a little more before Elton jumps in—I can see him over there dying to stand and talk. "If Christianity was something we were making up, of course we could make it easier. But it's not. We cannot compete in simplicity with people who are inventing religions. How could we? We are dealing with Fact. Of course, anyone can be simple if he has no facts to bother about" (1960, 129). Therefore, mystery, paradox, and the need for faith are givens of our human existence, and also should be well represented in our theology.

Elton: Thanks, Jack, for recognizing us "heavyweight" Quakers. We've been called many less complimentary things. I titled one book *A Place To Stand*. An outcome of "more than forty years of mental struggle" (7), it represents my trying to say something important for the assistance of "the ordinary seeker who is trying to be intellectually honest" (9).

I think that at least one thing about my struggle is important for approaching Christian theology. I'll put it simply, and aim it mostly at your "progressives," Clark. One must be determined to speak meaningfully to the present age *without* being "over-impressed by it" (7). I guess that classes me as a "moderate."

Tom: Great point, Elton. Anyone not engaged with today can hardly be an effective theologian for our times. Nonetheless, to be an effective Christian witness requires a Christian message rooted in more than the thought fads and religious experiments currently on the scene. We have a real message deeply rooted in a real history, one well tested by a long tradition. There is a wonderful yesterday waiting to impact a hurting today.

Elton: Yes, yesterday is full of rich and still relevant wisdom. There are many great Christian minds of the past, like Blaise Pascal. He hoped to tell the thoughtful seeker how he had found a center of stability in the midst of his intellectual perplexity. My goal has been much the same. The usual plan in developing a theology is to begin with an extended discussion about the existence and nature of God. I suggest a more experimental approach, focusing on the historical reality of Jesus. I call on serious seekers and beginning theological students to do something daring.

Dare "to live with the Gospels every day for a solid year. . .it may change your life. Christ's first followers were drawn to him before they knew who he was.... Pascal's defense of the Christian faith is a powerful one, but he well understood that neither his nor any other approach could make headway with those who were afraid to be open-minded about Christ. 'Men despise religion,' he said. 'They hate it and fear it is true'" (58).

If Christ turns out to be trustworthy, then God really is, and is really like Jesus. Learning that much is a stable base from which to live the life of faith and probe all other theological issues, no matter how paradoxical.

Tom: Yes, and the great minds of the early Christian centuries reflected carefully on the God who really is just like Jesus. Doing good theology today pays close attention to this treasury of ancient wisdom.

Henri: There's much wisdom in what you men are saying. Pascal named and worked with many paradoxes, even using paradox to highlight core Christian truths. For instance, he once announced that there is nothing so much in conformity with reason as the rejection of the ultimate adequacy of reason. That's a paradox dripping with wisdom!

Let me put this in personal terms. I have taught in a few of the great academic institutions of the world—Notre Dame, Yale, and Harvard. I value the life of the mind, obviously. In approaching Christian theology, however, I have learned something that sounds like reason rejecting reason, although it isn't, not really. Let me try to explain. I'll have to use reason, of course, to point to what surpasses reason.

"If there is any focus that the Christian leader of the future will need, it is the discipline of dwelling in the presence of the One who keeps asking us, 'Do you love me?'... It is the discipline of contemplative prayer.... The central question is, Are the leaders of the future truly men and women of God?... The original meaning of the word 'theology' was 'union with God in prayer.' Today, theology has become one academic discipline alongside many others.... For the future of Christian leadership, it is of vital importance to reclaim the mystical aspect of theology so that every word spoken ... comes from a heart that knows God intimately" (1989, 28-30).

James: Beautifully put, my brother. The role of reason in our theological work must be related to and even grow out of our spiritual experience. To know God well with our heads requires knowing God intimately with our hearts.

Henri: As a former seminary dean, James, I'm sure you know this well. Being prepared to minister for Christ requires both a disciplined brain and a matured relationship with God through Christ. That's a tough dual assignment for any graduate school of theology to accomplish.

This mystical aspect is why the curriculum of a quality theological education necessarily involves a primary focus on the *spiritual formation* of ministerial candidates. To understand Jesus requires getting acquainted with him very personally. I presume this is why your group conversation last time focused on the spiritual life. Apart from that, the doing of theology is merely an academic exercise, reason trying to comprehend what goes beyond the reach of mere reason.

Tom: As I reflect on the later part of my life, I see one great paradox. Christianity in the West has tended to send missionaries to "dark" Africa, supposedly so backward a place in every way. And yet, I now have well documented that out of Africa came Christianity's most brilliant early intellects, Tertullian, Cyprian, Clement, and Origen.

And here's another paradox. My life has been so absorbed in teaching and scholarship and writing, and yet more recently I have found great growth and joy inwardly through practicing ancient personal disciplines, finally writing *In Search of Solitude: Living the Classic Christian Hours of Prayer*. The importance of spiritual formation has been lacking in many modern seminaries with their excessive commitment to the academy as a top priority.

Barry: There's no doubt in my mind that people today must get more comfortable with paradox when they approach Christian theology. The intent of my *Caught Between Truths* is to seek theological balance, hold together what should not be separated, and think and believe both straight and whole (a disciplined and generous orthodoxy). When the fullness of truth is found in paradox, a pairing of parallel teachings, the challenge for us is obvious.

We must have the patience to avoid abortive choices and recognize and even celebrate being caught *between* truths. There's a lot of wisdom in a little humility. And that includes Tom pointing us back to the classic Christian tradition and my recalling the Old Testament theological themes that are basic to any real New Testament understanding (2015). Contrary to the assumption of our capitalistic times, the newest car model isn't necessarily the surest transportation that we must have in order to be happy.

To the extent that we go back appropriately in order to go forward wisely, "the church will become more of a foretaste of God's *shalom*, a welcome alternative to the destructive dividedness of our world.... We are to rejoice in the goodness of the gracious God who is both biblically revealed and yet beyond our full knowing. To be caught in this *knowing-unknowing* is to be human; to grasp it by faith and live it to the full is to be blessed forever!" (2007, 13, 136). And the greatest of all paradoxes, the heart of Christian believing, is the God-man, Jesus. As a group, we will be addressing this ultimate paradox in our next conversation.

Clark: I like the honesty and humility that's characterizing this conversation. These are admirable qualities that I've found sadly lacking in some circles of evangelical theologians. They function mostly as stalwart protectors of the truths they're convinced they know for sure, truths not to be questioned by others. Let me refer to my friend Stanley Grenz who will be our guest later and, happily, is a true believer who nonetheless is not the rigid-protector type.

You speak of being "caught between truths," Barry. Stan approaches the same territory by discussing the nature and certainly of "truth" as viewed through the eyes of today's "post-moderns." He stands solidly on the following traditional Christian conviction: "We believe not only that the biblical narrative makes sense for *us*, but is also good news for *all*." Even so, he is very aware of how common it is for people today (post-moderns) to assume three things about religious truth: (1) knowledge is not *certain* and cannot be determined by our rational capacities; (2) knowledge is not *objective*, that is, passionless, detached from the knower; and (3) knowledge is not *inherently good*—what we think we know we too often put to evil purposes (1996, 165-166).

Where does this leave us in the goals of our theological work? Stan sees these assumptions as necessary correctives to the "Enlightenment" mentality that's been the base of Christian fundamentalism for generations. He projects the contours of a "post-modern gospel," adapting to the times without forfeiting the gospel itself.

Stan concludes: "Our task as Christ's disciples is to embody and articulate the never-changing good news of available salvation in a manner that the emerging generation can understand. Only then can we become the vehicles of the Holy Spirit in bringing them to experience the same life-changing encounter with the triune God from whom our entire lives derive their meaning" (1996, 174). So, in Stan's wise work, I see much of the *why* and *how* of our approaching Christian theology today. He's a "moderate" at its best.

Will: I agree that Stan speaks helpfully, Clark, and I'd like to add a final comment of my own. We've been reminded that many church people aren't particularly interested in theology these days, regardless of how we do it.

We've also heard about conservatives who are afraid that Henri, Paul Tillich, I, and others want to dispense with an authoritative Bible and the classic creeds of the faith so that we can "do our own thing." The fear is that we too easily allow modern times to dominate, resulting in our theological work being anemic, even heretical. I insist that, at least for Henri and me, and I think for all others in this room today, that fear is baseless. We care about yesterday precisely because we care so much about today.

Here's a critical point I think should be made. It's not *whether* but *how* Scripture and church tradition function authoritatively today. The Bible should be our "living book," not a "dead letter." Scripture is indeed a gift from the gracious hand of God. "We are to carry the scriptures with us as we walk; and, with their help and the inspiration of the Holy Spirit, we are to wrestle with them in relation to the contexts, promises, and difficulties of our times" (1999, 97). This wrestling is our doing of Christian theology.

Elton: In service of such enlightened wrestling with the Scriptures, we should applaud Tom for his substantial helpfulness in being the general editor of the *Ancient Christian Commentary on Scripture*. That was a big and crucial job well done.

Henri: Yes, indeed, and may I also slip in a final comment or two? As I see it, the basis of all Christian theology and ministry rests in the mystical life. The challenge is not to go *out* and live the best we can; it is to go *in* and let our lives find their source in the divine life. Our true conversion experience is gaining the knowledge that God is the center of things, not us. I become able to love myself and my neighbor only because I come to know deep within that God has loved me first. We call that revelation. I can know God's thoughts only because God first had them and now has graciously enabled me to apprehend them in at least a modest but saving way.

I echo your observation, Clark, about the importance of honesty and humility in our theological work. I am pleased to say that appropriate theological modesty has been exercised well in this conversation. I also am pleased that the conversation has included me.

I'll end with this: "Dealing with burning issues without being rooted in a deep personal relationship with God easily leads to divisiveness because, before we know it, our sense of self is caught up in our opinion about a given subject. But when we are securely rooted in personal intimacy with the source of life, it will be possible to remain flexible without being relativistic, convinced without being rigid, willing to confront without being offensive, gentle and forgiving without being soft, and true witnesses without being manipulative" (1989, 31-32).

Clark: Henri, that's the best description of a theological moderate I've ever heard. I'm so pleased that you are my brother!

Barry: With that well-put wisdom, gentlemen, we now must end today's conversation. Many thanks to you, Henri, and to you, Will, for your presence and excellent contributions. You have enriched today's Christian community with your teachings and lives, and now you have blessed us as well.

Questions Related to Conversation #4

1. Are Barry's opening comments correct? Do many church people today think that theology is unimportant? Are they not as "brand" (denomination) conscious as believers used to be? Does that make theological work especially difficult?

2. Will emphasizes being "conversational" as the preferable way of doing theology. What does he mean by that? How does his meaning relate to a common emphasis of "conservative" theologians that the task is a simple receiving, organizing, protecting, and proclaiming of fixed divine revelation? Apparently, Will sees the simplicity and rigidity of this four-step approach as the error of those proudly "perched on a mountaintop."

3. The twin tasks of Christian theological work are said to be linking divine revelation and current relevance. How did Paul Tillich seek to do both through his process of *correlation*—and why would conservatives think he was prejudiced in favor of relevance?

4. What about the role of *paradox* in the theological enterprise? Explain what Barry means by being "caught between truths." Is that "between" place a potentially productive theological arena or a trap that somehow must be escaped?

5. Do you agree with Henri's suggested twin directions? He speaks of truth and real Christian ministry being found in the mystical life, not going *out* but going *in* to find our lives in God's life.

6. Look again at the opening quote of Walter Brueggemann. If the Bible is basic authority for Christian theology, then how do we deal with the claim that the Bible is both a *human* product and the carrier of *divine* revelation?

7. Is theological work ever finished as times keep changing? Can you balance having strong convictions and a humble heart? Can you be a true witness without being manipulative of others?

Conversation #5

FAITH'S SOLID CENTER

Life, Cross, and Resurrection
of Jesus, Christology, Suffering
and the Role of Hope

> The tested language of the church speaks in its own unrelenting ways to modern minds struggling with the follies and limits of modern consciousness.... I have sought to listen to and speak with Baptists without abandoning dialogue with Catholics, with charismatics without losing touch with fundamentalists, with the holiness revival traditions without demeaning pietists. How? By seeking the shared rootage of early exegesis out of which each has grown (Oden, *JETS*, 1991, 80). And that common rootage takes us straight to the feet of Jesus.
>
> The church confessed that Jesus is the eternal Word, not merely a teacher with a word.... Jesus, the teacher of the word, is the Word. The church confessed that Jesus is the promised messiah of the kingdom, not simply one who preached about it.... Jesus, the preacher about the kingdom life, is the very essence of this new life.... The church confessed that Jesus is the eternal Savior. He is the one who heals what is wrong at the center both of our being and of world history. He is not merely another healer of physical infirmities, but the Savior who takes away the sin of the world (Stafford, 134-135).

Barry: Great to see you all again, good friends. We have talked so far about the identity of God, our own identities as seekers after God, and how best to approach the task of being serious and thoughtful Christians as we do our theological work in this present time. Now we focus on what traditionally is understood to be the center of the

Christian faith, the real heart of the matter, the person and work of Jesus Christ. The two quotes above, from our own Tom and from Gilbert Stafford, insist that our unity is to be found only in affirming the shared ancient tradition of biblical revelation that makes amazing claims about the person and work of Jesus Christ.

Tom: Since I'm quoted above, and I now tend to distrust theologians of recent generations when they're trying to be novel, thinking to "improve" the ancient tradition of our common faith, let me share a little history lesson to get us going.

Some Christian leaders today want to take the spotlight off of Jesus and shine it directly on God. I'm sure we'll hear much about this later when John Hick is our special guest on the subject of the world's religions. Being Theo-centric rather than Christo-centric is a popular attempt to relax tensions between Christianity and other monotheistic faith communities by deemphasizing the unique Christian claims about the divinity of Jesus.

Fewer people get upset when little is claimed as absolute truth about Jesus. The nineteenth century saw numerous attempts to locate a common base for all religious belief in our human reasoning or intuitions or sense of morality. Then, early into the twentieth century, there was a strong reaction to this move to find the lowest common denominator.

Barry: Say just a little more about this, Tom, and then we'll get right to our guest of the day who surely will have much to say.

Jürgen Moltmann (1926-)—fountainhead of a theological movement dating from the 1960s that features the power resident in the Christian hope. He was a German soldier and then Allied prisoner during World War II. Later he received a first-class theological education and in 1963 accepted the prestigious German professorship of systematic theology at the University of Tübingen, a prominent post he held until his retirement in 1994. He was catapulted into the world's theological limelight with the publication in 1967 of the English translation of his book *Theology of Hope*.

Jürgen became a popular theological figure in the United States in the 1960s, a time when the religious public seemed fed up with both secularism and Christian fundamentalism. His fresh voice and "theology of hope" were open to many dynamic currents on the contemporary scene, including its social radicalism. It also was historically rooted in Jesus Christ and his resurrection. Much of this is chronicled in Jürgen's detailed 2008 autobiography, *A Broad Place*.

Tom: Gladly, Barry. This new theological movement in the twentieth century was begun by Karl Barth and later called *neo-orthodoxy*. It reacted strongly to 19th-century liberalism and drew focus back to the biblically revealed Word of God in Jesus Christ as the sole center of divine revelation. Most other movements that have followed have interacted with Barth's, affirming it or seeking to reject it in various ways.

Today we are back to this question that never goes away. Who is Jesus and how central and indispensable is he to Christian faith? In my opinion, the Stafford quote above, representing traditional Christianity, puts Jesus right in the center where he belongs.

Barry: Thanks, Tom, for the historic perspective. Before we begin trying to sort this out, let me introduce our special guest for the day, Jürgen Moltmann from Germany. Note on our screen above the fireplace a little information about him.

Welcome, Jürgen. I remember well my first meeting you at Duke University Divinity School in 2008 when I had the privilege of formally responding to a lecture you delivered to that joint meeting of the Wesleyan Theological Society and the Society of Pentecostal Studies. Our autobiographies had each just been published and you kindly autographed a copy of yours for me. I'd admired and quoted your work for years. It was a pleasure to be with you then and to have you with us now.

Jürgen: That was indeed a great time at Duke and today should be good too.

Barry: I now have read in your autobiography, Jürgen, about "Operation Gomorrah" and your eventful years as a prisoner of war (2008, chaps. 2-3). It's quite amazing that you spent more than five years in barracks, camps, dugouts, and bunkers and could still report that "this time is for me so important that I would not have missed a day of it" (2008, 34). In the middle of all that danger, misery, and loss, help us understand what became so important for you?

Jürgen: I understand why my comment about my soldier and prisoner years seems surprising. You might also recall from my autobiography, Barry, that I said: "What I have been sure of ever since my early experiences of death in the firestorm in Hamburg in 1943 was, and still is, the need to find an answer to the question, Why am I alive, and not dead like the others? Everything I have begun in my life was an attempt to answer this question" (2008, 381).

The war survivors of my generation of Germans came home inwardly shattered. No weak, liberal, bourgeois theology would have been meaningful for us. I went home from a prisoner of war camp to study theology in the hope of establishing a strong faith for myself and some source of hope for a new and better Germany and its churches. I had come from suffering and discovered the sturdy center of Christian faith in the suffering of Jesus Christ and in the liberating and hope-producing power of his resurrection.

Elton: As a man of peace, I'm grateful that something good came out of that awful time of war. Rarely does it, I'm afraid.

Jürgen: I'm deeply grateful to some kind chaplains and Scottish families, and to Norton Camp in England. Louis, you would appreciate this. The Norton Camp functioned for me as almost a closed monastic existence where some of us prisoners had time, books, and encouragement to seek a new faith and find hope and our humanity again. You have your Gethsemani and I have mine. People who weren't in that situation can't imagine how much we had lost and how wonderful it was to have a chance to start coming back to life, soon to arrive at a new future in Jesus Christ.

Jack: Thanks for your kind words about England, Jürgen. Those were indeed dreadful days. How good that some positive things emerged in spite of everything. Please relate for us more of that experience and exactly what emerged for you as the right way to view Jesus Christ and the hope he brings to this sometimes tortured world.

Jürgen: Sure, Jack. I know that your last group conversation was about how best to approach the task of Christian theology. Here's what I'd have said if I'd been here then. During my long time as a prisoner of war, I began working out an approach to theology that is biblically based, eschatologically oriented, and politically meaningful. I learned that the role of theology is bringing "the future to bear on the hopes and anxieties of the present" (1975, 8).

One thing is sure. We had plenty of anxieties in those troubled years of the 1940s, but I slowly began to see light. Hope was born from the promise of God's future, a promise based historically on the cross and resurrection of Jesus. This hope has immediate implications for our present historical reality through the ministry of the Holy Spirit. The future of God draws the present of humans forward to new levels of possibility. Theology for me is the attempt to penetrate and explain all of this.

James: What do you think of the Gilbert Stafford quote up on our screen that helps keynote today's conversation? Gil was a long-time colleague of mine and Barry's, and an admirer of yours.

Jürgen: I agree with it fully, James. Our Christian faith is Jesus crucified and resurrected—that's the very heart of the matter. We have little if we don't have belief in Jesus as more than a good preacher and first-class moral model. He actually was God with us, and through his Spirit he is still with us. I point straight to Jesus Christ and the power of his resurrection. That's what gives me hope!

It was pointed out in your last group conversation that today one might easily be attracted to the "liberal" agenda that tends to undercut Jesus as the center of the faith. In our modern setting, I insist that "it is not helpful to relate the Christian message only to the liberated subjectivity of modern men and women, as Rudolf Bultmann, Karl Rahner, Paul Tillich and many other modern theologians have done so impressively.... Within the bounds of the 'bourgeois religion' of this society which has become so dangerous, Christianity has no chance of unfolding the critical, liberating and healing powers of its message....

In the original and essential biblical testimony to Christian faith, theology finds the one who makes it *Christian* theology: Jesus, the Christ of God. His messianic mission, his surrender to death on the cross and his resurrection to new eternal life are the sources for any relevant Christian existence today. Jesus Christ is not an *object* of theology but the one and all-determining *subject* of any theology which claims to be Christian" (1988, 87, 39).

Tom: That's a clear and powerful statement of your view of our faith's solid center, Jürgen. For you and me, Jesus really is the heart of the matter. I once was focused on humanistic psychology, but now my personal reflection happens in the context of "the personal reality of the Word made flesh in whom our human personhood is most completely realized" (*JETS*, 1991, 84).

I hear clearly your strong focus on Jesus, but let me ask this. I have dialogued with Buddhist leaders in Asia and found richness in the exchange. Is it true that, even with Jesus as absolutely central, you have found theological help in another dialogue context, conversing with Marxists?

Jürgen: Yes, Tom, I have, and I think this helped me influence the revolutionary and political theologies of the decades of the 1960s and 1970s. For instance, I engaged my Tübingen colleague, the Marxist philosopher Ernst Bloch. He argued that humans are instinctively hopeful and strive to resolve the alienation found in ourselves. What drives history toward positive change is this quest for a hoped-for utopia. I agreed with much of this thinking of Bloch, but rejected his atheism.

The Christian's hope functions as Bloch's ideal, but it's not as groundless and shallow as his Marxist delusion. The Christian's hope goes beyond an abstract idealization of utopia; it is a passion for the future rooted in the real resurrection of Jesus in our actual human history. With Karl Barth, I am Christ-centered; with Ernst Bloch, I am hope driven; with Jesus Christ, I am historically grounded and heaven bound.

Clark: I observe that your theology also has a sturdy biblical base, Jürgen. The hope our faith generates, so far as I understand your position, comes from the actual presence of Jesus with us historically as that presence is biblically reported and interpreted by God's Spirit. I personally am pleased that your Trinitarian theology, so obvious in your books, has gone beyond *The Crucified God* and *The Way of Jesus Christ* to your *The Spirit of Life*.

You and I both have engaged scholars of the Pentecostal movement and have witnessed and maybe helped them avoid some theological pitfalls. We have wanted them to mature into a significant theological force on the contemporary evangelical scene. Christian theology, I would say, should be both rooted solidly in Jesus Christ and enlivened by the presence and power of the Spirit—as I tried to explain in my *Flame of Love* book.

By the way, Jürgen, in that book I observe that you have distanced yourself from Karl Barth's polemic against religious experience (10). I'm very much with you there. Tell us about that.

Jürgen: Thanks for those kind observations, Clark. You read me correctly. I venture that the foundation of Christian faith, while rooted in Jesus, is our human experience of the working of the Spirit of God, who is the Spirit of Christ and the Spirit of life. Why did Jesus come and what is the fruit of his death and resurrection? The answer is the outpouring of the Holy Spirit, who is none other than God remaining with us.

As Athanasius once said, "God became the bearer of a body so that human beings might be bearers of the Spirit." Speaking of the Holy Spirit should mean speaking of God himself, never merely one of God's gifts to seeking believers. Nor should the Spirit be separated from the historical Jesus. "The Spirit is the giver in what he gives. He gives himself.... The Spirit sets this life in the presence of the living God and in the great river of eternal love" (1992, 47, x). This setting of us before God is necessarily in light of Christ and seeks to reflect Christ in our lives.

By the way, Elton, I've reviewed your earlier comments about a "sacramental universe." That concept rightly opens the door for universal and present applications of the will and power of God in relation to the physical dimensions of this creation. Going through that door is so needed by the church today.

Elton: Thanks, Jürgen, for using my thoughts in a highly appropriate way. In my mid-eighties, I wrote a pivotal *Yokefellow Letter* (29:4). I was leaving my home in Richmond, Indiana, for retirement in Pennsylvania. As I made this big transition, I highlighted the importance of a "rational evangelicalism," evangelical because it is Christ-centered and rational because it holds that every conviction must face full examination. The older I had gotten the more I'd become convinced that "the closer we are to Christ the more sure we can be of intellectual and spiritual maturity" (Dec., 1987).

I believe more than ever what I wrote years ago: "A Christian is a person who, with all the honesty of which he is capable, becomes convinced that the *fact of Jesus Christ* is the most trustworthy that he knows in his entire universe of discourse. Christ thus becomes both his central postulate and the Archimedean fulcrum which, because it is really firm, enables him to operate with confidence in other areas" (1969, 38).

I admit to not being fully convinced myself early in my career. I talked much about Christ, but didn't emphasize his uniqueness. In reading some of your work, Jack, I was shocked out of my unexamined liberalism. I became a C. S. Lewis fan. What I had to face was the "hard fact that if Christ was only a teacher, then he was a false one since, in his teaching, he claimed to be *more*" (1974, 99). I was impressed, Jack, at how you turned the intellectual tables and put the unbeliever on the defensive. If Christ was not "the image of the invisible God" (Col. 1:15), then he was an imposter and charlatan.

Jack: Well Elton, I never knew until now that I had shocked you out of your unexamined liberalism. Good for me! I also got shocked like that once. We all must be daring in our thinking and keep Christ central. Here are some of my Jesus-inspired insights. "Nothing that you have not given away will ever be really yours. Nothing in you that has not died will ever be raised from the dead.... But look for Christ and you will find Him, and with Him everything else thrown in" (1960, 175).

So, here's the heart of the matter for me. The central question keeps confronting us. How should we think of Jesus? The Son of God? I finally came to speak of the Son as the one "streaming forth from the Father, like light from a lamp, or heat from a fire, or thoughts from a mind. He is the self-expression of the Father—what the Father has to say. And there never was a time when He was not saying it" (1960, 151).

Louis: For a Trappist monk committed to silence, I admit to the strangeness of a speech coming on. Here goes, Jack and Elton. I too once needed shocked, and out of worse than theological liberalism. I was little more than an ignorant and arrogant atheist. Then, like the two of you, I came to believe that in finding the Christ one also finds all else. There was a time when I didn't know who Christ was. Finally, I learned to believe that Jesus Christ, coming to us especially in the blessed Sacrament, is the living Christ in our midst, sacrificed by us, and for us, and still with us as the loving and revealing and redeeming God.

It is Jesus alone who holds our world together and keeps us all from being poured headlong and immediately into the pit of our eternal destruction. There is a power that goes forth from that Sacrament, a power of light and truth, even into the hearts on behalf of those who have heard nothing of Him and seem to be incapable of belief. This is the bottom line for me, the true heart of the matter. Getting our faith about Jesus right involves keeping our eyes open, our hearts at peace, and our souls planted deeply in the joy of Jesus Christ, our eternal Lord.

Barry: A wonderful testimony, Louis! A few minutes ago, Elton, you mentioned Colossians 1:15. I recall once being helped to focus on the true center of Christian faith by an assignment I received and greatly enjoyed fulfilling. The Wesleyan Publishing House asked me to write a commentary on the New Testament book of Colossians. When I got to the pages I was to write on this pivotal 1:15 verse, I said:

"Paul insists that Jesus Christ is none other than God now becoming human for our salvation. This Christ is the creative purpose that initially shaped all creation, remains supreme over all its orders of being, and is the unifying principle that underlies the whole cosmos and continues to hold it together. In short, Christ is the visible expression of the invisible God. To know the heart of God, look at Jesus" (2007, 288).

Earlier I had written what for me is the very heart of Christian theology. "The Christian faith makes a particular claim to truth. It centers in a belief that the salvation of humankind and of all creation already has arrived in Jesus of Nazareth.... Rather than lining up in the pantheon of the world's spiritual heroes, this Jesus is said to be the embodied presence of the sovereign God, the God who voluntarily chose, in Jesus the Christ, to assume incarnate form and suffer among us humans for our salvation" (1996, 182). What a story, the greatest story ever told! That's the one we have to share with all people in all cultures at all times.

Jack: It certainly is, Barry, and we are to tell it in varying ways that communicate effectively. What I now want to throw out is a particular caution since most of us have been deeply involved in the academic world of higher education.

I once wrote a narrative poem I called *Dymer*, the name of a young man I pictured being raised in an idealized city where I said its shapers had tortured into stone "each bubble the Academy had blown." This writing was early in my career when totalitarian states were emerging in Europe. I was concerned about how academics and politicians harden their fragile and sometimes premature and even perverted theories and then try to translate them into dramatic schemes of social engineering.

Here's my caution. We academics must remember that we rarely get the last word about anything. Even so, as we have been saying in this conversation, it may be that there are some sure words about some things that are more central than all others. It's focusing on those that keeps us from being mere relativists, and it's also the awareness of our intellectual fragility that should keep us from becoming tyrants! What an amazing model Jesus is—both the dramatic self-revelation of the sovereign God and the gentle and self-sacrificing heart of God who loves and comes to right where we are in Jesus, suffering with and for us. That's the beautiful heart of the matter for me.

Jürgen: That suffering is indeed the key to all Christian theology. One of my doctoral students, Miroslav Volf, once asked me which of my books I liked best. I told him *The Crucified God*. That's where I introduced the notion basic for much that would follow for me, the notion of a God who would suffer in solidarity with afflicted creatures and redeem them through that suffering. So much for a passionless God, as you have made clear, Clark, in your *Most Moved Mover*. I said this in 1970:

> At the center of the Christian faith stands an unsuccessful, tormented Christ, dying in forsakenness. The recollection that God raised this crucified Christ and made him the hope of the world must lead the churches to break their alliances with the powerful and to enter into the solidarity of the humiliated.

The whole of Christian theology comes into focus in the cross of Jesus, which is where the suffering God comes into clear focus for us. Seeing Jesus hanging there is seeing God's heart wide open to us, as ours now should be wide open to all who suffer.

Tom: Such is the consensual witness of the church, Jürgen. Nowhere in nature is the heart of God so fully revealed as it is in the history of Jesus. God's transcendent power is "not so much displayed in the vastness of the heavens, or the luster of the stars, or the orderly arrangement of the universe or his perpetual oversight of it, as in his condescension to our weak nature" (Gregory of Nyssa).

We marvel at the way the Godhead was entwined in human nature and, while becoming man, did not cease to be God. The divine humiliation was not an impoverishment of God but an incomparable expression of the empathic descent of divine love (John Calvin). God never did anything in history more revealing of the divine character than to become incarnate and die (2009, digital, 262).

Barry: That's as basic as one can get, Tom and Jürgen. My own immediate church tradition resists creedalism in general, but consistently has focused on one dogmatic anchor. Here it is:

> Jesus Christ is the heart of Christian faith. Belief must focus on him, but with a humility of understanding open to the ongoing teaching ministry of the Spirit of Christ.... It is in him, and in him alone, that the Spirit of Christ can bring to believers a personal holiness and a corporate togetherness that will allow the

unity necessary to represent Christ effectively in this divided world. It all centers in Jesus Christ, yesterday in a cradle and on a cross, and today, through his Spirit, to be in control of all dimensions of church life (2009-C, 175).

Jack: Let me balance my strong affirmation of Jesus Christ with a touch of appropriate humility. In my little piece I called *The Voyage of the Dawn Treader*, I have Eustace asking Edmund if he knows Aslan, that giant lion of a Christ-figure. Edmund's response is that *Aslan knows him*! Many characteristics of Aslan were well known to Edmund. Nonetheless, Aslan is so awesome and wonderful that he remains beyond Edmund's ability to really comprehend. Likewise, Jesus is the awesome God made known to us in the flesh; even so, the mystery of that majesty eludes our best thoughts. We know and we don't know. So it is. So be it!

James: Precisely, and we shouldn't cover over our unanswered questions with a thick layer of sophistication. We know that real communication is blocked when the speaker fails to take into consideration to audience being addressed. I once heard of a preacher who fumbled through a series of sermons that were too "heavy" for his congregation. Finally, a wise member took him home for dinner and the sharing of some good advice.

The preacher needed to go more slowly, remembering what the people knew and cared about. His friend advised, "They taught you theology, psychology, and philosophy in the seminary, but you haven't learned any 'people-ology.' You've been trying to give us in three weeks what you learned across three years.... You know, it would be well if you preached on something you know about, too" (2000, 88). That last comment really hurt the preacher. How easy it is to rush abstractly and with a flood of language at life's questions that are really beyond our ability to fully answer.

In 2 Corinthians, Paul reflects on the redeeming glory seen in the resurrected Jesus. It is a divine light "of the knowledge of the glory of God in the face of Jesus Christ" (4:6). I once preached a sermon called "The Face of Jesus." That is where we encounter most fully and clearly the character and work of God. "It is his experienced, understanding face that accompanies us in our life and comforts us in our pain. It is his unselfish face that confronts us in our pride. It is his set face that calls us from our polarization and rebukes our tribal selfishness. It is his holy face that disarms and defeats the syncretistic notions urged upon us by the attempts of many to relativize the New Testament message regarding who he is" (2000, 77).

Louis: Great, James, but let's get back to you, Jürgen, and ask a fairly sophisticated theological question. Your earlier comments tend to highlight a criticism I've heard of your Christological thought. You rarely follow the usual categories of systematic theology or engage seriously with historical theology. In you're book *The Way of Jesus Christ*, for example, you manage over 300 pages on Christology without mentioning Chalcedon—quite an accomplishment since that's a classic theological anchor for most Christians.

Tom: That oddity also makes me a little nervous too, Jürgen. After all, the classic faith from the apostolic age and just beyond is our one sure anchor theologically.

Louis: That's my point, Jürgen. Your writings can be seen as a complex mixture of observations about religious experience, process theology, feminism, ecology, anti-semitism, theodicy, the peace movement, political activism, etc., subjects that are all of significant concern to you and us. But, rather than following conventional lines of theological debate, you seem to champion various "conservative" positions in the midst of interlocking discussions of topics honored regularly by "progressives." So, are you a progressive-conservative or a conservative-progressive?

Jürgen: I'm not sure that an answer to that question is clear to me, or important. As to your two suggested options, I can say this. Yes, probably, one or the other, or maybe both. Is that clear enough? You're right about my not trying to fit into clearly classic theological categories. I certainly could say that I wrote my *The Crucified God* with my lifeblood. I worked in categories that fit best, typical or not.

We see dramatically in that pivotal Jesus event the very heart of the bleeding God. I emphatically reject the "conservative" idea of divine impassibility—so I'm not a consistent conservative. This conversation group will later have as its guest Dietrich Bohnoeffer, a fellow German. He once wrote in his prison cell that only a suffering God can help. How right he was! God in Christ, God crucified, is God seen and known best. That's biblical revelation. If that's a progressive viewpoint, then I'm one of them. If it's conservative, then that's who I am.

Clark: I agree with you, Jürgen, on rejecting the "impassibility" idea. It's just not biblical to claim that God's perfection renders the Divine invulnerable to suffering. To the contrary, God chooses pain on our behalf (the cross of Jesus), but God is never the hapless victim and certainly not at the mercy of the creation. I've explained at length that God willingly suffers *because of*, *with*, and *for* his people. "The Father suffers the death of his Son and the Spirit feels both the Father's pain and the Son's self-surrender" (2001, 56-58).

The conservatives react strongly against this assertion, and I have been criticized for supposedly sacrificing a sovereign God for a lesser deity, one who lives at the mercy of wayward humans and thus suffers. But the criticism is poorly placed. Only a truly sovereign God whose heart is love could and would choose suffering on behalf of sinners. Would you like to elaborate further here, Jürgen? This is an important point, it seems to me. Any repetition is quite acceptable.

Jürgen: Yes, I would. I think we all should do our theology from the grateful awareness of the divine passion we are shown in Jesus Christ. We ought to shift our primary thinking from what the cross meant for Jesus the Son to a more fruitful preoccupation with what it meant for God the Father. God hardly was untouched by the horrible death of the Son on Golgotha.

I admit that my searching, especially when dealing with this central subject, was partly my attempt to discover a viable life in Germany after Auschwitz, and a viable view of God in the face of such evil. But I also insist that a suffering God is at the center of the biblical revelation, and a suffering God can be and indeed is the sovereign God.

Let me be clear about one more thing. God cannot ever suffer unwillingly, helplessly, or because of some deficiency in the divine being. If we didn't make that clear, our critics, Clark, would have us by the neck. Rather, God actively moves toward suffering because of the divine essence of reaching love. God is affected by us only because of God's deep affection for us. And God now expects us to receive the Son, mirror his loving image, and take up our crosses as faithful citizens of the Son's reign in this world and beyond.

Jesus is at the center of it all. "Anyone who gets involved with Jesus gets involved with the kingdom of God.... Anyone who looks for God and asks about the kingdom in which 'righteousness and peace kiss one another' (Ps. 85:10) should look at Jesus and enter into the things that happened in his presence and that still happen today in his Spirit. That is obviously and palpably true; for who is Jesus? Simply the kingdom of God *in person*" (1994, 7).

Elton: I love your emphases, Jürgen. If that is being "progressive," I apparently am one too. We will hear later that John Hick, a radical progressive in Clark's terms, wants to de-emphasize claims about Jesus as the divine Christ, the one and only way to salvation. That's his way of leveling out the religious communities of our present time. Presumably that way the differing religious perspectives can more comfortably blend together and mutually affirm the one God. I am enough of a conservative to resist that suggestion.

I stand with you, Tom. You have insisted on the necessity of the wisdom of classic theology from the church's earliest centuries. You have said that, if Christianity is to remain Christian, the history of Jesus must be the point of constant reference. After all Christianity is not merely about the *idea* of deliverance, but about *a person* through whom this deliverance has come. So, to attempt Christian theology with the assumption of the historic coming of God in Jesus is like trying to do mathematics without using numbers.

Tom: Thanks, Elton, for your clear thinking and careful remembering of my own thought. Let me repeat what I wrote in *Classic Christianity*. A shocking aspect of the New Testament is the frequency with which Jesus makes reference to himself, his mission, his sonship, and his coming kingdom.

"No wonder he is regarded as delusional by some amateur psychiatrists whose naturalistic assumptions rule out taking seriously his own explanation of himself. Compounding the irony, all of this was said by one who most earnestly taught humility and urged others to 'become as little children.'... Either he did not follow his own teaching at all, or there must have been something utterly unique about him that enabled him to teach from a very different premise of authority than anyone else. The most shocking hypothesis is simply to suppose that he was telling the truth about himself and that reports of him were substantially accurate. This is the faith of classic Christianity."

Louis: I agree fully, Tom. Christ is at the center of Christian faith. I also agree with Jürgen's pursuing his Christology in terms not necessarily limited to the classic categories of historic Christian thought—although not necessarily outside their intended meaning. For me, especially later in my life, poetry and symbolism have emerged as crucial for expressing my spirituality and theology. For instance, my prose poem "Hagia Sophia" was my lyrical expression of Christ being born into this world. It could be said that belief begins less in notion and concept and more in image and symbol.

Tom: I have no problem with that as long as "lyrical expression" is in the service of not meant to replace historical fact. A rich mysticism is great if it's not all there is.

Louis: I'm enriching, not replacing the Christ of history. There are rich Christological implications in a theology grounded in the experience of Sophia. It is a Christology based less on discussions about the historical Jesus and more on the ongoing experience of oneness with Christ.

The theologian speaks less of what has been studied and more on what has been experienced. The Christ presented in the New Testament becomes the Reality within our own reality, the Being within our being, the Life of our life. Knowing Christ this intimately provides the believer with a lens that enables a true perception of God in all creation. Sophia, incarnated in the man Jesus, is the hidden Christ that seeks expression within the course of all natural and human history.

James: Louis, the depth of your spirituality moves me, although I also admit some concern about any subtle suggestion that we separate Jesus from his firm historical roots or remove Christology from its classic formulations. Belief is much greater than mere notions and concepts, granted, but spiritual "experience" not deeply grounded in essential concepts easily becomes an extreme, vacuous, even dangerous individualism. So, Louis, I love what you say, and also am nervous about it standing alone.

In a profound sense, Jesus *is* the last word! St. Paul once wrote about the divine brightness that shines in our hearts "to give us the light of the knowledge of the glory of God in the face of Christ" (2 Cor. 4:6). A redeeming glory suddenly seen in the resurrected Jesus had captured this Jewish leader, granting a richer knowledge of God and a deeper experience than he had found as a student of Torah and life as a rabbi. In taking Jesus seriously, and as central for Christian faith, one should accept as authoritative what Jesus taught and, just as pivotal, *who he was*—and *who he still is* through the ongoing life and ministry of the Spirit of Jesus.

The center of the Christian faith is the teaching that Jesus came to help us on our own ground (1) to apprehend God and (2) to have our own personal histories altered redemptively. Since our minds and hearts have to apprehend by faith such unspeakable glory, I gladly share this witness of a twelfth-century pilgrim:

> Nor voice can sing,
> nor heart can frame,
> Nor can the memory find
> A sweeter sound than Thy blest name,
> O Savior of humankind (2000, 73, 76, 78).

Barry: This is a good place to end our conversation—which our time constraint is forcing us to do anyway. The centrality of Jesus has been affirmed clearly. Questions remain, however, about how the nature of the historical coming of Jesus is to be conceptualized theologically and related to our individual lives of spiritual experience and formation.

These remaining questions naturally lead to our next planned conversation. It will center on compassion, that of God expressed toward us in Jesus and that which ought to result in our loving relationships toward others less blessed than ourselves.

Thank you, Jürgen, for the hope you have brought to so many people through your life and ministry, and thanks for your gracious presence with us today.

Questions Related to Conversation #5

1. Do you see a natural tie between Jürgen having experienced great suffering in wartime and then choosing to focus his theology in a hope that emerges from a crucified and suffering God? Does the expressed faith of each of us grow out of our own life context?

2. How did Jürgen find hope in the midst of his negative war experiences? Is hope at the heart of the Christian faith? If so, about the Jesus of history? Is it necessary to believe that he actually lived with us, was crucified, and was resurrected?

3. Note the emphasis of Jürgen and Clark that goes beyond just placing Jesus in the center. They add the necessity of a robust theology of and experience with the Holy Spirit, who is the Spirit of Christ and God with us in our present experience. They both have interacted extensively with "Pentecostals." Whatever the extremes of the large Pentecostal movement in contemporary Christianity, is this movement recovering something central for Christian theology and church life?

4. Do you agree with Elton that the *fact of Jesus Christ* is the most trustworthy fact in the entire universe of discourse, and thus should be the "central postulate" and "the Archimedean fulcrum" that enables theological wisdom in general? This is quite a claim! How does Elton relate this claim to what he calls his "rational evangelicalism"?

5. The potential of God suffering is quite controversial. Can a truly sovereign God be affected negatively by actions of mere humans? Did God's heart break as Jesus died on the cross? What of a book title like Jürgen's *The Crucified God*?

6. What about the classic creedal formulations concerning the person and work of Jesus? Are they authoritative milestones never to be abandoned, or are they more time-bound formulations that may require constant review and revision?

7. Given all that is said in this chapter, try writing in one sentence what these conversation partners appear to agree is the *heart of the matter*, the very center of the Christian faith.

Conversation #6

HAVING TRUE COMPASSION
Spiritual Disciplines, the Social Gospel, and the Christian Way of Life

In our post-modern time, the credibility of the Christian faith will be established in the public eye far less by claims to universal philosophical truth and much more by demonstrating what a difference the Christian faith makes in the laboratory of our human history. The way of Jesus Christ must be embodied boldly and compassionately. "Theology articulates our commitments, while ethical practices constitute the lived version of those commitments. We must renew our understanding that the social dimensions of Jesus' work and teachings are essential to the gospel" (Weaver, 144-145).

To the extent that we live our lives participating in God's goodness, reflecting the love of God seen in Jesus, to that extent we will be Christ to the world and experience deep spiritual joy. "If we have received the love which restores meaning to our lives, how can we fail to share that love with others?... The great danger in today's world is the desolation and anguish born of a complacent yet covetous heart, the feverish pursuit of frivolous pleasures, and a blunted conscience" (Pope Francis, *Joy of the Gospel*, 2013).

Barry: It's always special to be together. Our topic today is the Christian life, particularly the role of compassion. What is the purpose of living in and for Jesus Christ? Is it more than gaining the forgiveness of personal sin? Who are Christians to be, individually and corporately in this world? How are we to live in order to be authentic Christians obviously following Jesus, our Lord and model?

The questions are many and very basic. What about Christian "ethics"? Is there a particular "style" of living, one sometimes called com-

Georgia Harkness (1891-1974)– pioneer Christian woman, chastened liberal, honored Christian scholar, and a pastor's theologian. From her girlhood in rural New York state, Georgia was grounded in "evangelical" Christianity, an inheritance she never forsook, even if she expanded its meaning during her long life. She has been guided by the fundamentals of the Quaker faith, with Methodism becoming her direct religious affiliation. Reared in the context of individualistic evangelicalism, she brought balance by eventually exerting equal stress on the more social dimensions of the faith. For her, theology should lead to inspired and compassionate action. Georgia choose to be an "evangelical liberal." Her academic title, Professor of Applied Theology, reflects her commitment to keeping theology from being merely abstractions in the academic marketplace of ideas. Her many writings are on spirituality and social responsibility, theology and ethics, poetry and mysticism. They always are expressed in language accessible to the layperson. She has defied social and church conventions about a "woman's place," becoming the first woman to teach theology in an American seminary.

Graduating from Cornell University in 1912, Georgia completed her Ph.D. at Boston University and became Professor of Applied Theology at Garrett Biblical Institute in 1940, concluding her teaching career at the Pacific School of Religion in Berkeley, California. Active internationally through the Methodist Church and the World Council of Churches, her numerous books came to include her 1964 autobiography, *A Special Way to Victory*. An outstanding 1992 biography is *Georgia Harkness: For Such a Time as This*, authored by Rosemary Skinner Keller.

passion, that should characterize Christians? We have most recently discussed as a group how best to approach the doing of Christian theology and where the true center of theology lies. Now we consider the most appropriate way to evidence in actual public life the theology we formulate in the study.

Louis: Those certainly are key questions, and thanks for highlighting some insightful words of Pope Francis as we begin. There's no question that he's a Pope full of compassion for the poor of this world. You Protestants in our group don't have to take vows of poverty to be ordained clergy, but all who claim the name of Christ must be "poor in spirit" and exceedingly generous with the less fortunate all around us. Otherwise you are following someone other than my Lord.

Barry: Well said, brother. The one lead quote is by Pope Francis of Roman Catholicism and the other by Denny Weaver of the Anabaptist tradition. They are two Christians from very different streams of the faith who find themselves saying much the same thing.

Now let me introduce our special guest, Georgia Harkness. We are honored by your presence, Georgia, and certainly our conversation will be enriched by your considerable experience and insights into the proper Christian life. A brief vita of our guest is up on our screen over the fireplace.

Thanks, Georgia, for a personal gift you unknowingly gave me. You helped me get started as a student in seminary. I remember studying your book on Christian ethics as a required text. And congratulations for being the first widely recognized female Christian theologian of modern times. You also were one of the more widely read theologians in the middle of the twentieth century. You exhibited clarity of expression on a wide range of subjects, showing the power to simplify without becoming simplistic. You have blazed a trail that has opened the way for many women in recent decades.

Georgia: Thanks, Barry. It's an honor to participate in this conversation with men of the highest caliber, and it feels good to be received as a full partner and not secondary because of my gender. I note that you've already had Rosemary Radford Ruether with you, so you've surely had practice in the delicate art of non-discrimination. She'd see to that! My being treated with fairness and compassion wasn't true for most of my life, as you know.

By the way, my nerve to stand against deep-set and very wrong social patterns runs in my family. Although a Methodist, I'll explain shortly why I really resonate with the lead quote by Denny Weaver, a good Anabaptist brother of mine.

James: Please explain, Georgia, including why it's also special for you to have Elton in our conversation group. I doubt that most would be aware of that connection, including Elton.

Georgia: Sure, James, and I'm surprised and pleased that you know. It happened this way. I was almost a Quaker. If it hadn't been for a red dress, the Methodists would have lost me to you, Elton, and the rest of the Quakers.

My great-grandfather, Daniel, was a good Quaker in up-state New York. Unfortunately, he fell in love with Abigail. The Quaker villagers called her "the woman in the red coat." She was not a Quaker; worse yet, she was a "worldly woman" who offended her Quaker neighbors by appearing in public "out of plainness." When Daniel and Abigail married in 1802, the Society of Friends presented him with a letter of dismissal for marrying outside the meeting.

So, "through this combination of feminine charm, masculine stubbornness, and ecclesiastical stupidity, Providence thus decreed a hundred and fifty years ago that I should be born a Methodist" (in Keller, 33-34). We all have our personal stories and they often take strange turns.

Elton: I didn't know that story, Georgia. I'm sorry that my Quaker forebears were so inflexible. In being valiant for the truth as they saw it, they didn't get everything right—although many of them did free their slaves almost a century before the *Emancipation Proclamation*. They didn't always make proper judgments, obviously, but nonetheless they are known for their compassion. In your case, we lost to the Methodists a great Christian thinker and moral voice. I hope the Methodists treated you better than we would have.

Georgia: Well, Elton, early in my career my treatment by my church was hardly ideal. I've been given many great service opportunities in the Methodist Episcopal Church but, like other women, I was ordained for many years before I finally was granted full membership in a Methodist conference. Gender discrimination was slow to die. We Methodists, like those old Quakers, have had our traditions, standards, and social compromises, and we have been slow to change, preaching Christian compassion but not always practicing it.

Barry: I'm glad to report, Georgia, that my church body, the Church of God (Anderson), has never had a policy of discrimination against women in church life. We have had an admirable set of ideals, but also have struggled against the influence of social contexts pulling other ways, making our actual practice a mixed bag. Every group seems to have its blind spots and subtle compromises. You have withstood a wrong and finally prevailed. That's part of why we are privileged to have you with us today.

By the way, Georgia, one of our earlier group conversations was about the important dimensions of the Christian spiritual life. While today our focus is on the responsibility of Christians to reach out in compassion to the pain of our world, and since you weren't with us for that earlier conversation, please say something about the Christian spiritual life as you see it, particularly relating it to our call to moral action in the face of injustice. After all, in 1973 you did write an entire book on the meaning of mysticism for today.

Georgia: Yes, I'd be glad to start us right there. We should be warned about thinking that the Christian life can be truly light-bearing in this troubled world if the believer's devotional life is neglected. It's so easy for us to appear compassionate and conventionally moral and quite altruistic in our actions, but that's not enough.

The "Social Gospel" people of the early twentieth century did well to point out a wide range of social sins and arouse our consciences and compassion. In the process, however, their emphasis on our personal rebellion against God receded into the background. My being sensitive to both sides of this personal/social issue is what made me an "evangelical liberal."

As such, I can't help but agree with one of your earlier conversation guests, Lama Surya Das. I hear he said while with you that the Buddhist "Dharma" is the way of "developing transcendental wisdom and loving compassion within oneself and eventually overflowing to others" (2009, 28-29). Without affirming all of his theological assumptions, or lack of them, I so agree that our spiritual wisdom, if authentic and properly nurtured, will spill over on others with waves of loving compassion. If it doesn't spill over, we have failed our Lord and the people around us who are in need.

Clark: Georgia, our previous conversation ended with Louis, Tom, and James speaking about Louis' affirming of *Sophia*, transcendental wisdom. There was strong caution expressed that our rich spiritual experiencing must not get detached from a crucial theological assumption, that of affirming the historical base of Jesus actually with us as God's redeeming love. Allow me to build on this as we now focus on compassion.

I have written about God as the "Most Moved Mover," the One exhibiting the greatest of all compassions. I see an urgent need to highlight the relationality of God as Scripture presents it. I hope that an awareness of such a loving and relating God "will liberate believers to love God more passionately.... Augustine was wrong to have said that God does not grieve over the suffering of the world; Anselm was wrong to have said that God does not experience compassion; Calvin was wrong to have said that biblical figures that convey such things are mere accommodations to finite understanding" (2001, 9, 27).

Compassion lies at the heart of God and at the center of a responsible Christian life. I thank you, Georgia, for writing so often and so well in this regard.

Georgia: You're most welcome, Clark. Our truth and lives must take their cue from the amazing self-giving of God. My Methodist and almost-Quaker traditions both have known this well, even if practice has been sporadic.

James: You're right, Georgia and Clark. Compassion is critical for understanding God and ourselves as redeemed and redeeming children of the heavenly King. Being an African-American, I join both of you in knowing what prejudice and lack of compassion looks and feels like. You have certainly gotten more than your share of abuse, Clark, as defensive "evangelicals" have reacted vigorously to your straightforward stance that Augustine, Anselm, and Calvin were just wrong on this compassion business, at least as it relates to God's essential nature. I admire you for not abandoning that crowd long ago when they would have been happy to see you go.

Tom: Friends, let's be careful about dismissing too quickly the ancient wisdom of our mothers and fathers in the faith. As a Methodist myself, I grant you that many Calvinists have gone too far in focusing on God's sovereignty in a way that seems to shut off the divine relatedness and compassion. The abuse that James and Clark have endured, and Georgia too, isn't excusable. A theology that is technically correct and yet leads only to abstractions and social irrelevance is not worthy of its name. We've seen this problem in every generation.

Jack: In the name of justice, and remembering the key role of England in the histories of both Quakers and Methodists, I'll say just this. The beginnings and many offshoots of these two Christian traditions are rich in social idealisms and practical ministries most worthy of note.

James: Amen to that. A particular discipline is demanded of those who would be agents of God's reconciliation in our world. It's a discipline that "demands realism in the face of divisive walls, hostility, and hate; a discipline that refuses to cower before the barriers that block harmony; a discipline that properly and steadily informs, encourages, and energizes one to engage in the divine process of reconciliation, that readies one to take responsibility and, understanding the necessity for forgiveness, seeks to effect it by touching the soul, repairing the wrong that injured, and establishing the needed relationship. This discipline demands an active love, a healthy self-image, willingness to risk oneself, and a sense of being companioned in the task by God" (2002-B, 18).

And this discipline isn't something that will allow the separating of the cultivation of one's own spiritual life from championing the social implications and responsibilities of one's faith. We talked earlier about the important role of paradox in Christian theology. Well, here it is in Christian ethics. To really *be* is necessarily to really *do*.

Georgia: That was a mouth-full, James. I thought you were about to burst into a great sermon. I've never had the privilege of hearing you in the pulpit, but I can sense why you have been called "the prince of preachers," and why you, Barry, would have pulled together that wonderful book on preaching in honor of James.

Sorry for this aside, but I have a personal question. Am I right, James, that you are a skilled pianist and gave up concertizing for preaching? If so, Barry, it's no wonder you titled that book *Sharing Heaven's Music*.

James: You're correct in your assumption, Georgia, although I'm a little rusty these days. Preaching itself is a communication art form that, at least in the Black tradition, can't be separated from music, joy, celebration, and compassionate ministry. It's out of that wonderful mix, all fed by the glorious grace of God, that we believers tend to gain and exercise compassionate hearts.

The Lord is so good! That goodness means that "in our Sovereign Creator and Sustainer there is a compassion that relates to our concerns, a helpfulness that relates to our hopes, and a nearness that relates to our needs.... Being good, the Lord wills our good, eager to show us favor, always available to sustain us, always ready to forgive us, and always gracious to guide us" (2000, 31-32).

Louis: Let me squeeze in here, a strange activity for a monk committed to humility and silence. Relating serious spirituality and compassionate social action in this world is a necessary and hard thing. We all know that.

World War II was raging when I first came to my Gethsemani monastic home. Many of my peers probably thought me a coward—they marching off to war and me entering the security of a monastery. I knew well the streets of London that by then were pitted with bomb craters. The horrors of war ate at me; and believe me, the peace I sought in the monastery wasn't a safe or a socially useless seclusion for me. I was really convinced that making prayer the main business of life would be at the center of history-making. I felt I could do more for peace at Gethsemani than on some battlefield.

Can you non-monastic folks see that? Hardly running from social responsibility, I intended to put my life right on the line. I had known a wealthy, cosmopolitan world in London's West End, and once had even found myself defending Gandhi in a formal debate in a British school. India, I insisted, had every right to demand that Britain withdraw, and I admired how Gandhi handled himself.

My parents had held some radical convictions, including simple living and pacifism. Later, after I had become an orphan, I decided that I would do the same for the sake of my own soul and that of the world. We humans are mysteriously interconnected and I believed then and still believe that faithfulness in prayer can enhance the repentance and compassion of others.

James: Your mention of Gandhi, Louis, reminds me of my pastorate in Detroit during the heat of the Civil Rights movement in the United States. I had several personal contacts with Martin Luther King, Jr., someone also impressed with Gandhi. Now that some time has passed, I think it's clear that their deep devotion to God and to God's peaceful ways of confronting social evil were effective.

King often said that everyone can serve as Christ's compassionate agents of reconciliation. No ordination to ministry or college degree is required, only a heart full of God's grace and a soul motivated by Christ's love.

Tom: We are interconnected, as you say, Louis, all of us. We are the recipients of the saving grace offered by God, and all are called to nurture and use the spiritual gifts that have been given.

Here's a key question. What are our motives for helping others? What will be the outcome of our efforts? Before risking being drawn inappropriately into current political agendas and social schemes that may or may not further God's compassionate will, we must concentrate on becoming the truly redeemed persons that divine grace makes possible. That grace is the sole source of our spiritual vitality and potential usefulness as agents of love to those around us. Babes in Christ need to become mature disciples guided into active ministry by the ministry of God's Spirit.

Barry: The beloved song says that it's "amazing grace." Again, before we *do* we need to *be* new in Christ Jesus.

I never knew King or Gandhi close up, but I've known and loved you well, James, and a reading of the New Testament makes something very clear to me, in part through your life. Christian compassion expressed in the social arena is a paradoxical and often painful business. Prayer as a tool of social effectiveness, Louis, absolutely. But what of most Christians who don't have the option of a monastery? They sometimes face the painful paradox of Romans 13 and Revelation 13. The secular state deserves respect and submission; it also functions on occasion as a beast determined to devour the faithful! We'll really get into that dilemma for believers in our eighth conversation.

Georgia: I never had direct contact with King or Gandhi either, but I did get the chance to go to Germany in the early 1920s. There I saw firsthand the monstrous social evils left from World War I. That helped to make me a pacifist forever. But I learned, like King and Gandhi, to be an aggressive pacifist, more of an activist than a detached mystic—and, Louis, I also agree that being a monastic like yourself is hardly to be detached from Christian ministry in the world. Prayer and active peace-making belong together. You have modeled that superbly.

My first publication in a church journal was a 1924 piece titled "The Ministry as a Vocation for Women." Then my academic thesis topic was on the church and the plight of recent immigrants. I called on the churches to address the spiritual and social needs of the flood of new immigrants to the United States, seeing no necessary conflict between the spiritual message and the social gospel of Christianity.

And James, you're quite right. As maybe only the discriminated against can really know, the two are inextricably bound together, deep personal faith and intentional social ministry. The gospel of Christ is one, whole, an all-life gospel.

Louis: My memory goes back to India and an amazing witness that once came from Malcolm Muggeridge—who will be one of our final conversation guests in a few weeks. His witness has it all, gender sensitivity, deep personal faith, and a "social gospel" at its best. When more than eighty years old, Malcolm was reflecting on his being received into full communion with the Roman Catholic Church. He wondered about how and when he had experienced "conversion." For him, it had been a series of happenings over time. He tells of one of the most memorable events, a visit he had with Mother Teresa in Calcutta.

This milestone visit was a working occasion for Malcolm, a professional journalist. He and a crew were filming *Something Beautiful for God*. Mother Teresa's home for the dying, a former Hindu temple, had very poor lighting inside. The cameraman reluctantly took a few shots in there, only to be surprised later to find that those shots were "bathed in a wonderful soft light" which Malcolm judged "could not be accounted for in earthly terms." Some wondered what terms there are other than earthly.

Here's Malcolm's testimony on the power of Christian compassion: "Holiness, an expression of love, is luminous; hence the halos in medieval portraits of saints." Said Malcolm specifically of Mother Teresa: "Her total dedication to Christ, her insistence that all our fellow human beings must be treated and helped and loved as though they were Christ is quite irresistible" (1988, 15). In fact, Georgia, I agree that divine light surrounds acts of loving compassion and shines as something incomparably beautiful. It does so only because it is from God and is shining with God's own compassion.

Georgia: Precisely, Louis. I have insisted over the years that the Christian life cannot be vital and an effective bearer of the light of Christ in this world if we neglect nurturing the devotional life of each believer. Acts of compassion "can be conventionally moral, highly respectable, even to a considerable degree altruistic without it. But it cannot be a Kingdom-seeking, cross-bearing, richly fruitful life that God requires.... And without this quality, the light of faith tends ever to flicker as the winds of life blow upon it" (1973, 130).

And while I have the floor among you men, let me add some wisdom from a dear Christian sister, Corrie Ten Boom. Despite the awful abuse she absorbed from the Nazis, her wonderful ministry of Christian compassion rings true only when her testimony is taken into consideration. She often would say things like, "Trying to do the Lord's work in your own strength is a tedious, confusing, and exhausting business. It works properly only when a disciple of the Master is filled with the Holy Spirit, thus allowing the ministry of Jesus to flow naturally through the committed life."

Barry: I have a feeling, Georgia, that you're braced to say more. Feel free.

Georgia: Indeed! I've been convinced since the social crises of the 1920s that a faithful doing of Christian theology is an act of social responsibility that an help to create a more just world. Barry, that's why I wrote that textbook on Christian ethics that helped you in seminary. And that's also why I have called myself a "liberal, unrepentant and unashamed" and gone on to make clear that my liberalism has been "chastened and deepened" by world events and theological trends I have seen. Mysticism, yes, to a point. Social gospel, yes, if properly grounded.

Jack: That combination, the joining of the personal and social, is part of what I meant when I titled one of my books *Mere Christianity*. When we get right down to the basics, Jesus "works on us in all sorts of ways, through Nature, through our own bodies, through books, sometimes through experiences which seem (at the time) *anti-*Christian.... But above all, He works on us through each other. Men are mirrors or 'carriers' of Christ to other men. Sometimes unconscious carriers" (1960, IV, chap. 7, 163).

And one more thing, Georgia and gentlemen. A deep piety may be the *heart* of the thing, but not necessarily the *head*. Piety gives the right motive, but hardly full wisdom on the most appropriate social applications of the faith in particular circumstances. "When Christianity tells you to feed the hungry, it does not give you lessons in cookery. When it tells you to read the Scriptures, it does not give you lessons in

Hebrew and Greek, or even in English grammar. It was never intended to replace or supersede the ordinary human arts and sciences; it is rather a director which will set them all to the right jobs, and a source of energy which will give them all new life....

The application of Christian principles, say, to trade unionism or education, must come from Christian trade unionists and Christian schoolmasters, just as Christian literature comes from Christian novelists and dramatists--not from the bench of bishops getting together and trying to write plays and novels in their spare time" (1960, bk. 3, chap. 3).

Elton: That's good wisdom, Jack. I'm all about heart *and* head. A loving heart is not necessarily thereby a wise social strategist. Here's something I wrote when I was 93 years old and rather sure that I had little time left on this earth. "How do I want to be remembered? Not primarily as a Christian scholar, but rather as a loving person.... If I can be remembered as a truly loving person, I shall be satisfied" (*Quarterly Yoke Letter*, June, 1994).

Just as the church is not merely a self-improvement society, we individual believers don't exist for our own self-aggrandizement. Our accomplishments and understandings are so fleeting and limited. Let's always remember that Jesus left us no library or palace or wall of honorary degrees, but a rugged cross of compassion. That cross is the center of our faith, the manner of life that we are called to live and share.

Jack: I love your imagery, Elton, and your point is so significant. The cross triumphs over our libraries, and palaces, and walls, even over our fancy theological words and elaborate church programs. I would add only that too often Christian compassion gets poisoned by self-interest that is neatly presented as love.

I used the character of Orual in *Till They Have Faces* to dramatize something important for us to remember. How easily we can blame others and see everything that is wrong as injustice against ourselves. We then rush out to serve others when, in fact, we are protecting and serving ourselves by trying to control others. As the Bible shows us, God allows us to cry out to him, even to blame him for all that's wrong in the world, allowing us at least to avoid denying all the wrongness. My point is that we must be aware of our motivations for compassionate involvement with others. Sin sometimes infects what appears to be the best of our social endeavors.

Georgia: Jack, before now I'd never heard of your Orual character, but I strongly agree with what you're saying through her. And, Elton, you're so right. The bottom line is love. Circumstances change, so

Christian courses of action must change also—that's where the head must come in. However, God's love in Jesus Christ certainly doesn't change, even when so much else does. Fortunately, we have not been left without help in this constant changing. What is stable is our adherence to "the type of obedient, faith-filled love which Jesus embodied and proclaimed" (1957, 66-67).

The second half of my Christian ethics book that you read as a seminary text, Barry, is devoted to taking this love principle and exploring its applications among the relativities of our present world. That's the big and ongoing process, holding firmly to the love principle and aggressively and creatively looking for its fresh applications to things as we find them now. Christianity is living out the loving compassion of Jesus Christ. We might say that love is a special way of being alive. Love is our destiny, and we find it only as we journey redemptively with others who are in need.

Let me bring another woman into this conversation. I gladly affirm aspects of the recent work of Karen Armstrong. Her extensive study of the great religions of the world has convinced her that the heart of the matter for them all is *compassion*. In personal and political situations, vengeance leads to never-ending strife. Loving your enemies constitutes the ultimate act of compassion. Acting selflessly in love requires a leap of faith. It is an act so against the normal human grain, and yet so central to the mystery of religious belief itself.

Louis: Well said, Georgia and Karen. The love principle certainly is at the heart of true compassion, just as compassion is at the heart of true Christianity, and apparently other faith traditions as well. Too often missing among the social protestors I have known was a loving balance of right attitude and needed action. They got so upset about the injustice and violence they saw that anger consumed them, making it difficult if not impossible for them to bring change to the wrong attitudes of others.

"We have to have a deep and patient compassion for the fears of men, for the fears and irrational mania of those who hate or condemn us.... We all have the great duty to realize the deep need for purity of soul, that is to say, the deep need to possess in us the Holy Spirit, to be possessed by Him. This takes precedence over everything else" (letter to Jim Forest, July 29, 1962).

Clark: That's so true, Louis, and recently I've become aware of a good example of balancing truth and compassion, love and action. It's from your own church tradition and on a delicate subject that troubled one of our earlier guests, Henri Nouwen. Although known only to those close to him and from his most private writings, it now is clear that he struggled with reconciling his priestly vows of celibacy with his human desire for physical and emotional intimacy. Most people now would probably refer to his sexual identity as homosexual. Tell us, James, about this balancing by your church. I've heard that it may be a good model for others.

James: Well, I can tell you that finding the balance was and likely will continue to be an uncomfortable and unfinished process. Many ministerial voices in the Church of God (Anderson) called for a strong statement against homosexuality, identifying it as an unbiblical lifestyle that could not be tolerated among Christian leaders. The result was the formal adoption in 1993 of a resolution by the church's General Assembly. It reaffirms the group's understanding of biblical holiness as one that "cannot accept, endorse, or condone homosexual behavior."

Having made that much clear, the statement goes on to sound strong notes of Christian compassion. "We are a redemptive body and seek to express love, compassion, and concern for those who struggle with sexual identity or homosexual orientation to assist them in a chaste relationship in Christ and to demonstrate love and provide counsel and materials to bring redemption and wholeness." That's one attempt to balance heart and head, biblical text and human struggle. A good friend of Barry's, Howard Snyder, has made a widely-respected similar attempt (2014).

We leaders of the faith are obligated to affirm our understandings of the faith's foundations, its teachings and applications, but only in a context of respect and loving reconciliation for those who see and experience things in ways other than our own understandings of biblical truth and expectations. Stances and strategies seem forever in flux. How we need the guidance and compassionate heart of God!

Tom: Indeed, indeed! Let me be personal. After many wonderful years of marriage to Edrita, I lost her in death. Now facing the future alone, it was my time to draw closer to God. My need was for "grace to live a full life of accountability to God.... It took me a long time to move from withdrawal to engagement.... There was no map for this inward journey" (2014, 325-26).

Too many followers of Jesus haven't followed him far enough. They have withdrawn inwardly and found new life in Christ. What they have failed to do is reach out, engage, and become the compassionate hands and feet of Jesus in their own time and circumstances. The saving love of our Lord sours and fades away when not released into compassionate mission.

Barry: Friends, your life and faith wisdom are rich. However, the available time for this important conversation is coming to an end. In our last conversation, we affirmed that Jesus Christ is the heart of the Christian faith. He is the pivot around which the whole of our theology and ethics should revolve. And now, with your help Georgia, we have affirmed that it is the compassionate, loving heart of Jesus that is to define our practical and socially relevant Christian walk in this world. We thank you for your presence and for your loyalty over the decades to Jesus and his mission of redemption and justice.

Let's conclude today with this. The whole idea of compassion is based on our awareness of the interdependence of all living things. We are part of one another; we need each other; we are to serve each other. And this truth leads naturally to the subject of our next conversation. It will center on the church, the essential togetherness of all Christian believers as we seek to be Christ's body in the world. That's next time; for this time we are in your debt, Georgia, and mostly in debt to our wonderfully compassionate God.

Questions Related to Conversation #6

1. Clark judges that some of the best-known Christian theologians of the past were wrong in their insistence that God is not compassionate, if that is defined to mean that God risks, cries, hurts, suffers for and with us, and can be impacted negatively by us humans. Would compassion in the divine heart rob God of full sovereignty?

2. Georgia insists that a neglect of one's personal devotional life can impact severely the quality of that believer's social expressions of Christian compassion. Do you see this necessary connection? What are you doing regularly to avoid that negative impact on your own social witness?

3. According to Jack, compassion involves heart and head. What does he mean by saying that bishops shouldn't write plays in their spare time? If God desires an outcome, does God provide details of the most appropriate strategy for achieving it?

4. Try to picture in your mind a great library or wall of academic degrees. Now remember that Jesus left none of these behind from his own life. Elton says that Jesus only left a rugged cross of compassion. Do your life values allow you to prioritize in the Jesus way the attitudes and actions of your life?

5. Can Christianity be defined rightly as living out the compassion of Jesus Christ? Do you agree with Georgia when she claims that, for Christians, love is our destiny, the special Christ way of being alive?

6. What about Karen Armstrong's conclusion that compassion is at the heart of all the world's great religions? If it is, why is there so much violence done in the name of religion? See conversation #9 for much more on this subject.

Conversation #7

WHAT ABOUT THE CHURCH?
Fellowship, Creeds, Denominationalism, Unity, Worship, and the Sacraments

> The church from its beginning has been shaped by a received tradition of holy writ.... The Spirit assists the community of faith in accurately remembering, rightly interpreting, and practically applying Scripture. This is why the clearest and surest expositions of Scripture are to be found in the community of faith guided by the Spirit and not among individualistic inquirers (Oden, *JETS*, 1991, 89, 91).

> Speaking sociologically, any community, including the church, needs to choose leaders, order its life, and maintain regular practices that keep its identity visible and support its mission. Speaking theologically, such ordering and practicing in the church need to relate closely to the gospel message that creates and sends this Christ community. The church's roots, fruits, and symbols should interrelate so that each supports and reflects the others. If authentic, they all are gracious actions of the Spirit and essential disciplines of the people of God. (Callen, 1996, 310).

Barry: It is, as usual, a pleasure to see you all again. Our topic today is the church, the contemporary Body of Christ here on earth. The quotes above speak of the necessity of community formation around the faith and the long tradition of biblical authority. Interpreting that authority depends on the ministry of God's Spirit working through the community of faith to rightly remember, read, and apply.

Tom: My quote above, I admit, is quite the contrast with who I was in the early 1970s when I had "long hair, bobbles, bangles and beads, and a gleam of communitarian utopianism in my eyes" (*JETS*,

1991, 83). I now love the church in its ancient frame and biblical vision, not in the frame of my earlier fancies.

Louis: Interesting, Tom, and quite a contrast indeed. You always add a dramatic touch to our conversations with reports of your long journey home from the excesses of our time to the church of all times. Where you are now is certainly more comfortable for me and the deep historic roots of Catholicism.

Barry: We've all been on our individual journeys. Our last conversation was on the relation of compassion to Christian identity and the nature of the life we are to be living in God's Spirit. It became abundantly clear that the effective expressions of compassion by God's people are not optional, and they require the wisdom, support, and strength of the whole body of believers on mission together. Thus, we now are going to talk more directly about the church.

Let me introduce our two special guests. One is Harry Emerson Fosdick and the other Geoffrey Wainwright. Welcome, gentlemen. By you both being with us, we have a helpful widening in the representation of the church's geographic life, time periods, settings served, and even theological approaches to understanding the church. If you regulars wish to glance at our screen above the fireplace, brief vitas of Harry and Geoffrey now appear.

Harry Emerson Fosdick (1878-1969)—a master preacher, liberal thinker, and prolific author. The ministry and preaching of Harry drew large congregations and radio audiences, as well as famous critics. A Baptist minister, he rose to prominence as the weekly preacher at New York City's First Presbyterian Church (1918-1924). Fundamentalist Christians nationwide attacked his view that "modern Christians" could doubt doctrines such as the literal truth of the Bible and the virgin birth of Jesus and still remain faithful Christians. In a sermon titled "Shall the Fundamentalists Win?" (1922), Harry spoke out against the exclusion of modernists and their views. He became pastor of New York's Park Avenue Baptist Church in 1925. The church moved in 1930 to a cathedral-like new structure in Upper Manhattan, built by congregational member John D. Rockefeller, Jr. It became the interdenominational Riverside Church.

Harry pastored the Riverside Church until his retirement in 1946, taught at New York's Union Theological Seminary, and his "National Vespers Hour" aired on radio for nineteen years. He drew the title of his 1956 autobiography, *The Living of These Days*, from a verse of the hymn of his own composition, "God of Grace and God of Glory." He appeared on the cover of *Time* magazine in 1925 and 1930.

Geoffrey Wainwright (1939-)—a theologian and ecumenist born in Yorkshire, England. Geoffrey is an ordained minister of the British Methodist Church who received his university education in Cambridge, Geneva, and Rome. He served as a minister in Liverpool, England, before becoming a missionary teacher and pastor in Cameroon, West Africa (1967-73). Returning to England, he taught Scripture and theology at the Queen's College, Birmingham (1973-79), before moving in 1979 to Union Theological Seminary in New York to become a professor of systematic theology. Beginning in 1983, he taught Christian theology at Duke Divinity School in North Carolina, and came to hold visiting professorships at the University of Notre Dame, the Gregorian University in Rome, and the United Faculty of Theology in Melbourne, Australia.

From 1976-1991, Geoffrey was a member of the Faith and Order Commission of the World Council of Churches and chaired the final redaction of the Lima text on *Baptism, Eucharist and Ministry* (1982). Since 1986 he has been co-chair of the Joint Commission between the World Methodist Council and the Roman Catholic Church. In 2004 he gave the opening address on behalf of "the ecclesial communities of the West" at the Roman symposium to mark the fortieth anniversary of the Second Vatican Council's Decree on Ecumenism. Among his many books, the most influential remains the classic *Doxology: The Praise of God in Worship, Doctrine and Life* (1980).

Harry, we'll start with you since much of your church experience predates that of Geoffrey. Allow me to remind you of a little story you tell in your autobiography about Quakers and the construction of the Erie Canal (opened in 1825). Would you share it briefly, please?

Harry: Sure, but with a touch of reluctance since Elton's in the room. I'm sure his generous spirit will let me get away with it. So . . .

In a Quaker meeting, a solemn voice spoke against the construction of the Erie Canal. The man said with deep conviction, "If the Lord wanted a river to flow through the state of New York, he would have put one there!" Then, after a profound silence that allowed an absorbing of this apparent wisdom, one contrary Quaker voice said simply: *"And Jacob digged a well!"*

To that biblical bombshell of another time, I observe this about myself: "I have often wished, in facing similar situations, that so brief and crushing a retort could be found to religious reactionaries" (8).

Elton: Why this story, Harry? What, in your view, is the big problem with religious reactionaries in the church, be they Quakers or otherwise?

Harry: Here's the problem I see, Elton. In my family, Christianity was natural, practical, livable. Not so elsewhere around me when I was young. "Some of the most wretched hours of my boyhood were caused by the pettiness and obscurantism, the miserable legalism and terrifying appeals to fear that were associated with the religion of the churches" (33). Communities of Christians seemed dominated with the attitude that things are as God wants them, period. If God had wanted things otherwise, he'd have done it that way in the first place. Reactionaries abort progress out of hand. It's a recurring and heavy chain around the church's neck.

Elton: So you're saying your theology and ministry were shaped considerably by your negative reaction to this pettiness and legalism?

Harry: That's exactly right my gracious and insightful Quaker friend. I was so turned off by it. Opinions in church may be mistaken, you know, but openness and love should never be in short supply, and here's exactly where I found a major dilemma that has marked much of my life.

All directions seemed of equal danger. That part of the church that sought an effective contact with the current culture was seen as capitulating to the prejudices of the "progressive" social movements of the time. And that part of the church that was so defensive in the face of the current culture chose to protect itself "in the armor of a rigorous biblicism," and thus was cut off and essentially irrelevant to the culture (144). Irrelevance is deadly to the church and its mission.

Tom: I have spent much of my professional life serving the church on university campuses, particularly in a seminary setting where I came to observe a disturbing trend. It was, in my view, an excessive preoccupation with the "progressive" side of things, as you put it, Harry. Many of the mainline seminaries had chosen to become "slaves to modern ideologies" (2014, 261). I tried to explain in my *Requiem* why I judged that they were in their death throes deservedly because they were failing to serve the church in faithfulness to its distinctive beliefs, not its narrow legalisms but its time-tested and biblical traditions.

James: For a time I also was deeply involved in seminary education. I am pleased to report, Tom, that my seminary was not one resisting the digging of any new wells, nor was it so preoccupied with progressivism that the very integrity of the church was put at risk. This balancing is indeed a delicate and critical process.

Back to our guest. When you became the successful pastor of a prominent New York City congregation, Harry, how did you deal with this dilemma in your approach to preaching?

Harry: Good question, James. Then, of course, I was on the spot. People come to church on Sunday with every kind of personal difficulty that we frail and sinful are subject to. I decided that "a sermon was meant to meet such needs; it should be personal counseling on a group scale" (94). So I let the people bring the questions and I sought from the pulpit to offer the gospel answers.

Clark: That sounds like a pastoral version of Paul Tillich's "correlation" approach to theology—one of our earlier guests was telling us about that. And something else. It's likely, Harry, that you aren't aware that a very bright and cultured young German theological student, Dietrich Bonhoeffer, encountered your preaching during his time of study in the United States (1930-1931). I'm sorry to report that he reacted negatively to aspects of your ministry. Dietrich will be our guest next time when we talk about matters of patriotism and pacifism.

Harry: Yes, that's news to me, and I'm sorry I wasn't more relevant to his particular needs. Preachers never reach everyone. I certainly became aware later of Dietrich's dramatic ministry back in Germany. Those Depression years when he was in New York were troubled times for sure, and Dietrich's struggle with the compromising church in Germany probably didn't set him up well to appreciate my emphases in our American setting. The church must always be reacting to its given time and place. Regardless, I admire the wisdom and courage he showed through that awful Nazi time. I hope I would've had the courage to join him had I been in Germany preaching the gospel.

Please greet Dietrich for me when he comes and tell him for me that his neo-orthodoxy, inspired much by Karl Barth, was "a courageous challenge" to the evil of that time, one that, by its very dogmatism, naturally made "any soft type of liberalism seem unrealistic and pale" (264-265). I confess some guilt here. My reaction against dogmatism set me up to be a little "soft" on the progressive side. Church life always travels in this delicate continuum.

Jack: As an Englishman, I frankly enjoy listening to a German squabble with an American. In those awful Nazi times we Brits were right in the middle between the U.S. and Germany, and in our case you Americans were most relevant to us English!

Harry: I forgive your little waywardness, my English brother, enjoying a good squabble. And I can imagine Dietrich seeing me as soft and evasive on unchanging truth just like his compromising church at home. I admit that I was anything but doctrinally dogmatic in those years. Meeting the felt needs of people is always close to letting those people set the agenda of the church.

Any of us so-called "liberals" who failed to learn something from men like Karl Barth and Dietrich Bonhoeffer "is not worth his salt" (266). Dietrich's pacifism was admirable. I made it clear in my well-publicized sermon "My Account with the Unknown Soldier" that I renounce war and would not sanction any, including that much later one in Vietnam that was based on the thin rationale that Americans were fighting for freedom.

Barry: Let's leave the morality and politics of war to our next conversation and keep our focus on the church.

Harry: Of course, except for one more comment. Once I spoke sharply to delegates at a meeting of the League of Nations assembled in Geneva, Switzerland. I told them that too often the church has tried to carry the cross in one hand and a dripping sword in the other. I admire articulate war protestors. I struggle, however, with the decision Dietrich finally made to participate in an assignation attempt on Hitler's life; nonetheless, I wasn't in his setting and shoes and probably shouldn't judge.

Louis: Thanks, Harry, for your graphic analysis and upfront honesty. I can see why people would listen to you. Those Vietnam years were hard indeed. I also took a strong stand against that war, and in some ways think I became its victim. But maybe we should go more toward our focus of today, the church. Preachers like you, Harry, rarely if ever adhere to the vow of silence, the one we monks at least idealize.

James: We are full of words, Tom, that's for sure, and, Harry, you have been especially good with them. Let me suggest a good place to start addressing our specific subject for the day.

Creeds appear to play good and bad roles in church life. On the good side, they are milestone occasions when the best of Christian thinking gets captured, preserved, and holds the church together with a proper grounding and respect for biblical revelation and church tradition, a stabilizing such as you, Tom, represent so clearly. Creeds are part of that process of the church ordering its life to maintain the corporate identity that you speak of, Barry, in your lead quote for this conversation.

However, there is anther side, like your Erie Canal illustration, Harry. Too often creeds are grasped as ultimate wordings of wisdom and used in ways that restrict further thought and even justify sharp divisions among Christians who may hold slightly differing perspectives. What right did Jacob have digging a well that God had not provided at creation?

This danger of the misuse of creeds and other church traditions is why the church body that has been my home, the Church of God (Anderson), has never formalized any creed as its official and fixed stance. We would rather be in the position of learning and growing than using stances from earlier times as available weapons of division. Granted, this opens the door to possible confusion, but it also keeps available the possibilities of innovation, relevance, and progress.

Harry: That's a good application of my story, James. I wish I'd gotten to Detroit to hear you preach back in the 1960s.

James: You'd have loved my congregation, Harry. But, staying with my point, let me add a word of clarification about the ministry of Martin Luther King, Jr. Critics are very wrong when saying he was out to spread division among believers of different skin colors.

"His words flashed a stirring dream across the screen of every mind, a dream that he was concerned enough to tell and courageous enough to live.... His concern [was] for *community*. Again and again King tried to help us understand the nature of community, the need for community, and the concern of God that we work at being open to experience community.... His ministry was filled with 'showdown situations,' but his motive was not divisive" (2000, 167-169).

King was a man of the church, the whole church, a united church, one committed to grace and justice for all.

Harry: Good for your church group, James, and thanks for your clarification of King's true motive—you can't always trust what you "learn" from the newspaper and television reports.

Let me say this to us all. No theology can be understood "apart from the conditioning social matrix in which it is formulated.... Theological trends are partial, contemporary attempts to formulate great matters. To take the best insights of them all, to see the incompleteness and falsity in them all, to trust none of them as a whole, to see always that the Reality to be explained is infinitely greater than our tentative, conditioned explanations—that seems to me wisdom" (232). That humility should characterize church life.

Here's what I once said in welcoming new members to our great Riverside Church in New York City, as reported by my biographer, Robert Moats Miller (1985, 214):

> There are in this church many members of many denominations and many faiths. In welcoming you into our membership, we do not ask you to give up any belief or form that is dear to you, but rather to bring it to us that we may be enriched thereby. We invite you not to *our* table or the table of any denomination, but to the *Lord's* table.

In that declaration you can hear my ecumenical commitment to the whole Body of Christ, something I know that you, Geoffrey, care about deeply. The church is to be *unified* without necessarily being *uniform* in thought or practice.

Jack: OK, that's a good and gracious transition, Harry. Let me get our other guest into this conversation. We Great Britain folks need to have our say!

Geoffrey, your upbringing was not in American fundamentalism, but in British Methodism. Tell us something of your experience and resulting view of the church.

Geoffrey: Thanks, Jack. Well, Harry speaks of his Riverside Church and its creedal openness. All of my adult life as a Christian has been spent in ecumenical contexts, whether in Great Britain, Europe, Africa, or North America. For me, "What makes the church see clearly its true face is meeting with Christ and learning from him what sort of Bride it is that he loves" (1980, 65).

We learn the answer to the church's true identity in open relationships with our brothers and sisters worldwide. My English Methodism has its roots in the ministry of John Wesley, of course. He had an exceptional ecumenical spirit.

Tom: My own Methodism and worldwide interaction with the church, in both its establishments and on its frontiers, make me so glad you're with us today.

Elton: Geoffrey, you tie effective church mission to a necessary ecumenism. Apparently, we can't be productive in mission to a lost world without open, constructive, and worldwide relationships with our brothers and sisters in the faith. I'm sure that contemporary relevance is always part of what Christ intends for his church, and Jesus did pray so earnestly for the unity of his disciples as an important condition of mission effectiveness (Jn. 17).

Now let me comment back to you, Harry. You say in your autobiography that from your youth you have endeavored to be both an intelligent modern and a serious Christian (vii). My own passion has been that deep faith and rigorous intellect require each other.

I thank you for your generous evaluation of my book *Philosophy of Religion*. You wrote this about it: "In these days when the dogmatic belittling of reason afflicts so much of our current thought, this book is a God-send."

I have argued for decades on behalf of a "rational evangelicalism." When it comes to the Bible, a wooden literalism isn't good enough. "We are required, not only to read, but also to think" (1996, 66). Church members should be free to think deeply and speak honestly, gaining needed benefit from and yet not throttled by whatever blindness exists in the faith community.

As you reported in your boyhood story, Harry, old Jacob did indeed dig a well. Maybe that remains an apt symbol of our freedom today to look freshly at things that are unprecedented in our experience. The living God is always on the move. So, his people should be moving with him—and digging wells if they wind up in dry places.

Harry: Yes, Elton, indeed. To be relevant to our world, we need our brains in full gear. By the way, thanks for your advice on choosing the title of my autobiography. I had intended to call it *What a Generation!* but you wisely suggested that I use words from my own hymn "God of Grace, and God of Glory." Some of the words, really a prayer, are "Grant us wisdom, grant us courage, For the living of these days."

So I called my book *The Living of These Days*. In fact, at the dedicatory service in February, 1931, for the Riverside Church in New York City, we sang my words as an urgent prayer:

> God of grace and God of glory,
> On Thy people pour Thy power;
> Crown Thine ancient church's story,
> Bring her bud to glorious flower.
> Grant us wisdom, grant us courage,
> For the facing of this hour.

There's the church's heart, God's grace poured out on a grateful people prepared together to face the hour at hand.

Elton: Great words, Harry. You'll recall that most of our books were published by Harper & Row. You and I have had a delightful relationship—we even shared the same editor. And you're so right with your emphasis on "Thy people" in the hymn. I also have stressed the idea that it is not possible to be a Christian *alone*.

To use one of my book titles, we are to be "the company of the committed." To throw in a little of my Quaker tradition, and certainly to follow Jesus, we should be liberated from heavy concern about ecclesiastical systems and offices of church power. It's a long way from human pomp and circumstance to the simplicity of the humble and serving Jesus.

As we Friends have long said, Quakerism is "Christianity writ plain." I have worked over my many years to create ecumenically-based fellowships of the truly committed, fellowships that transcend denominational differences and work for spiritual renewal and social transformation. That's what motivated me to found the Yokefellow movement.

Barry: We might think that it's a long way from the simplicity of the Quaker church tradition to the "pomp and circumstance" of the Roman Catholic Church, but now we have Pope Francis who is sounding and acting a little like Elton's tradition! We are all learning to really be the Body of Christ on mission in relevant ways, allowing ourselves to be the people on whom divine power is poured and through whom that power flows to the world.

Clark: Indeed. I want to call our attention to the first thing our risen Lord did. He breathed his Spirit on the disciples and then sent them out as a special missional community. Therefore, the effectiveness of God's people, the church, does not rely primarily on its competency or programming or the sophisticated structuring of its life, but on the power of God's Spirit at work in and through us.

"The church rides the wind of God's Spirit like a hawk endlessly and effortlessly circling and gliding in the summer sky. It ever pauses to wait for impulses of power to carry it forward to the nations.... The main rationale of the church is to actualize all the implications of baptism in the Spirit" (1996, 114).

Given that, here's my concise view of the church. It's "a foretaste of the new race, the colony of heaven, the embodiment of the koinonia that God is and that the world will become.... God's love overflows in creation and redemption, and God seeks a community into which he can pour his Spirit" (1996, 47).

Barry: Those statements, Clark, strike me as both biblical and eloquent. It's been common, at least in many Protestant circles, to say quite simply that "the true church exists wherever the sacraments are celebrated and the word of good news in Jesus Christ is preached faithfully." Since the church is sustained from generation to generation by telling, hearing, receiving, and living out the biblical story of God in Christ, the church could not exist without that story.

Certain practices within church life are intended to keep presenting the story in a way that has the grace-filled potential of constantly forming the church into the image of Christ. These practices "are sacred, not in themselves, but only as the Spirit works through them to form, strengthen, and send the church on Christ's mission" (1996, 311). I speak particularly about Baptism and the Lord's Supper. Does anyone want to comment here?

Geoffrey: Yes, I do, Barry. The cross of Jesus always must be central. "The Johannine Christ promised that when he was lifted up from the earth on the cross, he would draw all to himself (Jn. 12:32). The hymn of Philippians 2 proclaims that God has exalted Jesus to the heights and given him the name above every name, so that he should receive the worship of all as universal Lord....

The implied vocation of the church is to catholicity.... Within the church, moreover, there can properly be no divisive distinctions based on human differences" (1980, 132-133). The churches we know struggle with the church's intended catholicity and the divisiveness of the human differences among its members. Addressing this dilemma has been a preoccupation of my entire ministry.

Barry: I'm sure all of us would agree that the church God intends is located presently *between heaven and earth*, the deliberately paradoxical title of the chapter on the church in my *Caught Between Truths*. We, as God's people in this world, are both a collection of fragile humans and the divinely-enabled body of Christ. In this awkward dilemma, am I hearing from you, Clark and Geoffrey, that the holiness of the church rests on being Cross-oriented and Spirit-filled? Is that the heart of the church matter?

Geoffrey: It is in my view. According to the New Testament writings, "the church is holy on three counts: it is the people of God; it is the body of Christ; it is indwelt by the Holy Spirit. Baptism is the fundamental ritual sign of the church's holiness" (1980, 127). And there's one more thing to be said. Unity belongs to the core calling of the church. I think of the severe disunity of the church today as an "absurd situation" (1980, 123).

I appreciate the pivotal role of the sacraments in church life. I have worked on such matters with church leaders from all over the world for many years through the World Council of Churches. Finally, I had the privilege of chairing the final redaction of the Lima text on *Baptism, Eucharist and Ministry* (1982). So much tradition and latent spiritual power lay here. May the Spirit's ministry inspire and strengthen our own.

Allow me a quick word about my book *Doxology*. It's a systematic theology written from a liturgical perspective. My controlling conviction there is that the relationship between doctrine and worship is more deeply rooted and essential than often is recognized. "In the liturgy, and correspondingly in theology, we seek to be open not only to our human environment but also, fundamentally and ultimately, to God. We want God to shape and transform our vision and our entire being.... A function of the liturgy is, by word and sacrament, by image and rite, to invoke the future in which God's kingdom and our salvation will be firmly achieved" (1980, 437).

Louis: I want to thank you, Geoffrey, a Protestant, for speaking prophetically on the virtual disaster of the church's disunity. I'm aware of that wonderful occasion in 2004 when you gave the opening address on behalf of the "ecclesial communities of the West" at the Roman symposium to mark the fortieth anniversary of the Second Vatican Council's "Decree on Ecumenism." We've got to find a way to be the church that is more than "West" and "East," more than "Catholic" and "Protestant." We all must find our way back to the feet of our Lord and there be one on behalf of a lost world.

And a comment to you, Harry. I too lived through the time in the 1960s when the American society was pulling itself apart over Vietnam. Now that we have seen a similar military engagement in Iraq, one would think we would have learned a few things.

I echo the words of Parker Palmer: "If we had been able to hold the paradoxical complexity of the fact that the human heart sometimes yearns both for the sweet air of freedom and for the order, however oppressive, that a dictatorship brings, we might have been less cocksure about our mission and more constructive in response to our national dilemma and Iraqi realities" (1980, 2008, xxxvi-xxxvii).

The simple fact is this. Nations follow their own self interests and often intrude on the communities of others. The church also must take care here, being sure that it lives for God's interests and doesn't use "evangelism" as a pretext for churchly aggression.

Tom: You are a dear brother, Louis, and the church and world would be so much better off if your wise words and those of Geoffrey's were taken seriously. Here's my personal testimony about the church.

"I have discovered that I belong to a vast family of orthodox Christian believers of all times and places.... The Christian family is far wider, broader, and deeper than most of us have commonly thought of it as being. Those who can recite the Apostles' Creed with full integrity of conviction and live out Christian moral norms, as well as worship in spirit and truth, are all part of a consensual family of faith.... Since God's Word is addressed to all humanity, orthodoxy embraces a scriptural inclusivism that is much broader than a politically correct inclusivism" (2014, 299).

Elton: That's a lot to think about, gentlemen. Engaging this world as the church is a necessary and yet difficult process. We must be spiritually well prepared. I once listed some conditions for gaining knowledge of the living God. They are reverence, a childlike spirit, quietness, moral obedience, and a combination of aloneness and togetherness. It's the togetherness that is the church, and the aliveness that can give it power.

I have talked about the church's mission in terms of the "strategy of penetration." Jesus told his little company of disciples that they were to be the *salt* of the earth and the *light* of the world. The mission purpose is to penetrate and preserve and enlighten. The nature of the church is such that "it must always be engaged in finding new ways by which to *transcend itself*. Its main responsibility is always outside its own walls in the redemption of common life" (1961, 69).

And let me add one more thing since the church sometimes acts like its own worst enemy. "Love is the final test of orthodoxy.... There is no reason to suppose that there was a single pattern of organization in the life of the early church or a single way of worship but, whatever the variety, there was a recurring emphasis upon the mutual love of the brethren.... Nothing could be more effective in the effort to rediscover the true pattern of the church as a loving community than a serious acceptance of the lesson of the washing of the feet of the disciples....

We need to contemplate the present applicability of an act which combines humility and loving service, which renounces unequivocally all struggles for prestige and pre-eminence, and which indicates the radical nature of the break that must be exhibited between the standards of the church and the standards of the world" (1961, 98-99, 105-106).

James: My church fellowship has tried to maintain the practice of footwashing for exactly the reasons you suggest, Elton. While pastoring a large urban congregation in Detroit, I was privileged to be a friend of Martin Luther King, Jr., at first through various occasions related to the Detroit Council of Churches (2002, 246-250). I came to know well his heart. He surely was about your strategy of penetration, Elton. The church lives for more than itself or it's not itself.

In April of 1963 I was on the planning committee that organized the "Freedom Walk" in Detroit when King used much of the same speech that he would use in Washington, D.C., that summer. Some 200,000 people massed to hear King "flash a stirring dream across the screen of every mind, a dream that he was concerned enough to tell and courageous enough to live" (2000, 167).

That dream, friends, had much to do with the church. It was about *community*, constructive, person-affirming, God-inspired community. King was so aware of the effects of relationships and social processes on the shaping of the identity and destiny of persons and their groupings. We all are caught in a network of some mutuality, and King was haunted by the negative social network strangling so many African-Americans of that time.

King's methods of addressing the problems of injustice and disunity were daring, controversial, and quite effective, but they never were intended to be *divisive*. God's concern always has been to birth a church, a united church, a redeemed and reconciling church. We who are part of it by divine grace are to be open to the God-expected experience of building a redemptive community that frees, enlightens, and reconciles.

Tom: Yes, the church is "a covenant community bonded not by politics, race, blood, or ideology, but by covenant with God the Father as made known through his Son. Jesus regarded his disciples as sisters and brothers, the Christian community as a nurturing family, and the faithful as children of God" (2014, 200). That's King's "person-affirming, God-inspired community." It's the church of the Bible, the Apostles, and the great Councils.

Harry: I hear about this wonderful vision of the church and realize that I've rightly been accused of having mostly missed the doctrine of the church in my preaching and writing. I confess that the six key ideas in the Bible that I develop in my *A Guide to Understanding the Bible* do not include the church as such.

I was so busy working in the church that I never quite got around to constructing a doctrine of it. Even so, I served, built, and loved the church. I once said that the church should be "the point of incandescence where, regardless of denominationalism or theology, the Christian life of the community bursts into flame" (in Miller, 215). The Holy Spirit is the fire; the needy world is to feel its comforting warmth.

Jack: I'm not sure if I'm the church historian in this group, but I'll venture an observation anyway. There are three impulses that have appeared in Christianity over the centuries. We might call the first "orthodox" (the drive for theological correctness), the second "gnostic" (the drive for higher knowledge and wisdom), and the third "pietistic" (the drive for the personal experience of transformation). These always have been present to some degree, often in considerable tension with each other.

I've tasted all three of these along my own journey. These impulses are not mutually exclusive, to be sure, but they do carry seeds of their own destruction when any one is separated too far from the others. Church life always has had its political dimension, usually struggling over the primacy of one or another of these impulses. Finding a good balance is a never-ending goal of church life.

For instance, contemporary "Pentecostals" seem to have shown us that the early church may have made a mistake by overreacting to Montanism, choosing church order to the detriment of spiritual enthusiasm. On the other hand, excessive enthusiasm soon goes sour and calls for the stability of good order and the richness of tested tradition.

Tom: If I may brag for a minute, John Wesley was accused of being an "enthusiast," and he was to an extent, but never outside the context of a robust dose of church order and tradition. The right combinations of things is so important, and rather rare.

James: I come from a church context that has been freshly focusing on impulse number three, although without emphasis on things like "speaking in tongues." It has criticized human organizational overlays on God's church that often function to the detriment of the work of God's Spirit. The danger, of course, as you well point out, Jack, is becoming so anti-organizational that virtual chaos is allowed to emerge and swirl with the conviction that the Spirit works best in a volatile, free-form context. In trying to redress the "man-rule" problem of church life, the risk is running into the "no-rule-at-all" problem.

Louis: You would know, James, that I come from what your group likely would see as Jack's impulse number one having gone to seed. After all, the Roman Catholic Church has numerous layers of highly developed organization and tradition, although we have hoped that all of it is more of God than of us humans. We all want to minimize "man-rule" in order that God may be truly God among us—that's part of what the monastic life is all about. And we all have failed to some degree in our efforts at bringing into being communities of faith that have stability and longevity without a loss of their essential God-relatedness.

I think we should all keep this in mind, something many Protestants easily miss. Even we monks in the church are keenly aware that we very much need to be a *community* of faith. Every true hermit, regardless of championing aloneness, sees the divine call in the context of the church and in service to the church. All of our discipleship and ministerial vocations are *within* the faith community, even though a few of us occasionally withdraw from it physically for a time. Our withdrawal is for the sake of the whole.

Geoffrey: Absolutely, Louis. Allow me to make a few more comments about theology, the church, and one of the great church leaders of recent generations. Christian theology is (or should be) a practical more than a speculative discipline. Such speculation as it engages in, if done properly, stands ultimately in the service of right worship, right confession of Christ, and right living. Those designated "Fathers" of the church usually were early bishops who oversaw the spiritual, liturgical, and moral lives of the faithful. Sometimes they gathered leaders in councils to clarify doctrine, and even guided the mission of world evangelization.

Tom: Exactly, and these early bishops and their councils are a dependable base that still endures for anchoring and guiding today's church, even with its very different settings.

Geoffrey: Correct, Tom, and I want to point out such a wise church leader in our own time. I believe that "a figure of comparable stature and range in the ecumenical twentieth century was Lesslie Newbigin (1909-1998). He and I have shared interests and concerns, and our paths have crisscrossed numerous times. Finally, I authored *Lesslie Newbigin: A Theological Life*. There is so much there for the guidance of the contemporary church.

Jack: I must note that Newbigin is another stalwart son of the British Isles. You class him, Geoffrey, as a modern "Father" of the church, a leader sometimes said to be of patristic proportions. Talk a little more about your reasons for such a grand designation of our honored church brother.

Geoffrey: I'll try. Newbigin's ministry was comprehensive in scope. He was both a working evangelist and a missionary strategist. He was an intellectual apologist for the faith and an ecumenist seeking to restore the integrity of the faith community worldwide. And then, given our focus in this present conversation, he rightly understood the church to be "the visible, tangible, social community that had been constituted by Jesus Christ's choice of his apostles and friends, and empowered by his bestowal of the Spirit on them after his death and resurrection" (2000, 391).

The church's members are to be Christ again in each day's real history, seeking a practical renewal of itself on behalf of the coming kingdom of God. That grand task was wonderfully embodied in my dear friend. It's a challenge for us all.

Jack: You make a great case for him, Geoffrey, and reflect much of yourself in the process. In my book *Mere Christianity*, I try to make clear the sole purpose of the church. It is to draw people into Jesus Christ—who is the heart of the whole matter of our faith. If congregations are failing to do that, then all the clergy and cathedrals in the world are mostly a waste of time and money. I join you, Geoffrey, in celebrating a special brother like Lesslie Newbigin. But let me leave him and bring up a piece of my own work for a minute.

I once tried to create a metaphor for the church, the community of faith intended by Jesus. It's in the fourth volume of the *Narnia Chronicles*. In this piece that I call *The Silver Chair*, I tell the story of the church. A band is called out from their familiar worlds to journey together to restore the king's son to his rightful identity. They went when commissioned by the Lion's breath (by the wisdom and power of the Holy Spirit).

This sent faith community in my story was flawed, as the church always is in this world, and various mistakes were made. Even so, by the grace of Aslan, the Lion's will gets accomplished through them. So there it is, a picture of the church on mission, going in all of its human frailness and yet in the power of God's Spirit!

Barry: A wonderful summary statement, Jack. Our time is up, gentlemen, although this subject is far from exhausted. We are in debt to both Harry and Geoffrey for their outstanding ministries to the church, their great love for the people of God, and their willingness to be here and share with us today their considerable wisdom.

In our next conversation we will address key matters of church policy and strategy. Being in this world as God's sent people is as demanding as it is glorious.

Questions Related to Conversation #7

1. Are the churches you have known resistant to change in teaching, organization, and practice, saying, "If God wanted it differently he would have made it that way in the first place? Can you understand Harry's lifelong opposition to such thinking in church life? What's wrong with being staunchly conservative?

2. Harry strongly and graphically criticizes one frequent public policy of the church, that of carrying the cross in one hand and a dripping sword in the other. Is that a fair criticism? Should the church be involved directly in politics? Can evangelism be aggressive arrogance as well as spreading the seeds of good news?

3. The current culture of the West is highly individualistic, a trend that has impacted the churches significantly. How important is experiencing *community* in church life? Is the corporate life of the church essential to Christian discipleship and mission?

4. What of Harry's approach to preaching and King's to social change? Can members of the church hold differing opinions, even beliefs, without being divisive? How can we build a *community* of believers that are not merely separate groupings of like opinion (a divisive denominationalism)? Can the church be unified and yet diverse in thought and practice?

5. Can you recognize in your church fellowship the dominance of one of the three "impulses" that, according to Jack, have appeared repeatedly across the history of the church (orthodox, gnostic, and pietistic)? Should you work toward keeping that dominate impulse in your church from separating itself too far from the checks and balances of the others?

6. The church hardly exists for itself, but for its mission. What about Elton's "strategy of penetration"? How about Geoffrey's call to "open and constructive relationships with our brothers and sisters worldwide"?

7. Can you retell Jack's story of *The Silver Chair* in a way that opens for you the great meanings of the church of Jesus Christ on mission in the world today?

Conversation #8

IS IT GOD *AND* COUNTRY?
Patriotism, Pacifism, Power,
Church Mission and Public Policy

E. Stanley Jones (1884-1973) "combined his evangelical theology with a culturally sensitive appreciation for other people. He preached a message of religious universality—that Jesus is the Savior of all of humanity—but without the hegemonic cultural pretensions characteristic of so many missionary evangelists" (Strong, 77). Jones thus presented, in his own words, a "disentangled Christ—disentangled from being bound up with Western culture and Western forms of Christianity" (Jones, 110). Somehow, God and country must be separated for evangelism to be authentic.

Wrote Thomas Merton (Louis): "Prayer and sacrifice must be used as the most effective spiritual weapons in the war against war.... This implies that we are also willing to sacrifice and restrain our own instinct for violence and aggressiveness in our relations with other people. We may never succeed in this campaign but, whether we succeed or not, the duty is evident" (in *The Catholic Worker*, Oct., 1961).

Dietrich Bonhoeffer (1906-1945)—German Christian pastor, theological educator, pacifist and visionary, the son of a professor of psychiatry and neurology at Berlin University. Dietrich became a Lutheran German pastor, wartime double agent, neo-orthodox existentialist, a social visionary and a daring church reformer finally martyred by the Nazis. He graduated summa cum laude from the University of Berlin in 1927 and earned his doctorate in theology at the unusually young age of twenty-one. He was influenced by Karl Barth and placed priority on the sovereignty of God and the need for full allegiance to God's will, especially in the face of a wayward nation. Bonhoeffer's active opposition to National Socialism in the 1930s continued to escalate until his recruitment into the resistance in 1940. He was martyred by the Nazis just before the war's end and became famous for phrases like "cheap grace" and "religionless Christianity." Some used his emphases, somewhat out of context, to support the "God Is Dead" movement in the 1960s.

Barry: Great to see you all again, good friends. Last time we were together we spoke about the church. This time we want to talk about an area of persistent problem in Christian theology and church life. How do Christians live as both members of the church and citizens of particular nations, especially in crisis cultural circumstances?

Louis: Our two lead quotes above, mine included, suggest that somehow we must disentangle our home cultures from our evangelism and restrain our instincts to violence to accomplish even our highest purposes. The church is trans-national. Can we be both Christian and patriotic?

It's the old God-Caesar tension that often troubles church life. All of us were impacted greatly by World War II, reacting to it in a range of ways. There was nowhere to hide. Millions of Christians made hard choices between national loyalty and the kingdom of God. Sometimes we do what the times seem to demand. We accommodate or pay a high price.

Barry: Thanks, brother. Let me introduce our special guests for today, men much experienced with this dilemma of God and country, church and culture. One is Dietrich Bonhoeffer, a German probably impacted by that 1940s war more than any of us. The other is James Cone, an American greatly impacted by racial discrimination and determined to relate the faith constructively to this human crisis at whatev-

James H. Cone (1938-) is an ordained minister in the African Methodist Episcopal Church and the Charles Augustus Briggs Distinguished Professor of Systematic Theology at Union Theological Seminary in New York City. Having earned the B.D. from Garrett Theological Seminary and the M.A. and Ph.D. degrees from Northwestern University in the 1960s, he soon emerged into the theological spotlight in 1970 with his pacesetting *A Black Theology of Liberation*.

Deeply influenced by both Martin Luther King, Jr., and Malcolm X, his many writings have been eye-opening and occasionally abrasive. His involvement with the Ecumenical Association of Third World Theologians has broadened his awareness and concerns beyond only the Black experience of oppression in the United States. With books like *The Cross and the Lynching Tree*, he forces us all to look hard at the themes of suffering, oppression, and ultimately redemption. Rather than merely recounting the tragedies of the past, he hopes to open conversations that can lead to the healing of very social wounds.

er cost. Brief vitas of each are now on our screen.

Dr. Cone, I must ask a favor. Since we have a James among our regulars, may we use your middle name, calling you "Hal"?

Hal: Indeed you may. It's nice to be asked. I've been called many things, often without anyone caring about my preference.

Barry: Great. Our topic of the day takes many forms. One of them is seen in the Jones quote above, the cross-cultural tension inherent in the Christian mission. Another is the frequent clash between national citizenship and allegiance to the kingdom of God. Still another is how we humans discriminate against each other through prejudice based on skin color or ethnic identity and turn that prejudice into church and even public policy if we can.

Hal: I've been so absorbed in my American context that I'm anxious to hear from you, Dietrich. You lived in a dramatically transitional and violent time in Germany, and you managed to blaze your own trail under God, one that now has been evaluated in sharply different ways. That happens to us "radicals."

Barry: OK. With Hal's obvious interest, we'll begin with Dietrich. When I was a doctoral student in Chicago in the late 1960s, your name and writings were highly respected—they gave rationale and inspiration for engaging constructively in what at that time was a troubled American culture. But then I read "conservatives" who, while respecting your stance against the Nazis, judged your thought to be a dangerous arena of not-so-subtle heresies. Could you begin by telling us who you really are?

Dietrich: Indeed I will. And it's good to be here, back in the United States after so long. My identity is complex, I admit, so the confusion about me is understandable. Let me start in an awkward place. I was not here for your last conversation, the one on the church. If I had been here, I would have made some sharp observations about your guest, Harry Emerson Fosdick, and then apologized for my premature arrogance.

Barry, you told Harry that I encountered him when I spent 1930-1931 in America as a young man. By then I was a convinced disciple of Karl Barth and a stout opponent of liberalism. I saw Harry marginalizing traditional Christianity, replacing it with an ethical and social idealism filled with faith in human progress. He was pastoring a wealthy church in a time of economic crisis, a congregation that looked to me less a fellowship of devoted believers in Jesus and more a religious corporation working for some wholesome social and personal ends of the people's preference.

But enough of that for now. It was a long time ago and much has changed. You asked who I really am. I grew up a culturally privileged and well-educated young man in Germany who was both fascinated with and frustrated by what I saw on my trip to America. I also was increasingly dismayed by what I saw developing in my own country.

Louis: If it helps any, Dietrich, here are two things to note. Harry told us that later he reversed some of his early liberalism and understands your negative reaction to his ministry. And now there is a professorship in theology and ethics named in your honor at Union Theological Seminary. Things can change for the better.

Only a few years after your time in New York City I began a short tenure of teaching English at St. Bonaventure in Olean, New York. At that time, I too was haunted by the expanding war in Europe and decided to write a novel titled *My Argument with the Gestapo*.

I had a poet return to war-ravaged London, obviously autobiographical on my part. He was a stateless person who had "lived in too many countries to have a nationality" (1969, 21). I had registered for the Selective Service in the U. S. as a conscientious objector and was prepared to serve as a medic, not being able to kill people made in the likeness of God.

Germany had started the war, of course, but my poet character senses something painful. The war was partly his fault too. He (I) was facing guilt, and soon would be facing a different kind of battlefield, the Trappist monastery in Kentucky and my own troubled, inward journey.

Tom: Your monastery a battlefield? That calls for some elaborating, Louis.

Louis: Gethsemani was a little nation all its own where we all were conscientious objectors. I had to fight with myself and contend with God, hopefully on behalf of all humanity. I once began a class as novice master by saying, "Men, before you can have a spiritual life, you've got to have a life!" (in Palmer, xxvii). I meant that our spiritual lives must function and grow in the midst of our messy earthly realities. Despite the difficulties of life in the political arena, the church must work within "the wideness and wildness of God" (xxviii).

Dietrich: Louis, your long life at Gethsemani makes me remember my time at Etlal, the Benedictine monastery outside Munich, Germany. I worked there on my book *Ethics*, trying to understand and explain an ethical basis for my being involved in the resistance against the Nazis. I knew that at some point I likely would be performing extreme actions, even political assassination. I was trying to justify such a thing as a responsible Christian person.

Participating in a bloody overthrow of the Third Reich and at the same time being a loyal follower of the lowly Jesus is demanding to think through. I understand, Louis, that you wrote while at Gethsemani in protest of another war, the terrible one in Vietnam. Maybe we really do understand each other.

Louis: Yes, I did, and with passion. You and I faced the same evil in the 1940s, Nazism. I concluded back then, unlike you, that what Hitler represented could not be defeated by the same violent methods it used—raw power. The only adequate Christian response was sanctity. "There is only one defense: to take the Gospel literally, and to be *saints*" (1958, 267). I intended to disappear into God, me a pacifist and monk with a brother who was part of a bomber crew in the Royal Canadian Air Force.

But I hardly disappeared, Dietrich. As I wrote in the prologue to my *The Sign of Jonas*, "like Jonas himself, I found myself traveling toward my destiny in the belly of a paradox." You and I had to deal with a dreadful dilemma, and do so the best way each of us could. We did it differently. Who's to judge which was best, or if both can be justified equally, or whether neither was best in the end.

Anyway, here's my question for you, Dietrich. I understand that you were a disciple of Gandhi and his credo of non-violence, and yet you also became part of a wartime conspiracy to assassinate Hitler. I admit to struggling over how one man puts that together—pacifism and deliberately planned murder. It's true that I resisted the U. S. war in Vietnam with passion, but I never got involved in acts of outright violence or encouraged anyone else toward violent protest. How was that for you, and how did you justify your actions?

Dietrich: You, of course, know that I faced false churches deeply compromised with a wayward state. I tried to explore the church's nature in my doctoral dissertation and in my post-doctoral work *Act and Being*. The German Evangelical Church had been shaped by nationalism and obedience to state authority. Influenced by this tradition, and with a strong new leader like Hitler emerging from the chaos of the Weimar years, many Protestants in Germany welcomed the rise of Nazism. One group within the church, citing the Aryan laws that by 1933 barred all non-Aryans from the civil service, proposed a church paragraph to prevent non-Aryans from becoming ministers. I opposed this bitterly as something surrendering sacred Christian precepts to a poisoned political ideology.

Protestantism was born as a protest against the excesses of the Roman Catholic Church. In the 1930s, I turned this inspired church history against another accommodating church that was denying the priority of the gospel truth of Jesus Christ. I had to rethink the nature of the true church and I started a small seminary for the new Confessing Church, virtually an underground operation. It was to be something of a Protestant monastic community where seminarians would live as students and growing disciples of Jesus.

Pastors must be active Christians, you know, just like the church must be active by speaking and acting on behalf of those unable to speak for themselves. And church seminaries must dare to resist modern ideologies that are overtly or subtly anathema to Christ.

Tom: A loud "amen!" to your seminary effort, my brother. My book *Requiem* is my own daring attempt in the American setting to call liberal, accommodating seminaries to accountability. Doing that doesn't always win you a host of new friends.

Jack: I was on the English side of that awful Nazi conflict, Dietrich. Since then I've learned about your passion for peace, daring role as a double agent, and many ecumenical contacts and efforts to gain an early peace. People living outside that horrible set of circumstances, and with no sense of history, would tend to judge you prematurely. Only a few years after the war there arose the "Death of God" theological movement. An Anglican bishop in my country, John A. T. Robinson, popularized it and credited you with its inspiration. I love mystery and paradox, and you, Dietrich, appear to be both. What do you have to say about God's "demise" and your role in it?

Dietrich: Forgive my smiling. I understand the confusion. German culture in the 1930s and early 1940s was inescapably Christian given the dominating shadow of Martin Luther, the fountainhead of Protestantism. Nevertheless, during the war I struggled with both an evil government and a church being seriously unfaithful to her Lord. They—supposedly my brothers and sisters in Christ--acted like God was dead, or at least was irrelevant to the evils of the situation. I reacted with vigor. I suppose you could call me a prophet of secular engagement, calling the church to drop her mask of false religion and become daringly "religionless" in the name of God—paradoxical, I know.

Let me put it this way. My call from God was to action, not abstraction. Religion can be a deceptive overlay that hampers participation with God's suffering in the world. That's why I called for a "secular" Christianity, not a Godless one, to be sure. I was calling for an end to a dangerous dualism. We Lutherans talk much about two kingdoms, man's and God's. I was rejecting those who shun responsibility for the world in the name of their hollow religiosity, trying to escape the dilemmas of the world and winding up being shaped and dominated by those very dilemmas.

In my book *Ethics*, likely my most mature work, I insist on Christian lives that allow themselves to be impacted by given situations, with decisions being made in part by the loving obligations demanded by the moment. God lives and his children are to be alive to the dramatic needs around them.

I see my approach as only being responsible; my critics see it as violating the unalterable standards of the Bible. As a Lutheran, I always have insisted on salvation by faith through God's grace alone. Bible reading, sermonizing, and disciplined prayer have been central to my life of faith. It's out of that spiritual matrix, in conjunction with the world as it's encountered, that one must discern and apply God's will and ways.

Karl Barth's views came to impact me significantly. Rather than my abandoning belief in God, I began breaking liberal and compromised molds and choosing instead the sovereign God known in Jesus Christ. False gods have to die.

In the late 1930s, I saw numerous Lutherans practicing what I came to call "cheap grace." In my *The Cost of Discipleship* I speak out against such perverted grace. I believe in resisting the "powers that be" when they flaunt what's right, even if the resisting costs me my very life. Pious prophets with radical biblical messages rarely are understood and certainly not appreciated. My message was rooted deeply in biblical revelation. The Word of God has been at the center of my life.

Elton: Thanks for that glimpse into the depths of your heart, Dietrich. As for me, that big war in the 1940s caused me much concern about the American society. I saw the United States trying to live in a dungeon of subjectivity, cutting itself off from the living God, denying the very existence of any objective moral order. I wrote *The Predicament of Modern Man* to emphasize that a "cut-flower civilization" may look fresh for a time, but faces the terrible danger of premature death because it is severed from its sustaining roots. We just cannot "maintain the dignity of the individual apart from the deep faith that every person is made in God's image and is therefore precious in God's eyes" (1944, 59).

In a sermon I preached in 1956 at the National Presbyterian Church, and with president Dwight Eisenhower in attendance, I lauded the Supreme Court's desegregation decision. There is an intolerable inconsistency between segregation of the races and a Christian commitment to living out the love of Jesus Christ. I once wrote to my friend Richard Nixon, then the vice-president and a fellow Quaker, urging him to follow his religious tradition by taking a strong moral stand on civil rights. I too was in a church-state struggle.

By the way, Jack, by then I had begun studying your works and was being influenced by your depth of thought and even style of writing. I want to thank you for that.

Jack: I'm flattered, Elton. Certainly I agree with you about the worth of every person. Even so, I remind you and the others that I'm no pacifist. All people are of infinite worth in God's eyes, to be sure, but protecting that worth—unfortunately—sometimes calls for violence in our fallen world. That's where I can connect with you, Dietrich.

We find ourselves as believers always searching and experimenting with how best to live effectively as Christians where we are. "The practical problem of Christian politics is not that of drawing up schemes for a Christian society, but that of living as innocently as we can with unbelieving fellow-subjects under unbelieving rulers who will never be perfectly wise and good and who will sometimes be very wicked and very foolish" ("The Humanitarian Theory of Punishment," *Res Judicatae*, June 1953).

That's why, Dietrich, I lament the need for your violent resistance to the Nazis, but I feel forced to affirm the possible Christian legitimacy of such a stance because of the sheer necessity of the occasion.

Elton: I hear you, Jack, although I stop short agreement. You and many Christians can create a reasonable case for a "just war," although others of us continue to struggle with that possibility being an acceptable expression of the Jesus life we meet in the Gospels. I do want to admit that there is the paradox of the unloving pacifist, the one "who condemns all of those in the armed forces and maligns his opponents.... Christian pacifism is a great and needed witness, but when separated from the love of Christ it seems inevitably to become cruel and bitter" (1996, 98-99).

Affirming pacifism and also admitting its occasional weaknesses, Dietrich, and thinking biblically, I would like to know how you concluded that violence can be an option for the serious Christian?

Dietrich: Thanks, Elton, for the honesty of your own introspection. It's so easy to hold a purist position when standing on the outside of a horrible set of circumstances like I faced. I don't expect most people to understand.

I learned that there are basically three ways for the church to respond to a society that has given itself over to evil. (1) It can try to help the state by questioning its wayward actions. (2) Or it can go further by actively assisting the victims of state actions—and for me that included the Jews. (3) Or, and here is the bold step I finally felt forced to take, the church might have to go beyond bandaging victims lying under the state's wheels. It might feel obligated under a just and loving God to finally jam a rod into the spokes of those wheels to save a mass of other soon-to-be victims. For me, the perversely spinning wheel was Hitler and we finally tried to jam a rod into him for the sake of humanity.

I think it was William Blake who once said: "The strongest poison ever known came from Caesar's laurel crown." Well, whoever said it, I saw this poison dripping from Hitler's head, and I learned instead to drink deeply of the living water flowing from the head of the gentle Jesus. The terrible question was how to confront Caesar on behalf of the goals of Jesus. I made a choice, hoping to sacrifice one evil man for the sake of so many of God's innocent children.

Barry: Tom, I hear that your break with pacifism was inspired by the Hungarian Uprising against communism in 1956. If so, that's an interesting coincidence since the first of my writing ever submitted for publication was about that very uprising.

Tom: Interesting indeed. Yes, my pacifist spell was broken by that uprising, and by Reinhold Niebuhr's critique of pacifism and Robert Batchelder's dissertation on Hiroshima. "Hungary was the first crack in the repression that had silenced freedom in Eastern Europe. As I watched students resisting tanks, I realized that unjust power had to be met with justified resistance. Those intrepid students on the streets of Budapest offered me a model of courage completely different from my earlier pacifism. I realized that moral decisions required something more than theories and ideas" (2014, 67). So, Dietrich, I thoroughly understand the tough decision you made in resisting Hitler with more than holy abstractions.

Jack: Well, let's face it. People often judge from their armchairs without ever having been in the game. The boldness of your third step, Dietrich, seems too far to go—unless you actually were there and it wasn't. By the way, Elton, let me state my view clearly to avoid any misunderstanding. It doesn't quite fit with yours, as Tom's doesn't either.

St. Paul appears to approve of capital punishment when he says that "the magistrate bears the sword and should bear the sword." It's recorded that soldiers came to John the Baptist asking, "What shall we do?" They were not told to leave the army. "When our Lord himself praised the centurion, He never hinted that the military profession was in itself sinful. This has been the general view of Christendom. Pacifism is a recent and local variation. We must, of course, respect and tolerate pacifists, but I think their view erroneous" (*Letters of C. S. Lewis*, Nov. 8, 1952, para. 9, 248).

Barry: Let's recall that one of our earlier guests, Jürgen Moltmann, also came through the terrors of Word War II and emerged with a strong Christian faith that includes a political dimension. He modified Barth's polemic against religious experience. He heard Rudolf Bultmann give a lecture in 1951 in which he rejected social legislation as a Christian option, and that lecture ended Jürgen's interest in existential theology with its insistence that faith is a private matter separate from politics.

Rather, Christian faith should send us into this world with hope and as agents of change in the name and manner of Jesus. Jürgen joins his friend John Cobb, another of our earlier guests, not so much in his Whiteheadian orientation as in his concern for a politically and ecologically relevant theology.

James: At the height of the Cold War in the early 1950s I was drafted into military service. I made up my mind to avoid complaining, believing "that God would help me to handle the experience wisely" (2002-A, 80). I had heard General Douglas MacArthur give a dramatic radio speech galvanizing the national will to resist Communist aggression. It affected me deeply and I was ready to serve my country.

Soon I was sent to Austria, became a chaplain's assistant, and had opportunity to visit Dachau and the former concentration camp there. I cringed at the pictures of that past horror and wrote in my diary, "I hereby pledge myself to the utmost defense of the personal freedom of those for whose protection I am currently engaged."

Being in the very place where "the blood of Nazi victims still cries out from the ground to be avenged, I felt what I vowed. Although valuing the primacy of human life, I have never been a conscientious objector, but standing there in that place of previous torture, if there had been any residue of an unqualified pacifism left in me, the visit to Dachau destroyed it" (2002-A, 98).

Elton: But, James, you know that no human government is fully righteous and just. Are you a subtle slave to human governments? You surely know that they often are perverse, and the best of them is capable of setting up new Dachaus of one kind or another.

James: I'm very aware of that danger, my friend. My ultimate citizenship is always the kingdom of God. Don't forget that my later involvement in the American Civil Rights movement, and certainly my friendship with Martin Luther King, Jr., with our deep commitment to non-violence in actively addressing injustice. I often have written and preached on reconciliation, without for a minute ignoring injustice.

Jesus tells us that God's kingdom is not promoted by human violence, that peace-making is the way to shape the best future, and that those who do this work of effecting reconciliation are God's true children" (2002-B, 20). Absolutely. Even so, and you would appreciate this more than anyone else, Dietrich, there seem to be limits to "unqualified" pacifism when an evil like Jew-exterminating Nazism is on the loose in this fallen world!

I'm sure we all are aware that the New Testament itself gives us a dramatically mixed view of human governments. The book of Revelation concludes the library of biblical materials by combining carefully the apocalyptic and prophetic traditions found sporadically throughout the Bible. Joined there is a sober realism about the roots of power, the fruits of idolatry, and a stern call for Christians to be keenly aware and ethically responsible.

Human history is indeed the arena of evil, the place of persecution; it also is the arena in which God has worked out human salvation and God's people are called to live redemptive lives. The "how" of living redemptive lives, especially in cases of extreme injustice, is not spelled out in detail and in advance.

Barry: The short of it, James, is that we are caught between what appear to be "contrasting biblical views of human governments—they are deserving of our obedience (Rom. 13) and revolting in God's eyes (Rev. 13)" (2007, 117). Be respectful of human governments, yes, particularly when respect is deserved. But equate loyalty to nation with loyalty to God? No!

That kind of dangerous practice lies at the base of today's cruelest religious reactionaries around the world. We see the proper balance in 1 Peter 2:11. Believers are people inclined to civil obedience; they also are "aliens and exiles" in our ungodly world. Let me try to shed some light on this dilemma with a little fiction—an unusual manner of theological communication that you have tried, Louis, and you have mastered, Jack.

My first novel featured an American submarine in World War II. During his first war patrol, the sub captain had his head and heart full of "an especially hideous sight of war, including desperate men diving off decks into the water that was near freezing and now ablaze with spilled oil" (2009-B, 95). He had been the victor in this violent sea confrontation—although victory was an ugly sight. Soon his sub slipped into a safe harbor and time for reflection.

As the victorious captain saw the lovely hills of Scotland moving slowly by, a prayer welled up in his troubled soul. "Thanks, dear God.... These last days have been frustrating, frightening, both successful and very sad. My God, forgive our sin for dealing death to others. . .unless there was so sin, just our duty. If you are really listening, God, please bring me rest of body and conscience... (2009-B, 97-98).

After the war, Admiral Dönitz, head of Germany's submarine service, was given a relatively light sentence at the war trials. The judgment was that he had fought a hard but generally "clean" war at sea. My novel reflects: "But let's face it. 'Clean' is such an empty word when one wanders through the wreckage and contorted bodies left after each battle.... Are some wars clean and others dirty, some just and some unjust?... Isn't there some other way for humans to address their differences? Apparently not. Hopefully so" (2009-B, 219).

Clark: That's sobering stuff, Barry. At times I held what might be thought of as the traditional view of Christian evangelicalism. Significant social problems can be solved only by widespread conversions to

Jesus Christ. As the argument goes, only saved people tend to save sick societies. Politics is generally seen as a dirty business, tempting conservative believers to abandon evangelism and compromise in the public arena. For me, however, there was "one enormous zigzag" in the middle of my career. The early 1970s was a turbulent time in the United States. I realized that evangelical Christians have to practice the demands of the gospel, including in public affairs.

Your writings, Dietrich, were being read with appreciation at the time. I was tempted to adopt the stance of pacifism, Elton. I saw clearly the rightness in the anti-racism and anti-Vietnam rhetoric swirling around me. I wrote for the new *Sojourners* magazine. I felt a deep alienation from mainline American culture and resonated with a resurgence of the radicalizing elements of Anabaptism, such as seen in John Howard Yoder's book *The Original Revolution*.

But that awful war in Vietnam ended, finally. Soon the culture shifted, I moved back to my native Canada, and before long I was admiring the strong and stabilizing figure of Ronald Reagan. I had awakened from "my radical dream," backed away from my brief flirting with a pessimistic millennialism, and started hunting for ways to bring society under God's laws by a combination of evangelistic and political initiatives.

I grieved the obvious slip of the North American culture into a secular abyss and was thirsting after its Christian reconstruction. I know now that we "can't sanctify any social order," so I have come to appreciate again and also be critical of Western democracy. I went too far in both directions and still am seeking the proper middle way (in Callen, 2000, 118).

Barry: The history of the American people is symbolized well by the "Boston Tea Party," an active resistance against British domination of its colonies—sorry to bring that up, Jack. Much more recently, the year 2010 saw the rise of another "Tea Party" movement in U. S. politics, this one demanding more local control and less big, tax-and-spend government. This alternating of strong central government and local control seems constant in human affairs, and occasionally turns violent.

It's helpful for me, Clark, to hear of your own journey with this across the decades. You have admittedly shifted your own emphasis as the culture around you shifted. We all need to avoid absolutizing the viewpoint we currently hold on this or most any other subject.

Tom: It's clear to me that we've all struggled with this God-and-country issue, even if in different settings and in some different ways. Dietrich, are there one or two of you? Some critics insist that you are a religious humanist and practical atheist; others wince at that description and focus on your warm-hearted Christian piety, love of young pastors, and sacrificial call to suffer for Christ in this world. Which is it? You have been nearly a monk, somewhat like me, but also a political agent quite unlike me. Are you one or many?

Dietrich: The best answer, unfortunately, is "yes." Remember that my prison letters and papers were never edited or set in a larger context—the Nazis would hang me before I could do that. I was deeply conflicted, yes, which made me drawn in multiple directions. But I honestly believe I was only one man in my faith in the only God who is above all systems of mere humans. The struggle was how best to live out that faith in an extreme set of circumstances. My best judgments will all be accountable to God's final judgment.

Louis: I confess my considerable concern with the virtual worship of capitalism in the West. I went along with a little of it even inside Gethsemani. At first the royalties from sales of my autobiography helped get the monastery out of debt. I adjusted to the idea of being an economic asset to my brothers. But then I began to oppose the toxic fertilizers being used on our fields to maximize production.

As a monk committed to a life of silence, I detested the noise of our farm machinery and certainly the sense I had that our monastery was imitating corporate America. I was sure that dead birds and sick monks was an unacceptable price to pay for allowing crop dusting. Finally, I was heard and some changes were made, but the confrontation was not always without awkwardness. One has to act on behalf on one's convictions and pay any necessary price.

Barry: We must turn to our other guest, James Cone (Hal), and think through his experience about racism, justice, and Christian responsibility. As we do, we shift from genocide in Europe to racial discrimination in the United States. As an African-American who has suffered unjustly and spoken out strongly and influentially, we need to hear you now, Hal.

Hal: This conversation so far intersects well with my life and commitments. My heart broke as I listened to Dietrich and the Nazi's attempted extermination of the Jews. My people in the United States have been much like those poor Jews, except that they were gassed in chambers and we were hung from trees!

I wrote my *Black Theology and Black Power* in the context of the Civil Rights and Black Power movements. Martin Luther King, Jr., was the powerful symbol of the first and Malcolm X the voice of the second. I wanted to make them a single voice, one bringing the Christian identity and the other the "Black" into my theology. My question was, What does the Christian gospel mean for Blacks struggling for justice?

Dietrich: I can almost taste your struggle, Hal, and I'm still reeling from that image of people hanging from trees. What was your answer to your big question?

Hal: Just this, my new friend in suffering. The gospel is "first and foremost a story of God's solidarity with the poor, empowering them in the fight for freedom.... That was and remains my central theological point" (*BT*, 265).

And, Dietrich, just as Germany was a "Christian" nation doing all the Nazi dirty work, so the United States was the scene of all those Black lynchings usually being done by White Christians who sang on Sunday "Jesus, Keep Me Near the Cross." So you can understand the irony and pathos and even anger in my book *The Cross and the Lynching Tree*. Here are the two most powerful symbols in the Black mentality, two trees of horrible injustice, one smelling only of death and the cross shining with an amazing hope even beyond the awful injustice.

Let's remember that theology is hardly universal language about God. It is contextual language defined by the human situation that gives it birth. No one writes theology for all times, places, and people. There is no "abstract" theology worth its salt that is separate from real human experiences. I certainly have radiated mine. And the passion with which I have written has alienated many White theologians who either ignored or attacked me.

I'll say it again. "Theology is not only rational discourse about ultimate reality; it is also a prophetic word about the righteousness of God.... Oppressors never like to hear the truth in a socio-political context defined by their lies" (2010). I admit that the style of my writing has been influenced more by Malcolm X than be Martin Luther King, Jr. Even so, its truth is fully that of the liberator God in the suffering of Jesus Christ. Jesus is "the event of God, telling us who God is by what God does for the oppressed" (2010). He assures the oppressed that God's righteousness will someday vindicate their suffering. That assurance is how they survive.

James: I want to note how quiet it is in this room right now. Hal, you bring up the underside found somewhere in all of our traditions, times and places when the gospel of Christ has been badly perverted, with the Bible being quoted in support of the worst of human instincts. Justice and liberation certainly lie at the heart of the biblical revelation. And when it comes to patriotism, Christian loyalty to country finds it limits when a whole nation operates counter to the love and justice of God. Friends, we now have been given dramatic examples of such limits in Germany and the United States.

Hal: Let me break the silence only to say this, James. "Salvation" too often is understood by Christians as a mystical communion with the divine that will get you to heaven and out of the horrors of the present. Karl Marx had a point. Oppressive societies are glad for such an escapist understanding because it makes religion an opiate that keeps people from challenging the injustice. It's an effective tool of enslavement.

In the U. S. setting, Blacks "have sung songs about heaven until we were hoarse, but it did not change the present state or ease the pain. To be sure, we may 'walk in Jerusalem jus' like John' and 'there may be a great camp meeting in the Promised Land,' but we want to walk in this land—'the land of the free and the home of the brave' " (2010). I've written boldly to name the evil, decry passivity, and encourage my people toward a proud walking in the freedom God intends.

Surely, to believe in the God who creates heaven for us later is not also to believe that such a wonderful, liberating God wants us passively to accept a hell on earth. The Jews journeyed through the biblical story aided by the liberating God; I have sought to assist American Blacks to do the same in their own painful journey.

Elton: In at least a modest way, my Quaker tradition in both the United Kingdom and the United States became a leader in opposing slavery. Names like John Woolman, Anthony Benezet, and John Greenleaf Whittier were early forerunners of your heart-cry, Hal.

Even so, the shame is still there and your warning must be heeded. Quakers may have led in opposing slavery, but many of them also owned slaves at one point. We all get caught in cultures aimed at perverting our Christian identities. Once perverted, Hal, the need is great for a grating voice like yours.

Hal: Yes, unfortunately the prophetic voice must be loud and harsh. I wrote *God of the Oppressed* in response to critics, mostly but not all White, who challenged my reading of the biblical God as the Liberator of all in bondage. They were upset that supposedly I was too influenced by Malcolm X. The simple fact is that we all read the Bible selectively, my critics from the liberal White dominant viewpoint and me from the Black perspective of the marginalized. I admit in this book that "I am Black first—and everything else comes after that."

Dietrich: At least folks in the U. S. didn't jail and then execute you for challenging the religious and political establishments. That's slightly better than my experience with the powers that be!

Hal: I suppose, and I'm deeply sorry about your awful treatment. One way that was found to silence me was to just ignore my work, preferring to dialogue with what was more in vogue, Latin American liberation and feminist theologies. No matter. A lesson I and all must learn is that, beyond our own immediate location of interpretation and concern, we must broaden our vision.

We must work to make real the beloved community envisioned by Dr. King. The full humanity of any, Black folks and others, is possible only as we each champion such humanity for all others. One way I have tried to do this is joining the Ecumenical Association of Third World Theologians and traveling and dialoguing widely.

Barry: Dietrich and Hal, you both have sobered us, chastened us, and shown us a God of love *and* righteousness. We are grateful and uncomfortable because of what the realities our national histories actually are. The "Christian" nations of Germany and the United States, of all counties, have practiced and biblically justified slavery and even genocide.

For Christians, is it God *and* country? Apparently the answer depends in part on what the country is all about at any given time. Sometimes hard choices must be made by those faithful to Jesus. Dietrich and Hal, you have made such choices in differing ways and settings, and for that we honor and learn from you.

Hal says he has learned something significant in his Third-World travels. How does the revelation of God in Christ apply to people reared in other faith traditions, and to those who have never even heard of Jesus? Hal reports that "I cannot limit God's revelation to Jesus or to the fight against white racism.... No one people's language and experience are capable of capturing the full reality and presence of God" (Preface, 1997 ed., *God of the Oppressed*).

This report raises the big questions that we will pursue in our next conversation.

Questions Related to Conversation #8

1. Look again at the quote leading this conversation. Did E. Stanley Jones compromise his role as Christian evangelist or adapt wisely in different cultural settings, thus enhancing the authenticity and maybe even the effectiveness of his missionary work?

2. Pacifism appears in this conversation both as a worthy Christian stance and as one with likely limitations under extreme circumstances of social evil such as sometimes is encountered in this world. In your judgment, can both pacifism and "just war" be acceptable Christian stances?

3. Dietrich's approach to making decisions is sometimes called "situation ethics." To what extent should circumstances have a bearing on Christian decisions and actions? How should we relate biblical teachings and apparent societal necessities?

4. Dietrich says that there are three options for how the church can respond to the human society in which it finds itself. What are they? How can we decide which is best, or might the best choice vary from place to place and time to time?

5. Assuming the Bible is the fundamental guide to Christian decision-making, do you agree that the Bible presents mixed views on human governments—one, proper authority worthy of our respect and obedience, and the other perverted power deserving nothing other than our resistance in the name of God?

6. Clark admits to changing his mind more than once on the issues of Christian faith, patriotism, war, etc. Maybe he was influenced excessively by current pressures and trends in the culture around him (church and society), like many German Christians were in the 1930s and 1940s. How do we live *in* this world without subtly becoming *part of it*?

7. Hal presents a powerful challenge to passively accepting injustice. Is Christ Black? Must we wait on heaven and give up on the now?

Conversation #9

THE MANY RELIGIONS OF THE WORLD
Religious Knowledge, Exclusivism, Finality of Jesus, and the Validity of the Christian Mission Today

> In our time, when day by day mankind is being drawn closer together, and the ties between different peoples are becoming stronger, the Church examines more closely her relationship to non-Christian religions. In her task of promoting unity and love among men, indeed among nations, she considers above all what men have in common and what draws them to fellowship.... Men expect from the various religions answers to the unsolved riddles of the human condition which today, even as in former times, deeply stir the hearts of men (Pope Paul VI, 1965).

> We affirm that there is only one Saviour and only one gospel.... We recognize that all men have some knowledge of God through his general revelation in nature. But we deny that this can save, for men suppress the truth by their unrighteousness. We also reject as derogatory to Christ and to the gospel every kind of syncretism and dialogue which implies that Christ speaks equally through all religions and ideologies (Lausanne Covenant, 1974).

Barry: Hello good friends. Our topic today focuses on Christianity and the many religions of the world. There is no question about religious pluralism being a major factor in our modern world. There is question, however, even among some Christians, about whether Jesus Christ is the only path to salvation.

Remembering our fifth conversation, we affirmed Jesus as the solid center of Christian faith. But today's pluralistic setting places this affirmation under a cloud of doubt.

Most people are very aware of competing claims to ultimate truth. The heart of Christian identity, evangelism, and mission surely depends on whether or not Jesus is viewed as ultimate truth. This is why the above quotes, one drafted by the Roman Catholic Church and one by a worldwide gathering of "Evangelical" Christians, focus on this subject.

Jack: I doubt that our guest today, a fellow Brit, would have signed the Lausanne Covenant quoted above, as James and Barry did in Switzerland. So let me introduce him and let him speak for himself. A brief vita of John Hick appears on our screen. Welcome, John.

John: Thanks for the invitation and your focusing on such an important topic for Christians today.

Louis: Well, John, to get us started, I wonder about your life's journey. Would it be accurate to say that over the years you have moved from a commitment to "evangelical" Christianity to a much more "pluralistic" position—which would be why we doubt that you would have signed the Lausanne Covenant?

John: Yes, that's quite accurate. I have more of an affinity with the other quote

John Hick (1922-2012)--a prominent English philosopher/theologian and a modern prophet of religious pluralism. Born in England in 1922, John experienced an "evangelical conversion" to Christianity at age eighteen. While studying philosophy at Edinburgh University in Scotland beginning in 1941, with a view to later ministry in the Presbyterian Church of England, he was attracted to the philosophy of Immanuel Kant and began questioning aspects of his faith. World War II intervened and he served as a conscientious objector with a Friends' ambulance unit. After the war, he continued his studies, was ordained, and pastored for three years before returning to the academic world. John completed doctorates at both Edinburgh and Oxford and assumed teaching roles at Cornell University and Princeton Theological Seminary in the United States. He returned to England in 1967 to teach at the University of Birmingham.

Along the path of this professional journey, John shed many of his earlier "fundamentalist" convictions. Confronted in Birmingham with considerable religious diversity, and troubled by many Christians who were intolerant of other faith communities, he gravitated toward a pluralist position of the world's religious traditions. In 1979 he returned to the United States to assume a chair in philosophy of religion at Claremont Graduate School in California, which he held for some two decades. Authoring several widely-read books, he delivered the prestigious Gifford Lectures at Edinburgh, Scotland, in 1986-1987 and authored his autobiography in 2005.

from the Second Vatican Council. It feels like an attempt to reconcile God's love with the facts of cultural and religious diversity in our day.

My original commitment to Christianity was of the conservative, even at points of the fundamentalist kind. Eventually, however, I became troubled by the implications of such faith for the other religious communities of our world. Diversity is a dominant theme of our day and I decided that Christian theology must adapt to this overarching reality.

Jack: It's so easy to decide that all faith communities deserve respect and may even be as right as any other. So, John, please go on to explain your process of change.

John: How good to see you, Jack. Thanks for the open door. In the late 1960s I was teaching philosophy at the University of Birmingham in England and attended worship with Muslims, Hindus, Sikhs, and others. I observed all of them doing essentially the same thing. They were "human beings opening their minds to a higher divine Reality, known as personal and good and as demanding righteousness and love between man and man" (1980, 5).

It was the contrast that I began to find troubling. I observed a pervasive racism entrenched in the British mind, an awkwardness built right into the social institutions, likely a leftover of the previous imperialism. It extended right into the Christian community.

For instance, the university required every student, regardless of religious tradition, to study the doctrines of the Church of England. I soon went to work on curricular reform. I came to believe that one necessary adaptation of Christianity is an ending of the exclusivistic stance that insists that it or any faith system is inherently superior to all others. Such exclusivity is strongly implied in the Lausanne statement that Barry and James signed. In my opinion, this statement is reactionary, dated, and even dangerous in today's world.

James: John, just a note without our being defensive. Barry and I signed that statement not as a threat but as fresh hope for all peoples. It was an act of love that assumes we have good news and are obligated to share it for the good of others.

Now, one of our earlier guests, Georgia Harkness, called our attention to the current work of Karen Armstrong. Karen sees compassion as the common denominator among the religions, much like you see a common commitment to righteousness and love. Want to comment?

John: Yes, I admire the great work of Karen. And, indeed, compassion is part of the commonality.

Elton: Well, John, I hear you, but I'm not quite with you on this one. I do have a compliment to share, however. You are one of four major thinkers involved in our group conversations who have delivered a set of the prestigious Gifford Lectures. The others are Jürgen Moltmann, William Temple, and Alfred North Whitehead. The original bequest of Adam Lord Gifford (1820-1887) has been used quite well to promote serious explorations of the knowledge of God and God's relation to this world.

So, John, congratulations, and please give us a brief summary of the central burden of your particular lectures from the 1980s.

John: I'd love to, Elton—and you put me in quite the company! My book *An Interpretation of Religion* is an expanded version of those lectures of mine. What I do is lay out a case for a pluralist interpretation of religious experience.

Relying in part on the thought Immanuel Kant, I argue that the major religious traditions of humanity constitute diverse and yet equally authentic responses to the "Real" (my preferred term for the ultimate ground for all religious experience). The belief systems of the different religions are actually differing patterns of perceiving and experiencing the one Real. They, therefore, are not necessarily in conflict and should all respect each other.

A key question always brought up is the identity of "God." The fact is that God is "trans-categorical" or ineffable, and is to be distinguished from the forms of this Real that are manifested in our human conceptual frameworks and modes of religious experiencing. This allows us a constructive interpretation of the history of religions and requires some humility from us all.

Knowledge of God, and all the resulting truth claims, are historically and culturally influenced, and thus should not be considered absolute—at least, not for persons in other traditions. The Real is absolute; our human concepts of the Real are relative and partial.

Tom: Of course they are, John, we are only human. But, according to the consensual teaching of Christianity to which I subscribe, "the incarnation is what makes Christianity distinctive in the sphere of the history of religions. Non-Christian religions have distinctive features too, but only in Christianity is the promise of God to Israel fulfilled by God's own personal coming in the flesh. Christianity differs from the religions of the world in that its understanding of God comes, not from human striving, intellect, and will, but from God's own self-disclosure in human history, through the people of Israel, which culminates and clarifies itself finally *only in Jesus Christ*" (2009, 196).

John: I fully understand that claim. That's where I started in life, just not exactly where I've ended.

Elton: Let's get back to your Gifford Lectures, John. I have so appreciated this great series, including the set that William Temple gave back in the 1930s (published as *Nature, Man, and God*). There's no question that we now live in a world where Christianity is in close contact with other religious traditions and must find thoughtful and constructive ways of judging and relating. Your pluralist approach is one thoughtful way of dealing with the subject, although in my view not clearly the best way.

I have argued that the fact of God being active in all faith traditions is not a reason to avoid Christian distinctiveness and mission. I believe strongly that "no true Christian can be content to hold his faith to himself; whatever he really prizes he is bound to share. As I visited the brave fellowships of Asia and Africa, I understood better the words of Emil Brunner: 'The church exists by mission as fire exists by burning' " (1972, 82).

John, your approach, in my judgment, affirms other faith traditions to the excessive extent that witness to them about the claims of the Christian faith becomes virtually unnecessary and even arrogant and inappropriate. I have to join James and Barry in seeing legitimacy in the Swiss Covenant of the 1970s. It respects all people and is also anxious to share with them what is believed to be really good news.

Tom: I love that quote by Brunner, Elton, and I'm generally comfortable with your critique of where John has come out. Late in my career I became focused unexpectedly on the continent of Africa and its great significance for Christian history, theology, and biblical interpretation. Out of that came my book *How Africa Shaped the Christian Mind*.

Now I'm convinced that something is crucial for African church leaders who are and will face an aggressive Islam. I'm not saying that Christianity should be attacking Islam, only that it will not withstand Islam's assertiveness and absolutist claims "without an accurate memory of their own six centuries of pre-Islamic vitality as well as their history of courage, sacrifice, and determination since Islam" (2014, 321). The religions of the world, John, are hardly being respectful of Christians these days.

James: Your substantial work and concern on the African front is new to me, Tom. As an African-American myself, I thank you!

Barry: And since I work regularly with an AIDS-orphan ministry in several African nations, I too thank you. How blind we Christians have been to this large portion of our own history.

Louis: Enough of admiring Tom's work. Let's get back to the main subject. Are you saying, John, that Christianity is one of many religious communities and in part is the product of its own historical and cultural origins, as all others also are?

John: You're exactly right, I am, and the resulting pluralism is a big issue that can't be ignored. Christians have tended recently to take one of two approaches.

Exclusivism. This approach insists that Christianity is the only true religion and the singular source of salvation for all humans.

Inclusivism. Increasingly popular today among mainline Protestant denominations and the Roman Catholic Church is the other approach. Salvation is viewed as indeed through Christ alone by virtue of his atoning death on the cross. Even so, this salvation is not necessarily confined to "Christians," but is available through God's grace, at least in principle, to all seriously seeking human beings, *through* if not *because of* their given religious traditions or lack thereof. Good people outside Christianity can benefit from an implicit Christian faith, being "anonymous Christians," or at least will respond to Christ as their Lord when finally confronted by him after death.

This inclusive approach claims middle ground. At least it avoids the horrifying conviction that only Christians can be saved, while it still holds to the traditional conviction of the unique place of Jesus Christ in God's saving revelation and work. But even inclusivism has its negative side.

Inclusivism still holds that God is known most fully in Jesus Christ (the consensus result, I hear, of one of your earlier conversations). The benefits of this superiority may manage to trickle down, but only indirectly to others who remain outside the immediate fellowship of Jesus. We Christians are judged the spiritually rich ones in the world of religious knowledge and experience; others can manage to benefit by weakened reflections of this pure light.

Tom: So, where does that bring you on the subject of the salvation of humans from their considerable in problem?

John: Salvation is typically defined by Christians as forgiveness by God because of the atoning death of Jesus on the cross. I have come to think differently about salvation, viewing it more as the transformation of men and women from natural self-centeredness to a new orientation centered in the divine reality, the Real that we often call God. This transformation releases people to liberated lives of love and compassion for fellow human beings.

To put my view of salvation in New Testament terms, those being saved are those whose lives embody the "fruit of the Spirit." This opens up a more radical inclusivism that, among other things, can help diffuse the religious absolutisms that are being exploited dangerously in most of the major conflicts in today's world. I know this group already has had a whole conversation on compassion. I think that compassion is a central human goal, commonly affirmed among all the major religious traditions of the world.

Jack: Your view is very clear, John, and clearly noble. Inclusivism I affirm but, as a biblical Christian, I hesitate adding the word "radical" to it. It certainly is true that "if you are Christian, you do *not* have to believe that all the other religions are simply wrong all through. If you are an atheist, you *do* have to believe that the main point in all the religions of the whole world is simply one huge mistake. If you are a Christian, you are free to think that all these religions, even the queerest ones, contain at least some hint of the truth" (1960, bk. II, chap. 1, 43).

While this much inclusivism is true in my view, my faith says that there is something contained in the Christian revelation in Jesus that keeps just anything from being affirmed as truth. There is an objective historical reality, Jesus, whose coming to this world both shows us the true God as none other does and opens our way to renewed relationship with God as none other does. This stance leaves me compassionately open to others and yet rooted in Jesus Christ.

Clark: Agreed, Jack, and well said. And one more thing. I am moved by your story of Emeth in "The Last Battle" that's part of the final volume of your *The Chronicles of Narnia*. Emeth learns to his surprise that his worship of Tash is honored by Aslan.

"But I said, 'Alas, Lord, I am no son of Thine but the servant of Tash.' He [Aslan] answered, 'Child, all the service thou hast done to Tash I account as service done to me' " (1996, 205).

With that, it is clear to me, Jack, that you understand God to be a singular and redeeming reality, mercifully at work in the religious life of humanity at large and yet located centrally in God as revealed particularly in Jesus.

Jack: You judge properly, Clark. I view God through the eyes of a wonderful inclusivism, but one with a definite truth core whose historical name is Jesus. I don't view this faith stance as arrogant or closeminded or dangerous to those who believe differently, but rather a source of joy to my life and potentially to the lives of all others.

Clark: I thought so. And I hear you, John, but I can't give up the centerpiece of my faith in response to pluralism. I join Jack in continuing to affirm the central significance of God-with-us in Jesus, a divine revelation that should not lead us to the wrong-headed assumption that the work of the Spirit does not reach people who have not heard of Jesus, or have gotten a twisted view of him from faulty witnesses.

I'm not an expert on comparative religions, to be sure. Still, I believe deeply in the universal work of God's Spirit, work not in conflict with a high view of the distinctive person and role of Jesus in the overall work of God (1992, 74-80). Jesus is the only one who has died for all, and his Spirit surely loves and somehow seeks to mediate that finished work to the benefit of all.

And I'd like to make one more comment, although I'm sensing, John, that Jack and I have grabbed hold of this conversation too much, and maybe a little defensively. It's just that we're confronting a subtle assault on the very integrity of the Christian faith that we know and love, God fully self-revealed in Jesus Christ. May I make one more quick set of comments?

John: Go ahead, Clark. I understand the defensiveness—I used to do my share of the same thing. And I appreciate the ongoing effort to find some middle ground. I know this isn't easy since we're working on questions about the traditional heart of the faith and the very different world of today.

Clark: Thanks for your patience. The distinction you make, John, between the exclusivism and inclusivism approaches is clear enough, and I doubt there is one strict exclusivist in our conversation today. However, I see a third option. I think "it is possible, on the basis of the particularity of Christ, to propose a global theology. God has not left himself without witness anywhere, though he has revealed himself definitively in one particular human life. Moral and spiritual worth can be found in other faiths, yet God's revelation in Christ is of surpassing value" (1996, 207). This is my form of inclusivism, one that retains the surpassing value of Jesus Christ.

I think there's a viable middle ground here. I'm about where our earlier guest, Donald Bloesch, came out on this. Yes, there is a "hidden Christ" in the great religions and cultures of the world. And yet, this Christ "will invariably be misunderstood and confused with the idols of human imagination" (1992, 53).

James: Clark, does the confusion with idols extend sometimes even to Christians themselves?

Clark: Unfortunately, yes. In the end, God's self-revelation in Jesus Christ stands in judgment over all religions, including over institutionalized Christian faith. True religion emerges only as it is purified by the grace of God in Jesus Christ. So, here's an important question. Should Christians be busy proclaiming their faith's superiority over all other religions? No! What we should be doing is submitting our own inadequacies and ambiguities to the judgment of Christ so that we can present a more authentic witness to God's good news for the whole world. Even while needing repentance ourselves, however, we do have really good news from God that needs shared with everyone. We should share not because we wish to dominate but because we so deeply love.

John: I hear that, Clark. That's a good way of stating what I was saying is an increasing stance in mainline Christian denominations. It's a modified exclusivism, to be sure, but still not modified enough in my view. I think even the Jesus revelation carries its inherent limitations derived from its historical and cultural origins.

Elton: Well, John, I agree to an extent. Of course, all of our thoughts and beliefs are earth-bound. Even so, my faith tells me that God has broken through all of that in Jesus with a divine light that gives the needed orienting perspective. We humans don't perceive this Jesus light in its fullness, but there nonetheless has been an "incarnation" of God's presence and truth, and his name is Jesus. What I hear from Clark is a crucial message of caution to the Christian community. Let me build on this Jesus-based "global theology" of yours, Clark, always keeping in mind your good caution.

I tend to think that your view, Clark, is an adequately modified exclusivism. We Christians have been suffering from a distorted image of a missionary. We too easily conceive of a narrow-minded person who goes into another culture with virtually no understanding of or appreciation for it, and with a message that condemns its long-held convictions. So many contemporary Christians already have shed this missionary model and, unfortunately, sometimes with it even the mission altogether. But Christianity and mission are inseparable.

You, John, would appreciate at least the following point I'm anxious to make. The problem is intellectual. A critical task is to think carefully about all this. I say that sound thinking begins with the assumption that the only good reason for being a Christian is the belief that the Christian faith is right about its Christ claim.

Of course, Christianity has been captured by given cultures and at times has functioned in shameful ways toward others. Still, here's the core question: "Is the faith itself, rooted in divine revelation in Jesus, and apart from its poor performances, *true or not?*"

The champion of cultural relativity, like your more radical inclusivism, John, falls into inevitable self-contradiction, it seems to me. "If there is no objective moral order, and therefore no real right, then there is likewise no real wrong.... It is obvious that, though there may be elements of truth in all, the faiths cannot be equally true because some assertions are in direct conflict with others.... The ultimate and permanent case for the Christian mission rests directly upon the conception that the Christian faith is true" (1972, 52-53, 56).

And the truth to which I refer does not require defense of Western civilization, a particular church hierarchy, or a given set of creedal statements. The truth, the heart of the matter to proclaim is "that God really is, and that He is like Christ. Being like Christ, the One who is Lord of all, including all nations, all races, and all cultures, cares for every individual and has made every human being in His own image" (1972, 59).

John: Allow me to repeat, Elton, that I don't deny the existence of a single and definitive reality. I readily affirm the "Real" who is and stands above all. Nor do I claim that, since there are directly competing elements in the various faith traditions, they can all be true ultimately. What I am saying is that each of us responds to the one Real in our limited ways, including Christianity.

While I would go further than you, Elton, I do appreciate how you and Clark are sounding a note of genuine caution in the face of too much Christian arrogance. We are all limited humans responding to our inner longings and spiritual needs in the best ways we can within our given cultures.

Elton: Thanks for that reminder, John. Humility is required of all, and all certainly is by God's sheer grace. And there's only one true God. What I don't maintain is that other faith traditions are all wrong, because they're not; what I do maintain is that "whatever is true in all religions is genuinely consummated in Christ" (1972, 67).

I am aware of a difficult question that constantly arises among those of us who believe that salvation is through Jesus Christ alone. What about truly good people who, for whatever reason, have not explicitly accepted Jesus Christ in this life? I say that we dare not limit God's saving activity. Christ surely can reach such people in whatever their circumstances or time frames or cultural settings.

Two kinds of Christian theology have failed on the mission fields of the world. One of these is "the old-fashioned Fundamentalism and the other is the old-fashioned Liberalism. The former fails because it cannot meet the challenge of scientific thinking and the latter fails because it is too broad and syncretistic to have a cutting edge" (1972, 102). I, and I think we, choose neither of these failed approaches.

Louis: I agree, Elton, and I want to focus on Christian motive and method for its evangelism. We wrongly represent God if we wind up mistreating any person made in God's image, whatever his or her religious community.

The Roman Catholic Church made this clear pronouncement in 1965: "The Church reproves, as foreign to the mind of Christ, any discrimination against men or harassment of them because of their race, color, condition of life, or religion. On the contrary, following in the footsteps of the holy Apostles Peter and Paul, this sacred synod ardently implores the Christian faithful to 'maintain good fellowship among the nations' (1 Peter 2:12), and, if possible, to live for their part in peace with all men so that they may truly be sons of the Father who is in heaven" (*Nostra Aetate*).

James: That fine statement originated with Pope Paul VI, my good brother, and we must not miss the more recent exhortation of Pope Francis on primary Christian motives. He "summons each of the faithful to be Spirit-filled evangelizers who encounter Christ's love . . . and who are so convinced that life with Christ makes all the difference that they seek to share the gospel with others. They want to give their lives entirely to mission, living not for their own purposes, but for the Lord's" (Sri, 123). Our mission motive as Christians is to be love reaching out in order to increase the joy in others that we ourselves have found in Christ.

Barry: Reaching out in love requires a special skill so often lacking. We need to embrace the "other" in this world. Facing differing faith communities is a simple fact of our times. Others threaten our Christian thinking with their opposing truth claims. Competing faith communities sometimes even use religious rhetoric to threaten our lives. We seem to have two choices. We can open our minds and hearts to the potential that may lie in something new, or we can fall back on a flight-or-fight response.

Parker Palmer has made something plain for all teaching-learning settings: "If we understand the promise of paradox, our encounters with 'the other' have the potential to make our world larger, more generous, more hopeful" (1980, 2008). Our salvation comes from God's grace. In turn, we ought to approach others gracefully, openly, anxious to share, and also willing to learn. That goes against the grain of so many humans. We easily get defensive and then aggressive, so unlike our Christ.

Jack: The difficult question is clear enough, Barry. Pluralism presents problems and possibilities. Can we be open to such potential that is resident in other faiths and still remain true to the person and commission of Jesus? The quote of E. Stanley Jones that led off our eighth conversation would respond positively to this question. He says he presented in India and elsewhere a "disentangled Christ—

disentangled from being bound up with Western culture and Western forms of Christianity" (110). Our faith is always tangled to some degree with some culture. Our commission is to share Christ, not ourselves or our cultures of origin. We are to be ambassadors of love, not religious imperialists building private empires—was that a British inference on my part?

Clark: Sure was, Jack, and I liked it! Beyond proclaiming to others our deepest religious convictions, it's obviously humility time. We're all with you on that much, John. We don't have all the answers as Christians, and we aren't to act arrogantly as the divinely-appointed final judge of all other people. "Let us not be too sure who will be justified and who condemned. No one is automatically barred from heaven. We leave all people to the mercy of God. We are *good news* people—negativity does not become us" (1996, 190).

Rather than acting as though we know all the dim edges of the huge truth sphere, I go back to our conversation five that we called "Faith's Solid Center." I'll stand with Jesus as the center and allow him and his Father to determine the edges that I cannot see clearly. The basic truth affirmed by Christianity is a *Person*, Jesus, not a set of detailed *propositions* about theological matters seen differently by the religions of the world.

I've called my own position "inclusive finality" that functions within the framework of two axioms. (1) Salvation is only in Jesus Christ. (2) God's will is to save all people who are willing to receive his saving grace. We don't need to think of the Christian church as the ark of salvation, leaving everyone not physically in this boat with us to an eternity in hell. Instead, we should think of the church as God's chosen vessel for witnessing widely to the good news of the fullness of salvation which has come into the world in Jesus and for all people.

Elton: Well said, Clark. I once wrote the book *A Place to Stand*. My chapter "A Center of Certitude" keyed off this quote of René Descartes: "I shall be entitled to entertain the highest expectations if I am fortunate enough to discover only one thing that is certain and indubitable." Knowing the fate of all the faithful religious people of earth, the Emeths, Jack, is not what I can be certain about.

For me, John, "a Christian is a person who, with all the honesty of which he is capable, becomes convinced that the fact of Jesus Christ is the most trustworthy that he knows in his entire universe of discourse" (1996, 38). Standing in that solid center of faith should not place us in the mindset of the old British imperialism, as you so well said, Jack, but establish us in the mood of joy and witness that shares good news, like you said, Clark, without conveying announcements of the mass damnation of any people. As good Quakers, on many disputable subjects we should just keep our mouths shut!

Tom: The Bible and the consensual witness of the church over the centuries are quite clear. God is never left without witness in the world (Acts 14: 17; John 1:4). God is known in various and sundry ways in general human history, yet has come to be finally known in his Son (Heb. 1; 6: 59). The dialogue with the religions of this world has proceeded on this basis in classic Christianity.

"If the revelation of which Christianity speaks is only for Christians, then there is no compelling need for dialogue. But that does not square with Scripture. The Great Commission is to go to all nations and proclaim the gospel. Continuing dialogue with Islam, Buddhism, and Hinduism presents a vexing set of challenges to the Christian community to account for its statements about Jesus. Yet, in the vital dialogue with world religions, Christians are tempted to dilute the testimony to the universal relevance of Jesus' coming and instead focus more amiably upon the moral teaching of Jesus or his extraordinary life. It remains a pivotal Christian assertion that Christ is the truth even for those who do not recognize him as their truth" (2009, 244, Kindle ed.).

Jack: Defensive as I sometimes am about my native homeland, I fully agree that the old-style British imperialism is hardly a workable model for how Christians should view and relate to the people of other faith communities. They must have their freedom and dignity, regardless of our views. But I agree, Tom, that granting dignity to all does not imply failing to go to them with a witness of good news.

Tom: Amen, Jack. In recounting the Christian consensus on this topic in my *Classic Christianity*, I concluded this. Where we are headed as faithful believers is a house of "many mansions" being prepared for us. Although the Lord has sheep "not of this fold" (Jn. 10:16), their identity is not known to us now.

"There is immense diversity among the actual histories of persons who hear and respond to the gospel and vast variety in the levels of capacity that various cultures and personal dispositions allow. There is not in the real world a simple equality of opportunity to hear God's good news in Jesus Christ, however much it intends to reach out for all. Some of these many mansions may remain opaque to our view." I leave all that to the loving wisdom of God.

James: I am a Christian preacher who assumes that I need a clear message that can inspire faith and change lives. It's true that I'm a lover and reconciler of people and don't use the pulpit to deride the honest truth searchings of others. Nonetheless, I am convinced that there is good news for all people. Let me use words of a Lutheran friend to highlight the message I gladly proclaim.

"At one point in history God has communicated his reconciling love to and for the world—in the death and resurrection of Jesus Christ.... Christ stands as the essential representative between God and humanity, representing God for the world and the world before God.... Somehow Christ is the place where the contradiction between God and humanity gets resolved—actually and necessarily.... The only unique thing that Christianity has to offer the world is its witness to Christ; and by Christ we do not mean some anonymous Christ principle but the concrete reality and historical person of Jesus as the Christ" (Braaten, 76-78).

There's the heart of the matter. I don't proclaim this Christian distinctive arrogantly, but joyfully, not as a threat to anyone, but as a wonderful opportunity for any who will hear. For those who don't, I leave them in God's hands that are wiser and stronger and more just than mine.

Louis: Let me repeat for us what I once said to young monks in my role as Master of Novices at Gethsemani. It certainly suggests my openness to at least some of your thought, John. I said:

"Life is this simple. We are living in a world that is absolutely transparent and God is shining through it all the time. This is not just a fable or a nice story. It is true. If we abandon ourselves to God and forget ourselves, we see it sometimes.... God manifests Himself everywhere, in everything—in people and in things and in nature and in events. It becomes very obvious that He is everywhere and in everything and we cannot be without Him" (in Forest, 165).

Therefore, my time with the Buddhists, for instance, brought great spiritual richness to me, in part because I was open to it. I saw God among those devout people. And to be so grandly open to the ever-present God is not a violation of my belief in Jesus, the apex of the divine presence.

Where does that leave me about who will be "saved"? People like those Buddhists I visited might not be fully correct in terms of the revelation in Jesus, but they are far from being all wrong. How will God handle that at judgment time? That's for God to figure out. Our roles do not include being the final Judge. We are to be open, faithful to what we know, sharing gratefully, and learning humbly. While God shines in all, our sin spreads a blindness that isn't yet all removed. All have sinned, are blinded. God wants all of us to see again!

John: I'm tracking with you, Louis. Your open spirit is far from what I knew as a younger man. I now am a dialogue partner, not a

Christian missionary, but I am encouraged by the tone of this conversation.

Louis: Allow me just another minute—monks usually don't talk this much. I affirm at least part of what you're trying to get said, John. In our world, we must allow ourselves the privilege of slipping beyond the security of our well-reasoned definitions of religious things. We must give some space to the mystery of an intimately present God who yet remains uncaptured by our little minds. Let me elaborate with the words of a brother who has written so graciously about me.

"We need to have courage like Father Louis to take off the shoes of our own customary ways and walk among our brethren of the other faiths and paths, one with them in a common search for peace, harmony, and spiritual enlightenment. It will do us little good to have the right dogmatic answers (the devils know the truth, too) if we do not have that experience of the truth that calls forth from us a complete "yes," that calls us forth from our everyday earth-bound consciousness into the clarity of a compassionate universal love" (Pennington, 43).

John: Louis, your good brother's words resonate well with me. I have been heard today by you men and, to a significant extent, even appreciated. You have been gentle with me and I have felt your love, the very love we all should extend to religious communities not our own.

Barry: Thanks, John, and your comments, Louis, leave us quiet and humbled. I think all of us in this conversation group understand and appreciate John's sensitivity to unwarranted religious imperialism, even if we don't tend to go as far as he does into the relativistic pool of pluralism. Regardless, John, we are in your debt for joining us today.

My friend Delwin Brown, also a good friend of yours, Clark, once made this "progressive" observation. I think it reflects your view, John. "The incarnation of God means that all the world's religions are frail but fertile sites of the divine.... We may say with John's Gospel that no one comes to God except through Christ, but "Christ" is the Christian name for the logos of God in all of creation, including all religions" (2008, 38).

I honor this loving and sensitive observation, and respond to it only with the concern that it tends to forfeit the full and historical revelation of God in Jesus Christ, the core belief of classic Christianity, as you would quickly remind us, Tom.

Now looking forward to our next conversation, there come the many questions surrounding the final end of our historical experience as humans. When will the Judge call a halt to our ignorance and sinning and bring full justice to all of creation? How will that happen and who will benefit?

We will have two special guests with us next time. They will bring sharply differing perspectives to help us sort things out and discover the heart of this matter of final things.

Questions Related to Conversation #9

1. What exactly does John Hick mean by "pluralism"? Is this a major reality in the religious world of today, one that cannot be ignored?

2. Is the *exclusivism-inclusivism* distinction clear to you? What of the varieties of inclusivism that are increasingly prominent among Christians, for instance, the "radical" and "inclusive finality" types?

3. Do we Christians know enough from biblical revelation to make sure judgments about the eventual fate of those people who never declare faith in Jesus Christ for their salvation? If you think we do, why do so many biblical scholars not see it that way?

4. Recall that little story about Emeth's surprising encounter with Aslan. Does that describe well the biblical story of God's attitude toward those "good people" not committed specifically to Jesus?

5. Tom says that having all the right answers, even the right view of Jesus Christ, is hardly enough if our hearts and attitudes toward others remain wrong. Think about that seriously as you relate to people of other faith communities.

6. Are you ready to embrace the big paradox? On the one hand, Jesus is the full and final revelation of God to humans. On the other hand, as Tom puts it, "we must give some space to the mystery of an intimately present God who yet remains uncaptured by our little minds."

7. Are you sure about who will be "saved" and who will not? Should you be a "missionary" to the lost world, or is that too much religious arrogance?

Conversation #10

ARE THESE THE LAST DAYS?

Biblical Prophecy, Resurrection, Millennial Theories, Heaven, Hell, and Eternal Life

> The human story is a proper topic for the doctrine of last things because the divine saving activity transpires within the flow of events in time. In fact, seen in its entirety, history is the narrative of God at work in the world. In this context, the doctrine of last things is a systematic-theological reflection on history as the narrative of God's activity in bringing humankind to God's intended goal (Grenz, 1994, 780).

> But if the Christian hope is reduced to the salvation of the soul in a heaven beyond death, it loses its power to renew life and change the world, and its flame is quenched; it dies away into no more than gnostic yearning for redemption from this world's vale of tears (Moltmann, 1996, xv).

Barry: How good it is to be together again. Our topic today is "end times" and beyond, those topics called "eschatology" by the specialists and heatedly argued over by numerous interpreters of the Bible. We want to explore such subjects in light of the insights of our faith, in continuity with our previous conversations, and possibly in response to the daily headlines of today's turbulent world.

The thought of John Hick shared in our last conversation is viewed by many conservative Christians as one of the signs that the Christian community has deteriorated badly. Some even say that this deterioration is so advanced that God will tolerate very little more—thus, the

Stanley J. Grenz (1950-2005)-- the son of a Christian minister in Michigan, Stan graduated from the University of Colorado at Boulder in 1973, Denver Seminary in 1976, and the University of Munich, Germany, in 1978. His dissertation was done under the supervision of Wolfart Pannenberg. A prolific author, he was Professor of Systematic Theology and Christian Ethics at the North American Baptist Seminary in South Dakota from 1981 to 1990, and then Pioneer McDonald Professor of Baptist Heritage, Theology and Ethics at Carey Theological College and Regent College in Vancouver, British Columbia, Canada.

An ordained Christian minister who ministered in various roles in local churches, Stan also served as president of the National Association of Baptist Professors of Religion and as a member of the national board of the American Academy of Religion. Beyond numerous articles published in journals ranging from *Christianity Today* and the *Christian Century* to *Christian Scholars Review*, *Theology Today*, and the *Journal of Ecumenical Studies*, his influential books include his systematic theology, *Theology for the Community of God* (1994), and his book on eschatology directly relevant to this conversation, *The Millennial Maze: Sorting Out Evangelical Options* (1992).

end is surely near and will be full of divine judgment on our human waywardness.

James: That's so true. Popular TV preachers and books on the nearing judgment abound. Let me point us back to the two lead quotes on our screen.

Stan, one of our guests today, sets the historical frame of the subject, and a previous guest warns that becoming preoccupied with the future jeopardizes our church mission to the present time and world. That should give our conversation a good start.

Barry: Thanks, James. A paradox seems to be embedded in every topic we address. In this case, "How should believers balance what is hoped to be *near* with what is known to be *already here*? (1997, 24). How do we live in hope for tomorrow without allowing that hope to erode our mission for today?

Now, let me introduce our special guests, Hal Lindsey and Stanley J. Grenz. We have extended this double invitation for today because Hal and Stan represent contrasting views of the Christian approach to the subject at hand. Exploring this contrast should bring more light than heat— we hope! Welcome, friends. Please, everyone note the brief vitas of our two guests now on our screen over the fireplace.

James: Being a musician myself, allow this opening illustration. Josef Strauss substituted once for his ill and more famous musical brother, Johann, writing a new waltz for the occasion. Not having done this before, and not intending a musical career, he called his waltz "The First and the Last." But it was so well received by the waltz-loving Viennese that he composed another one, calling it "The First After the Last."

Well, that's it, isn't it? It's the arena of theology that we call "eschatology." When the last of earthly life is done, what if anything comes next? Is there anything after the last? How should what Christians expect after death impact how we should live in the present? Personally, I like the title of one of Barry's books, *Faithful in the Meantime*.

Barry: Thanks, James. Let me address you first, Stan. I remember well the lectureship on the Anderson University campus which you and Delwin Brown co-delivered in 2000. You were a guest lec-

---

Hal Lindsey (1929-)—a Christian Zionist and dispensational premillennialist who studied at Dallas Theological Seminary and is proudly called a "fundamentalist." He served with Campus Crusade for Christ before his book *The Late, Great Planet Earth* (1970) became a bestseller. Coming on the heels of the Six-Day War in which Israel quickly captured vital territory from its neighbors, this book fueled the popularity of dispensationalism that identifies the founding of the modern State of Israel as a key to biblical prophecy. Many of Hal's later writings are sequels or revisions and extensions of this first book. He currently maintains a major internet site, "The Hal Lindsey Report," featuring daily addressing of breaking news headlines interpreted in the context of biblical prophecy. He has led dozens of tours to Israel.

Some of Hal's editorializing has been inflammatory in nature, such as an essay on the American web site *WorldNetDaily* that pictured Barack Obama as paving the way for and demonstrating the world's readiness for the Antichrist. Hal has had a long relationship with the Trinity Broadcasting Network and serves on the executive board of *Christian Voice*. Once referred to by the *New York Times* as "The Jeremiah of Today," in 1969 he helped organize a Bible School next to UCLA named "The JC Light and Power Company."

turer in my class on Christian spirituality during that time. I was grateful then, and it's a pleasure now to have you join us.

Stan: Thanks, Barry. I recall those days in Anderson fondly. And Hal, I look forward to this conversation that includes you. I've tried for years to find some middle ground on which evangelicals can stand together on these tough eschatological issues. Maybe this conversation can help.

I stretched in one direction by working with Delwin Brown who was a process-progressive theologian. Today I have an opportunity to stretch in the opposite direction with a prophetically focused fundamentalist. I trust that in all this stretching I grow rather than break!

Usually, Hal, you and those of your style of thought have been excluded by the mainstream evangelicalism. But exclusion gets us nowhere. In fact, the whole subject of eschatology too often gets pushed to the sideline as too controversial and relatively unimportant. Some just say, "Who knows?" and "Whatever we think, what will be will be."

But I view eschatology as "at the heart of what the Bible intends to teach.... The Bible presents history as meaningful in that it is directed toward a goal.... The Bible, therefore, presents history in the form of a narrative, the recounting of the acts of the Sovereign Lord of history accomplishing his goal" (1992, 27). And I think Moltmann is right in his lead quote. Talking about tomorrow should enhance and not undercut today. So our conversation is important and I'm pleased to be part of it.

Tom: Hal, allow me to add to Stan's comment about exclusion. You should be aware that inviting you to be our guest today was not an automatic decision by this group. Some if not all view you as a representative of the "extreme right," likely not a good listener to alternative views and one who has not produced a body of serious theological literature such as Stan and others of us have in abundance.

Sorry for sounding so arrogant, an attitude many tend to toss at fundamentalists. And I understand how that must feel since many of my academic colleagues have accused me of falling over the cliff to the right.

Nonetheless, your being here indicates that this group is open to sharp differences of opinion and recognizes that you have demanded much public attention. In fact, Hal, your *The Late Great Planet Earth* is one of the best-selling books of non-fiction in recent decades. Congratulations! Ours sometimes haven't sold nearly as well. What would you say is the reason for your book's unusual popularity with the Christian public?

Hal: Well, first, I'm used to the prejudice against conservative thinkers like me, and I thank this group for at least inviting me and being open to hearing some biblical truth as I understand it. Thanks, Stan and Tom, for your gracious spirits. If finding "middle ground" requires any compromise with plain biblical truth, you know that we won't find any as far as I'm concerned—but I'll listen and try and see where this conversation actually goes.

Now to your question, Tom. Why the great popularity of that 1970 book of mine? I told my readers that I was "attempting to step aside and let the prophets speak." After all, the politicians, educators, and biblical "scholars" had talked long enough, often in evasive circles. I wanted to "give God a chance to present His views" (6). To me that just makes good sense.

People seem to appreciate straight Bible talk that appears to have direct relevance to the world they are experiencing. I once worked as a tugboat captain on the Mississippi River. You might say that now I'm tugging at the biblical text and finding wonderful and sometimes alarming truths that mark our times and point straight to God's soon-coming future. I can't allow anyone to pull me down the river the wrong way, any anti-Bible way. Our fallen world is going straight down the river of sin to a well-deserved hell.

Jack: Hal, I love your images of rivers and tugboats. People read and understand good stories and graphic images. I've made a living at that, and maybe you have too. But now to your point.

I'm all for allowing God to speak—I'm sure we all are. The divine message about the future, if we can locate it, is surely the right message. But there is a prior question that complicates the issue. Can we humans set aside our humanness so easily, managing to allow God to speak without our own interpretive limitations inevitably entering the picture?

I suggest the likelihood that you, and possibly others of us, may be the victim of some questionable presuppositions about the nature of biblical prophecy. Let's begin there in our quest for clarity.

Hal, let me ask you a question. Shouldn't a proper reading of the Bible take seriously the relevant literary and historical considerations that lie in and behind the text? Otherwise, don't we risk descending into an anti-biblical subjective speculation driven by modern times more than biblical texts?

Hal: Of course, Jack, in principle. The problem is that so-called "scholars" have a tendency to accept working assumptions that are non-biblical in nature and are accepted from secular sources, like a prejudice against the possibility of actual miracles and direct revelation and prophecy from God.

I see such interpreters as the ones often descending into subjective speculation, proudly calling it enlightened biblical scholarship. They sink biblical teaching deep into a maze of big words that they coin for each other, leaving the majority of Christian believers completely in the dark about God's specific intentions for today and tomorrow.

I'm pleased to report that it's different with me. My writing is simple, straightforward, biblical, and with obvious relevance for our immediate times and the lives of average believers. Since there are far more of them than there are the "scholars," my books sell really well, informing and inspiring the general church. I praise God for this simple truth being given to the hungry masses.

People listen when I say things like I once did about Barack Obama. I said on *WorldNetDaily* that Obama was demonstrating and paving the way for what the world now is so ready for, the Antichrist. We are ripe for a messiah-like figure as the end nears, and I'm not one to avoid saying the obvious and even naming names. It's not time to dialogue and theorize, building tenure credentials for some university or seminary by publishing sophisticated articles and books; it's time to repent and be ready!

Louis: According to Jesus, Hal, it's always time to be ready. Readiness and informed biblical interpretation are not mutually exclusive things. I think you and I would agree that book success in the marketplace, pleasant as it is, is not a fair judge of what is true. The public can be very gullible, something counted on by big marketing firms. Jesus also said that the way to destruction is very broad, and on it may travel some "scholars" and biblical interpreters.

The majority is often wrong about many things. Speaking your mind plainly is a good thing, and I've also done that many times, although not in as dramatic and "prophetic" a way as you. As a good monk, and I think a good scholar, I'd rather be silent until I was much more sure of what I was saying about current events and their relation to biblical revelation.

Hal: But I'm sure already, Louis. My *There's A New World Coming* is an in-depth analysis of the Book of Revelation. Here we learn considerable detail about what will happen before the millennium, and it's near and certainly not pretty. Armies of the world will gather in the area of Israel, "at least 200 million soldiers from the Orient, with millions more from the forces of the West headed by the Antichrist of the Revived Roman Empire (Western Europe). Messiah Jesus will first strike those who have ravaged His city, Jerusalem" (1984, 193).

Elton: Fascinating, and likely fanciful so far as I know. Waiting to speak until one's quite sure reminds me of Barry's uneasy memory of my comment to a class in which he was my student. I said I hate fog, especially of it's inside the head of a speaker. I'm aware of TV and pulpit prophets who forcefully announce coming events on God's timetable. I say that, if only they had waited a few years to speak, actual events would have stopped their premature predicting. There are dozens of such examples solidly on the books of history.

Louis: Anyone who knows me, Hal, knows that I have no fear of speaking out. Let me give you an example, something I judge not speculative and certainly lacking the kind of graphic detail you think you find in the last book of the Bible.

As a young Christian I spoke out against a popular trend that was insisting that a good God and a hot hell can't both be true. I sharply disagreed. After all, it's not compulsory for anyone to go there. Those who do go travel by their own choice and against the will of God. In damning them, God is only ratifying their own decision. Mine wasn't the popular view, but I spoke out with courage, like you do. And I sure wasn't building tenure somewhere. In the monastery, tenure comes only by faithfulness, commitment, and serious attention to the Word of God.

Jack: Well said. In a similar way, I once wrote a book called *The Problem of Pain*. In it I said that "the damned are, in one sense, successful rebels to the end; that the doors of hell are locked on the *inside*" (127). In my judgment, such a statement resonates well with the whole of biblical revelation, not just a fragment being lifted out of context. And, Hal, let me speak to your caution about ivory-tower and self-serving biblical scholars. I certainly can identify to a point with your concern, but only to a point.

I too have criticized the shortcomings of closed academic communities that are blind to their own sophisticated irrelevance. I did some of that myself early in my unbelieving career. And Tom, you have written *Requiem*, recounting clearly the failures of many mainline seminaries. We are all church leaders here, and none of us is afraid to speak our minds; it's just that some of us are reluctant to equate our minds with that of God.

Much like yourself, Hal, I have tried to reintroduce Christianity to a largely secular audience, making old truths relevant to people where they live. You introduced dispensationalism to its widest audience ever and enhanced its immediate appeal by suggesting its possible connections to current events—like your identifying the Antichrist's with a revived Roman Empire in the form of the European Common Market.

Such an identification is a political observation that at best is highly suspect biblical interpretation. You have wanted readers to accept Jesus Christ as Lord and Savior and thereby escape the wrath to come. The escape is fine, if it doesn't wind up being irresponsibility based on bad Bible reading.

James: While I don't agree with the details of many of your biblical interpretations, Hal, I do affirm your basic evangelistic agenda. Even so, I note that, ten years after your extremely popular 1970 book, your focus had changed considerably. Your newer *The 1980s: Countdown to Armageddon* carries a full-blown political agenda. You blame America's ills on groups of liberal conspirators who, as you saw it, were dismantling the military and undercutting the free enterprise system. It was time to clean house in Washington.

My point is that I have seen you being carried along by the shifting winds of the times. You have made significant adjustments when what you once thought was biblical prophecy just didn't work out in fact. I fear for any of us who read the sacred pages and move quickly to unknowingly printing and preaching our own social and political agendas.

Stan: I agree, Jack and James. And Hal, you and likely the rest of us do tend in some ways to be reflections of our times, and usually more than we realize or want. We are tempted to read history in an unfair light. So, allow me to sound more cautionary notes, and please don't take them personally. We all might be guilty at points.

The first caution is about not reading our own agendas into the past. Hal, at least in my view, your picture of postmillennialism in your books is mostly a caricature—it was not the construct of starry-eyed utopian liberals. On the contrary, it was the dominant position among American evangelicals in the late eighteenth century and throughout most of the nineteenth.

Post-millennial, of course, means that Christ will return only *after* great advances of the divine agenda in this world. The Christian leaders influenced by this view, often Wesleyan by tradition, were full of optimism about the overcoming grace of God when the church is a faithful agent of God's Spirit. They were not wide-eyed liberals.

To the contrary, "their optimism was born out of a belief in the triumph of the gospel in the world and of the work of the Holy Spirit in bringing in the kingdom of God, not out of any misconceptions concerning the innate goodness of humankind or of the ability of the church to convert the world by its own power" (1992, 66).

In addition, I urge further caution since "the most notable forerunners and early leaders of evangelicalism—Luther, Calvin, Wesley,

Whitefield, Edwards—said nothing explicitly about premillennialism, much less a rapture. They likely would be rather puzzled by these teachings of yours because "such beliefs are relative newcomers to the history of Christian beliefs about the end times" (Wilkens/Thorsen, 47).

Hal: Their being puzzled is no surprise, Stan. The great church reformers of past centuries knew little about prophecy. After all, "they were primarily interested in unlocking biblical truths desperately needed for their generation. They therefore didn't spend much time studying truths about the future. Possibly they sensed that their age would not witness the fulfillment of the Book of Revelation" (1984, 11).

Stan: That's an interesting "theory"—you have those too, Hal. Wesley, Calvin, and others did extensive study of the whole Bible, not excluding the Book of Revelation. But on to my other cautionary note. It's about attitude.

In my view, difficulties arise whenever we attempt to pinpoint the eternal situation of the lost and then become insistent that we know, expecting others to agree. The simple fact is that we don't know exactly what eternal punishment will be like and precisely when it will happen and for whom.

We can learn something helpful from all three of the main millennial theories concerning Christian living between the *already* and *not-yet* of Christ's two advents. That was the point of my book *The Millennial Maze*. Such learning would keep us balanced and humble about speculations beyond our ability to really know. We must be careful not to build whole belief systems out of fragments of biblical materials.

Hal: You speak of "millennial theories." That's the voice of a "scholar," Stan, someone who may be avoiding the plain teaching of the Bible by living in the world of maybes and alternatives. If you're having trouble finding the rapture in the Bible, you had better look more carefully. Paying attention to what the Bible is trying to say gives God's Spirit the freedom to push our prejudices aside and hear God's real voice. That's been a central burden of my whole ministry. And, Clark, your annihilationism, I just have to say, is only a clever way to avoid a full-blown biblical doctrine of hell. Sinners won't be wiped out but punished forever!

Clark: Well, Hal, I've explained at length in my writings the biblical basis of my doctrine of annihilationism, so I won't argue that here. You are correct that it is *a* way (a "theory") to balance God's love and justice in light of the fullness of biblical teaching. It's not the only way, but the most biblically balanced way in my view. And note that I'm open for more dialogue on this; I'm certainly not trying to insist that you agree with me. Most evangelicals don't.

I certainly want to hear God's voice on all matters, and I believe strongly in the ministry of God's Spirit and the authority of God's Word. I also believe, however, that considerable discipline and lots of information are required for our responsible interpreting of the Bible.

After all, the Bible a massive text that is millennia old, composed in non-English languages, in cultures so different from ours, sometimes using styles of writing not familiar to modern readers, and at points based on assumptions of the ancient Middle East foreign to the Western mindset of today. If probing carefully and compensating for all of that is being "scholarly," then so be it. I'm a careful reader and interpreter because of my love for God's Word.

Now, I'd like us to get back to you, Stan. Let's hear these potentially helpful learnings you hinted at.

Barry: Yes, please, and be sure, Stan, to bring some clarity to some specialized words we've started mentioning that likely are not familiar to some of our young listeners in the room.

Stan: Of course. And, Clark, to illustrate your point, we can't assume that most Bible readers today understand the nature of "apocalyptic" literature and how that kind of ancient writing bears on the proper interpretation of the Book of Revelation. That's part of the reason that this final book of the Bible has become such a fertile place for conflicting claims about detailed knowledge of the future.

Let me venture a few "learnings" briefly. Common definitions of key words will help us avoid talking past each other. The basic options of the many readings of God's plans for the future key off of the concept of "millennium," a perceived future time when God's peace and justice finally will reign supreme. This concept is mentioned only briefly in the Book of Revelation, nonetheless it is used extensively by many Bible interpreters.

Postmillennialism sees Christ returning to launch a wonderful thousand years of peace, years on earth after (post-) the faithful work of the church is complete. It projects an optimistic mood that calls us to confident engagement with this world's evils as inspired agents of God's Spirit and mission.

Premillennialism features a more pessimistic tone, reminding us that any progress in our engagement with the world's evils ultimately will have to be God's doing, not ours. In fact, things tend to be judged as so bad that Jesus will have to return before (pre-) any wonderful thousand years can possibly begin. The dispensationalism of Hal is a complex variation of premillennialism and quite new in Christian thinking.

Amillennialism features an attitude that "lifts our sights above the merely historical future to the realm of the eternal God. It reminds us that the kingdom of God is a transcendent reality that should not be confused with any earthly kingdom prior to the final transformation of creation. No earthly city can ever hope to become the New Jerusalem, except through a radical transformation both of human nature itself and of the universe that through the Fall unwillingly participates in the human predicament" (1992, 214). The "millennium" is seen as the age of the Spirit's reign that began with the first coming of Jesus and increases as the church becomes more Christ-like. It is not a political kingdom like those of this world, just as Jesus said.

When I graduated from high school in 1968, my parents gave me a leather-bound *New Scofield Reference Bible*, an early tool for popularizing the dispensationalism that you represent, Hal. When I entered Denver Seminary in 1973, I learned that not all evangelicals are dispensationalists, in fact, few Christians ever had been until recent times. As the result of my studies, even in a premillennial seminary, I graduated a convinced amillennialist. I had encountered the work of young German scholars that led to my doctoral study under Wolfhart Pannenberg, and to the realization that eschatological perspectives impact deeply the attitudes of God's people regarding their place and role in this world.

James: Stan, your review of controversial subjects like the multiple millennialisms help us consider the alternative positions held by serious Bible believers. I applaud your sensitivity to the history of biblical interpretation and your willingness to leave unclear matters in doubt, exactly where the Bible leaves them. As to these theories of future events, you see a key lesson to be learned from each, but without absolutizing any of the theories themselves as the biblical one. I see that as wise and biblically responsible.

Here's what else I see. The Bible provides divine foundations, impulses, intents, and assurances, but not calendars and grand political schemes with contemporary nametags. Hal, you bring to our conversation a strong faith as we try to get to the heart of a difficult subject. But I have seen too many preachers with inflated confidence in their biblical interpretations who, in fact, were skating on thin ice as they proceeded to build elaborate systems of future expectations and call the end result "exactly what the Bible says."

Barry: Hal, we often don't see ourselves doing what we actually are doing. That's partly why group conversations like this one are so important for mutual checking and correction. When it comes to reading the morning news of the world and then relating it specifically to biblical images and supposed predictions of end-time events, I'll say only this. The entire history of the church is full of dramatic examples of failed attempts to determine precisely where we are on God's calendar. Might you, Hal, be the first to have it all correct? Possibly, of course, but probably not.

Hal: I will say only this, James and Barry. I see what I see, read what I read, and don't hesitate to say what I say, all to the glory of my God who once came in Jesus and is soon coming again! I don't see myself dealing in theories, but in plain biblical teaching which should stand above question. It's happening and the rest is about to happen. Since the Bible says so, I guarantee it!

Clark: My heart follows your love of the Bible, Hal, but my head won't let me follow you very far beyond that. Your last statement was excellent, James. I hope you've all seen Stan's book *The Millennial Maze* and Barry's book *Faithful in the Meantime*. They cover the territory well and strike the right chord about Christian eschatology in general.

And there's also that book *The Scripture Principle* that Barry and I co-authored. We do want to know what the Bible says, and we'll believe it when we know. But, Hal, the simplistic approach of "I read what I read" is just not adequate for interpreting the biblical text as it has come to us.

Having said that, you're certainly right about one thing, Hal. The Bible must be viewed as authoritative for us Christians. What I want you to do, however, is become more aware of the divinity *and* the humanity seen in the biblical texts themselves, and clearly in their very human writers, readers and interpreters—including you and me and all of us.

The Spirit inspired the writings originally and now must bridge the changed cultures, languages, and centuries to illumine us to the intended meanings and contemporary applications. This divine-human interaction should bring a humility that forces us to rely heavily on the present ministry of the Holy Spirit, and to do so within the community of faithful readers and with the assistance of the believing scholars in the church. As isolated individuals with our own prejudices and limitations, we must not risk reading bits of the Bible, fail to listen to the community's readings, and move quickly to knee-jerk pronouncements about the Bible's direct relationships to the events of our day.

Tom: I heartily agree and want to make sure that the community of faithful readers in view is not just our present churches but the skilled Christian interpreters of the earliest centuries.

In recent years, I have acted as the general editor for a major community reading resource, the *Ancient Christian Commentary on Scripture*. Those interpreters of apostolic and post-apostolic Christianity never heard of communism, the European Union, or one world church, but they knew the Lord and the Bible. Their wisdom is generally more reliable than reading with the Bible in one hand and today's newspaper in the other.

Hal: I'm willing to look through any books you note, Clark and Tom, but truth remains truth, the Bible is clear enough as it stands, it seems to me, and the dramatic events of these years appear to almost speak for themselves. I'm uncomfortable with any Christian who chooses to hide behind the claim that there is "humanity" right in the biblical texts. These texts, all of them, are God's inerrant Word!

I read the Bible; I don't change it according to my personal thoughts and preferences or because "the scholars say...." I may be a human reader, but one blessed with the divine Word in my hands and the call of the Spirit to proclaim it without change or apology.

Louis: Let me emphasize a point that has been hinted at more than once. How we think about lots of things is influenced by our times. When I was a young man, Communism was in fashion and I was attracted to it. I saw Europe and America in the grip of "bourgeois ugliness." Clearly, "I was the product of my times, my society and my class" (1948, 133).

So here's my point. I see much of our eschatological speculations as extensions of our particular times and personal experiences. And, Hal, when you get very political in your views of current events as fulfillments of biblical prophecies, I see more of you than anything necessarily biblical. You'll please excuse a poor monk for being so honest.

Clark: Is there more you could share on this personally, Louis?

Louis: Yes, unfortunately. I'll be honest about myself. When I was young, I was anything but a saintly monk. For instance, I loved movies. My great heroes were Charlie Chaplin, W. C. Fields, and Harpo Marx. I'm glad I didn't look for them in the books of Daniel and Revelation. With your approach, Hal, and if I had been looking for them, I likely would have found them somewhere! It's not that they would have been there, understand, it's just that I would find them because I was sure in advance that they were there, and finding them would have been so meaningful in my eyes. That's just how things work—and shouldn't work.

Elton: How about a Quaker moving a monk off the stage for a minute? Apart from all of our human limitations in trying to read the Bible properly, the real subject of eschatology is the resurrection of Jesus. Apart from believing in this, the Christian movement wouldn't have endured at all. Christianity is the gospel of the resurrection. It is *the* event of the past that makes possible our hope for eternal life in the future.

And why do we believe in Jesus' resurrection? Because of historical evidence, not archaeological but historical, not so much what those first disciples said when they reported the resurrection, but more "what they *became*" (1996, 36).

A beaten, broken, and deeply discouraged group of nobodies was transformed within days into vibrant and courageous proclaimers of the resurrection, and they remained so for the rest of their lives, despite intense persecution. What could possibly account for that? The answer is quite straightforward. Jesus *had risen*, he had risen indeed! And with him, some day, as he has promised, so shall we. That's the heart of this matter. I don't know exactly when or how, only that it *will be* because God lives and loves!

The position of Jesus is that "because God really is, and because the whole world, both present and future, is under His fatherly care, we shall be objects of His affection just as much after the death of the body as we were before. Because we could not be objects of His affectionate care if we were not alive, then those who love Him will continue to live" (1969, 110-111). If we believe in God at all, we cannot "believe in His defeat; therefore, we believe that there is another and fuller life in which the justice that is denied here may be finally achieved" (1969, 119).

My concern, Hal, with your prophetic announcements goes beyond the obvious issue of questionable biblical interpretation. In my view, such speculations—and that's exactly what they are-- are out of character with the early disciples of Jesus. Those men and women were very confident of God's loving care of His own beyond their graves, but they were most careful to avoid claiming more than what was given to them—and Jesus, the giver, was modest indeed in what he said about the future beyond God's faithfulness, continuous love, and the absolute divine trustworthiness. I'll take the Master's lead and be cautious about details he refused to share, even when pressed by his disciples.

Hal: To my numerous detractors over the years, and to you gentlemen who at least are trying to be civil, I have said this in my book *There's a New World Coming*. To the skeptic who says that Christ is not coming soon, I would ask him to put the Book of Revelation in one hand and the daily newspaper in the other, and then sincerely ask God to reveal where we are on His prophetic time-clock. There is the book of God, the clock of God, and the soon-returning Son of God! I'll leave it at that.

James: Fair enough, Hal. Your stance is crystal clear. Let me take us back to you, Stan, and your emphasis on the importance of eschatology—despite all the disagreement and conflict surrounding it. What exactly is its deep significance for today's Christians.

Stan: The significance extends well beyond dealing with questions like the nature and timing of a "millennium" as referred to in Revelation 20. The systems of millennial interpretation, based on very little biblical material, can still shape helpfully our attitude as the people of God in this world. As I said before, the optimism of one (*post-*) should be tempered by the pessimism of the other (*pre-*), while both should be controlled by the third's realism (*a-*).

Having said that, here's the caution. The role of eschatology is not primarily to speak about the details of the future and the discovery of events that must come to pass in the last days. Rather, it is to provide zeal for worldwide evangelism, holy living, constant watchfulness, and courage in the face of persecution. "Our knowing that God stands in the future, beckoning us onward, provides a source of hope. In hope we can direct our efforts toward the advance of God's reign on earth. We can be steadfast in our efforts at each step en route to the consummation (1 Cor. 15:58)" (1992, 209).

Barry: Friends, one of our earlier conversation partners, Jürgen Moltmann, has written wisely on the subject at hand (*The Coming of God*, 1996). So has another of our previous guests. Let me quote some words of Georgia Harkness that end her book *Foundations of Christian Knowledge*:

> When we have finished our theologizing, we shall not understand all mysteries. We are but human pilgrims following the pathways of knowledge, and to the end of the earthly way we shall still "know in part." Yet our faith in Jesus Christ our Lord can give us the *assurance* of things hoped for, the *conviction* of things not seen. And is not that, after all, the object of the quest? (153)

James: Georgia was wise, Barry. Maybe no one has put it better than Frederick Douglass, born into slavery and then an influential abolitionist. Near the end of his life, he remembered that God reigns in eternity and that whatever delays, disappointments, and discouragements may come, truth, justice, liberty, and humanity will prevail. Indeed, they will!

And further, I have thought much about the mystery of just being alive, and I've stood in awe of us humans facing the world and perceiving even slightly what God is and will be doing in it. We know and we don't know. We see through a glass darkly, and yet, because of Jesus and through the eyes of his Spirit, we do see enough to go on in hope and joy.

Elton: Blaise Pascal once reported in his *Pensees* (no. 205) that he had stood astonished at the immensity of things and at his own ignorance about most of them. Like Pascal, I have been overwhelmed but nonetheless steadied by my biblical faith that has led me to a passionate engagement with the world as a thinking self alert to responsibilities, alive to God, and humble before the mysteries of being and time.

And there's the question of beyond time. We must keep coming back to our conviction that the decay of the flesh is not the end. Knowing Christ leads to the belief that what will be later will at least be the best we know now, and surely so much more. "We have good reason to suppose that the love of Christ will not change and that it will dignify our little lives, however different they may be from anything we now experience" (1969, 128).

Louis: It's easy to criticize believers like you, Hal, for reading into the Bible your own political perceptions of the current day. Even so, I insist that being heavenly minded does not necessarily make us of no earthly use. In fact, check out the facts of history. Christians who did the most for this poor world were ones who were thinking much about the next one.

"The Apostles themselves, who set out on foot to convert the Roman Empire, the great men who built up the Middle Ages, the English Evangelicals who abolished the Slave Trade, all left their mark on Earth, precisely because their minds were occupied with Heaven.... Aim at Heaven and you will get earth 'thrown in'; aim at earth and you will get neither" (1960, 104). Good eschatology is not escapism. Those full of assurance about tomorrow are freed to make a real difference today.

Barry: Well said, brother Louis. So, as this conversation closes, let's all determine to "aim at heaven," redeeming our time here on earth, all the while joining that heavenly chorus that we are told cries out: "Hallelujah! For the Lord our God the Almighty reigns. Let us rejoice and exult and give him glory" (Rev. 19:6). And let us be reassured by the New Testament writer: "And now I commend you to God and to the message of his grace, a message that is able to build you up and to give you the inheritance among all who are sanctified" (Acts 20:32).

Clark: One ministry of the Spirit of God is to assist communities of Christian faith to discern the truth in what they read in the Bible. There is a "divine reading" in which the mind descends into the heart, and both are enveloped by the love and goodness of God. What the Spirit does is enable the Word to be exposed in the words as the spiritually open reader moves beyond information to spiritual formation (Pinnock/Callen, 2009, chap. 9).

Jack: Whatever the details of the future, these "last days" have one clear agenda in God's eyes. We are to be formed into the image of Christ and function selflessly as agents of Christ's reign in this present world, inspired and strengthened by our faith in the world yet to arrive. We live as believers *in the meantime*; we have mission responsibilities now, bolstered by the assurances that Christ is raised from the dead and will provide for us now and always.

Stan: On that note, I'd like to make a concluding comment. "God's eternal community has dawned, is dawning, and will one day arrive in its fullness. The God who has reconciled us to himself through Christ will one day bring us into full participation in the grand eschatological community of his divine reign." This vision should inspire us in the in-between era to seek to be God's community in the present, "proclaiming in word and deed the good news of the coming eternal community in which God himself will dwell with us" (1994, 859). To that end, I surely commit myself, and I know that all of us do. The glory now and always belongs only to God!

Hal: Amen to that, Stan. You men have let me have my say, and I've tried to listen, so it's been good to be with you today. What God has planned will surely come about, however well we understand it. We should live and speak boldly in that light.

Barry: Indeed, and thanks Stan and Hal for being with us today. We are brothers on a journey. We are better together than apart. We titled this conversation "Are These the Last Days?" Well, are they? In one sense, all times for the church are the last days, and have been so for many centuries. Jesus said as much to his first disciples as he warned them to live as though his return might happen suddenly at any time. But his focus was on the challenges of present ministry to a broken world, on being "faithful in the meantime," however long that turns out to be.

Let me emphasize something we appear to agree on. "Yes, there will be a consummation to the biblical story of salvation history. The primary biblical concern, however, is hardly to satisfy human curiosity about the future. It is to highlight that God's reign and future intent already have broken into our history in Jesus Christ and should make a difference *now*, as it certainly will *then*" (1996, 276).

Friends, we have only one more conversation scheduled. We've given it the strange title "Tramps for the Truth." As all of us journey in the present in light of God's assured future, what should be our daily mindset? See you next time for the answer.

Questions Related to Conversation #10

1. How do you explain the public popularity of the subject of "eschatology" (final things)? Have you read or seen the "Left Behind" materials or encountered the books by Hal Lindsey? Is that which is fascinating and dramatic necessarily true? On the other hand, does the fact that so many disagree with Hal's view of most things make Hal wrong?

2. Hal insists on the Bible as God's "inerrant" Word and reads the biblical text rather literally, making dramatic pronouncements, insisting that he has found "prophetic" truth being played out in current events. How can so many others read the same texts but come out at very different places of interpretation and application?

3. What is the essential difference between the two guests, Stan and Hal, in their approaches to Christian eschatology? Are such approaches easily reconciled? If not, is it healthy for the church if both are present at all times? They will be, healthy or not.

4. Elton summarizes what for him is the heart of this matter of Christian eschatology, the resurrection of Jesus. Do you find yourself agreeing? Is that what made the great difference in the earliest church?

5. Try to explain how assurance of God's future can be crucial in how God's people think about and act in the present prior to Christ's return. Is eschatology often used as a tool of worldly escapism?

6. Look at the 2009 book by Clark and Barry. What is the "Scripture principle" that they affirm as basic? Can you understand and practice the advice that is recommended by Clark—keep the Bible in your hands and God's assisting Spirit in your heart?

7. Are these "the last days"? What does that mean? If they are, how should we be living?

Conversation #11

TRAMPS FOR THE TRUTH

The Ongoing Life of Faith and a Pilgrim Theology

> The passing moments of a life in the setting of Eternity; the tiny planet Earth in the setting of the Universe; a loving God who has counted the hairs of all our heads, who cannot see a sparrow fall to the ground without concern; the wild, ferocious story of humankind—civilizations that come and go, leaving their debris behind for archaeologists to dig through and diagnose; wars won and lost and ongoing; philosophers who are credible and then scorned; today's beliefs, tomorrow's folly; today's hero, tomorrow's villain or idiot; Towers of Babel everlastingly being built and never finished (Muggeridge, 1988, 52-53).

> No matter what my story has been for others, for me it has been a story of providential leading along a long road (Oden, 2014, 334).

> I am a pilgrim still in progress. My eventual destination is to be fully at home with the Lord by whose side I already walk. In the meantime, I wait to hear new guidance from that gentle voice from above. Wherever it points will be pleasing to me (Callen, 213, 459).

Barry: This is it, good friends, our final conversation together. The topic today involves faith for the ongoing journey of our spiritual and theological lives. We are pilgrims facing unknown futures and the troubling issues of constant change and frustrating incompleteness. These necessarily impact our theological understandings and religious lives. How can be make the impact a good one?

Malcolm Muggeridge (1903-1990)-- prominent British journalist, author and satirist. Malcolm's life and work spans the twentieth century. It was a violent century which he chronicled with courage and matchless prose from bases in India, Russia, England, Algeria, and elsewhere. By the 1960s he had left his agnosticism for Christianity. In 1982 he became a Roman Catholic and began advocating the teaching of Christ as the key to recovering the moral stability in the modern nations of the West. A shrewd follower and skilled interpreter of world events, Malcolm has sometimes been mocked for his style and views, and at least once was called a "prophet." He responded to this designation, alluding to the biblical prophet Amos being called by God from pruning trees to announcing God's word: "I am no prophet, no, nor prophet's son. I was a journalist and the Lord took me as I sat at my typewriter" (1972, 2).

Initially attracted by Communism, Malcolm and his wife, Kitty, traveled to Moscow in 1932, where he was to be a correspondent for the *Manchester Guardian*. He became well known for his wit and profound writings, often at odds with the prevailing opinions of the day. He liked to quote this: "Never forget that only dead fish swim with the stream." He wrote two volumes of an autobiography that he titled *Chronicles of Wasted Time*. His last book, *Conversion*, describes his life as a 20th-century pilgrimage, an insightful spiritual journey rarely rivaled.

Tom: I titled my personal memoir *A Change of Heart*. Things in this life rarely hold still. I've heard that we can't discover new oceans unless we have the courage to lose sight of the shore.

What about lives of ongoing faith, new discoveries, willingness to dare and experiment, the openness to think new thoughts without forfeiting the wisdom of the past, the faith to leave the yet-unknown future in God's hands? What are we to do with the fixedness and fluidity of our best thinking and believing?

Jack: Those surely are the big and right questions, Tom. For a start, we should quit trying to rebuild the Tower of Babel! As our lead quotes for the day suggest, we are pilgrims still in process, always to be open to new leadings by our loving Lord.

Barry: Excellent! Now let me introduce the first of our two special guests for today, one of them the source of the Tower of Babel warning. He is Malcolm Muggeridge. His vita and that of Roger Olson are now shown on our screen above the fireplace.

How good to have with us two wise men well into their journeys of faith. Malcolm, a personal characteristic I hear you inherited from your father is what sometimes is called iconoclasm, a willingness to swim against the tide of established ideas and institutions. Is it correct to assume that you have been a constant seeker, one often out of step with the majority of others who belonged to the establishment?

Malcolm: Well, Barry, one of my earliest childhood memories is of feeling estranged, of being a sojourner in this odd world. So, what you've heard is about right. I surely have had my share of doubt and skepticism along the way, and I did kick up a lot of dust—and, to be frank, often enjoyed doing it. "For most of my life I have been on a quest for faith, and I knew what I disbelieved long before I knew what I believed" (in Hunter, 220). Let me be more specific. You eight fellow travelers in the faith can stand a little of my story—I'm here, so you've asked for it.

I have been a daring journalist blundering along, telling the truth as I saw it, and often paying the price. For instance, I was a leading figure in the early years of the British Broadcasting Corporation's television work, but the day came when I was banned from it. What awful sin had I committed? I had written my "Royal Soap Opera" article in 1957, saying straightforwardly that a materialist society, having ceased believing in God for the most part, is prone to hero worship—including the British royal family becoming almost a substitute religion in England.... I see your smiling face over there, Jack.... Soon I found out that saying that couldn't be tolerated.

To be fair, this problem isn't just in Britain. I let loose with another salvo in 1978. This one was aimed toward the United States. The most educated society in Western Europe may have elected Hitler in the 1930s, but the highest density of universities per acre and per person today is in California. Need I say more? School degrees and gathered wisdom aren't necessarily the same thing!

Jack: I'm still smiling and will slip in only this. Jolly good!

Malcolm: My journey has specialized more in truth-telling than friend-making. I've not been so good in the eyes of those happily building their own Towers of Babel. I doubt that I'm the prophet a few have called me but, to paraphrase Kipling, "I saw the sunset ere most men saw the dawn." A little arrogant? Maybe, but mostly true, I think.

Elton: Let me draw an analogy, Malcolm. "Life is essentially a journey. It is of the essence of reality that it should be process, and it is of the essence of our life that we should walk.... Each, as he journeys, keeps asking the way and watching for hints dropped by those who may have walked the same path.... Sometimes we are forced to retrace our steps, and frequently we find the pathway rough" (1951, 213). That's been my ongoing experience, my gathered wisdom, and apparently it's yours too.

Malcolm: Exactly, Elton. And my steps have covered the pathways of many of the biggest world events of the twentieth century—and sometimes as a journalist it's been very close up. The whole thing's been quite a ride, one that—of all things--finally brought me to faith in Jesus Christ.

Louis: I've felt much the same way, Malcolm, as I bumped along on my strange journey to faith. I lived a long time in a monastery, but my superiors knew well that at points I was about ready to move on. Occasionally I got that vagrant itch. Something in my nature made me dream of being a tramp.

I wasn't above idealizing those flea-inhabited holy wanderers of old. My travels, and certainly my books have come to wander the world, but I faithfully remained at Gethsemani. One needs roots as well as visions and horizons. Don't any of you doubt, however, that I've kept journeying, even when well rooted and behind monastic walls.

Jack: As a literary man, Louis, I'm still relishing in your phrase "vagrant itch." Let me offer this advice as we each scratch along with our personal itches. Roots, yes, we need roots but not *anchors*. We all tend to be limited by our private provincialisms from which we need to escape as we can. We need to travel away from our prejudicial homes and be informed and humbled by the wider world of ideas and perspectives on life. "That is always the way it is with stay-at-homes. If they like something in their own village, they take it for a thing universal and eternal, though perhaps it was never heard of five miles away" (1933, bk. 8, sec. 7, 146).

Clark: I want to admit, and with pride, that I've always been a pilgrim, always have sought to grow on my journey of discovery. Many of my "evangelical" Christian brothers and sisters in the Christian faith think that confession is in order for me since I've done this changing. They put revealed truth in a static and protected category where even slight change is judged intolerable.

My changes of mind on various theological matters over the decades have brought the criticism that I'm intellectually unstable by allowing previous commitments to shift—something quite unacceptable to rigid theological gatekeepers. But I now report without apology to this special group of friends that I'm a fluid fellow traveler.

Tom: Let me repeat that my memoir is titled *A Change of Heart*. Believe me, folks on the more liberal academic side of things can also be staunch and critical gatekeepers!

Clark: So I hear. I have strong convictions, as you all know. But all of them are open to examination at any time. Growing usually means some change if one is honest, and I've tried to keep growing. So have you, Tom. And you're right, Jack. Things can look different when you wander outside your little village and actually listen to the thoughts of others. I have tried to do that, and at a price.

By the way, Malcolm, I once studied in England and was not guilty of worshipping the royal family. I hope you're proud of me. We must be careful of our priorities. One's theology is "a work of human construction, even when based in divine revelation.... It would be helpful if we discussed matters as seekers after truth rather than as gatekeepers obsessed by who is in and who is out of the evangelical movement" (2001, ix, xii).

Barry: I note that Roger Olson, our second guest today, hasn't yet been invited to speak. So at least let me slip in here, Clark, that Roger once put you in the "post-conservative" category. He had reference to your 1979 article where you clearly affirm classical Christian orthodoxy and just as clearly insist that even ancient and tradition-tested doctrines need to be reconceived and reappropriated for contemporary people. You said that "fidelity does not consist in simply repeating old formulas.... It includes the creative thinking required to make the old message fresh and new" (28). That's a good example of Jack's earlier comment about our needing roots but not anchors.

Louis: Roger, you are so patient with us. You'll get your chance shortly to tell us about your love-hate relationship with Pentecostalism. But for now, let me report how lucky I've been on several fronts. I've never struggled with the royal-loving British like you, Malcolm, or the reactionary Evangelical movement like you, Clark, or the liberal academics like you, Tom, or even Pentecostalism like you, Roger. Still, I've had a long love-hate relationship with Roman Catholicism. I've scratched that vagrant itch on several occasions and have some little scars to prove it.

In 1938 I entered Columbia's graduate school of English and soon wrote my thesis on one of the great dissenters of the eighteenth century, the mystic poet William Blake. I'd loved his poems for years. My father had wanted my mind "uncontaminated by error or mediocrity and ugliness and sham" (1948, 9). But Blake encouraged me to listen to my own drummer and "live in a world that was charged with the presence and reality of God" (1948, 189, 191). So, I finally listened and now have traveled through life outside and inside the church, but always reaching, longing, looking for God's authentic presence.

Malcolm: It's just as I suspected. You men are all my fellow travelers. Since I've never been known as conventional, let me go ahead and be unconventional again. I'll stick my nose into previous conversations of yours where I wasn't invited. I know that you've had as conversation guests both Dietrich Bonhoeffer and Hal Lindsey—now there's a strange pair! I want to say something about end times (hardly like Hal), and about one of the greatest witnesses of all times to the future (clearly like Bonhoeffer).

As I look back on that terrible war in the 1940s, it was Bonhoeffer who was executed, but the Third Reich that really died violently. I ask, where in the murky darkness of this sordid world does any light shine? My answer is: "Not among the Nazis, certainly, nor among the liberators.... What lives on is the memory of a man who died, not on behalf of freedom or democracy or a steadily rising Gross National Product, nor for any of the twentieth century's counterfeit hopes and desires, but on behalf of a Cross on which another man died two thousand years before.

As on that previous occasion on Golgotha, so amidst the rubble and desolation of 'liberated' Europe, the only victor is the man who died [Jesus], as the only hope for the future lies in his triumph over death. There never can be any other victory or any other hope" (1976, 205).

Elton: Yes! That's exactly what I tried to say in the earlier conversation of ours about eschatology. The heart of the matter of end things, and of the Christian faith itself, is the death and resurrection of Jesus. The raw power of the world finally succumbs to the sacrificial love of God. As we stumble through this world living our little lives, our hope lies just there and nowhere else.

Malcolm: Agreed, Elton. In the early 1930s I saw firsthand the inhuman results of Stalin's social policies. The sight haunted me, helping me to say four decades later: "My disillusionment with the notion of a predestined progress towards a kingdom of heaven on earth led me inexorably back to the kingdom not of this world proclaimed in the Christian revelation" (in Hunter, Foreword to Muggeridge's *Chronicles of Wasted Time*). The Lord Jesus captured this journalist, leading to my highly autobiographical book *Jesus Reconsidered*.

Let me say a little more and then I'll shut up and finally let Roger talk. Pascal, despite being a Frenchman, was the most brilliant scientist of his time. He defended the Christian faith against the arrogance of those who believed they could live without God, or at least could mold God as they wished in the service of their own selfish goals. While not denouncing the methods of science, Pascal uncovered its pretentions, saying, "Like the old pagan gods, science has come to belong to man's quest for power, not truth."

Pascal skillfully takes us with him "on his own arduous mental and spiritual pilgrimage, delivering us at his destination, where we find the intersection of time and eternity in a Cross on which God dies in the person of a man, and a man rises from the dead in the person of God" (1976, 57, 81). We tramps in search of the divine find ourselves right there, at the foot of the cross of Jesus, mouths open, pride shattered, eyes fixed on the fullness of the truth itself. What we find is that God's love *has found us*. That's the heart of the whole matter.

Louis: Malcolm, that statement captures the vision I have sought in my years of contemplation. Beyond you and Pascal, both real tramps for the truth, there's another man of yesterday with wisdom for us. I mentioned that I wrote my thesis at Columbia on William Blake. I was attracted to this man because he was unwilling to adjust himself to a time that was pious, grasping, self-satisfied, and indifferent to the poor. Blake was not a shallow romantic, nor was he, in the name of reasoning, blind to God's gracious presence in this world.

Living with Blake helped convince me to be a special kind of tramp, one who knows that this world is "charged with the presence and reality of God" (1948, 189, 191). If Blake's thought is heterodoxy, it is the rebellion of a saint whose intense desire for God condemns the hypocrisy, skepticism, and materialism of cold and trivial minds. I've tried to be a modest saint in Blake's lineage, moving on with my conscience in the face of this world's many challenges.

Malcolm: Yes, Blake is one of my heroes too, Louis. He was a seeker after God who found ultimate reality beyond the mirage of time and matter. He viewed the heart of reality through the lens of imagination, being "profoundly distrustful of the intellect as a means of finding truth, and of science as a means of exploring it" (1976, 85). Blake certainly did say and write many things that upset Christians of his day, even while being a Christian himself. Establishments are never patient with prophets.

I've made a career of doing much the same thing. Blake saw the Enlightenment spreading like a plague, championing an age of human self-sufficiency that finally would destroy itself. For him, "doom would befall men if they came to believe they could shape and dominate their own destiny" (1976, 100). Humans keep trying and just can't do it.

Far into my own journey, I now can say at least this much. Despite everything, there is hope for us since, "in the stress of life, collectively in the chaos of politics, individually in the clamorous demands of the ego and the flesh, it is always open to us to wait on God. All we have to do, as it were, is make a little clearing in the wild jungle of our human will, and then keep our rendezvous with our Creator.... Peace is the acceptance of earthly circumstances; all the turbulence, doubt, conflicting devices and desires; crystallizing in one single prayer: 'Thy will be done'" (1988, 66-67).

Jack: None of this should be a surprise. "Our whole being by its very nature is one vast need; incomplete, preparatory, empty yet cluttered, crying out for Him who can untie things that are now knotted together and tie up things that are still dangling loose" (*The Four Loves*, ch. 1). So it's a process, a journey, a hint of bigger things. "If I find in myself a desire which no experience in this world can satisfy, the most probable explanation is that I was made for another world" (1960, 106).

Great literature is filled with stories of pilgrimage—Homer's *Odyssey*, Virgil's *Aeneid*, Dante's *Divine Comedy*, Abraham setting out by faith to an unknown destination. Blaise Pascal was right. For Abraham and us all, the thirst is for God. By faith we journey on, hoping for a city whose architect and builder is divine. An old hymn says that each of us is "prone to wander." Well, we indeed are tramps wandering in search of God's truth and God's coming tomorrow.

Allow me just another minute, with apology to our still-waiting brother, Roger. I have traced my own journey in the autobiographical book *Surprised by Joy*. I explain there how I came to see that the ultimate joy in life is still ahead, still about to be. I once retold the story of Orual from Greek mythology. She was angry at the gods because they refused to show their faces in the way and to the degree she wanted. The simple fact is that our present understandings of God and the divine will are always incomplete. Our best theologies remain our best approximations.

Roger E. Olson (1952-) is an Arminian theologian influenced by Pietism and his Pentecostal upbringing, which eventually he abandoned primarily because of its anti-intellectualism. Now a Baptist, since 1999 he has been Professor of Theology at George W. Truett Theological Seminary of Baylor University in Waco, Texas. Graduating from Sioux Falls Seminary, Olson earned the Ph.D. in Religious Studies from Rice University. He is the author of *The Story of Christian Theology: Twenty Centuries of Tradition & Reform, The Mosaic of Christian Belief: Twenty Centuries of Unity & Diversity, Reformed and Always Reforming: The Postconservative Approach to Evangelical Theology, How to Be Evangelical without Being Conservative*, and co-author with Stanley J. Grenz of *20th-Century Theology: God & the World in a Transitional Age*. He has served as editor of *Christian Scholar's Review* and been a contributing editor of *Christianity Today*. He considers himself "an evangelical theologian even if some of my critics don't!" His blog site is "a place for irenic exploration and conversation; it is not for insulting people or movements or inflaming them." Such an attitude fits him perfectly for this book.

Malcolm: Marvelous, Jack. Life too often is about like this. It's as though I'd been cued on to the stage only to find that I had forgotten my lines or had rehearsed for a different play. That's me, part of me anyway. So I call us to tramp on, believing regardless of our lingering confusion and unbelief, following the Master to death and resurrection!

Barry: Those observations, Malcolm, almost bring silence to the room. Now it's more than time to bring into this sacred silence our other guest, Roger Olson, a good Baptist brother. It's already been observed, Roger, that you once referred rather approvingly to Clark as a "post-conservative" and have yourself had something of a love-hate relationship with Pentecostalism. Moving beyond one thing, *post-*, and struggling with another sounds like you've been a bit of a tramp yourself.

Roger: Yes, I suppose, scratching my own vagrant itch as I have gone along. My itch has been an insatiable intellectual appetite, something that the Pentecostalism of my youth wouldn't accommodate.

Reluctantly, I finally had to move on. Maybe the bigger departure of mine was from "modernism," a mentality that assumes to sit objectively in judgment on all truth claims. So I had to become a non-pentecostal, post-modern conservative.

I once imagined a conversation between a radical and a moderate form of post-modernism, mine (*The Christian Century*, Dec. 15, 2009). The radical judged that all truth claims are mere power plays intending to oppress others. The moderate, myself, believed that there is truth out there, but that none of us has fully comprehended it. Therefore, the quest must go on and some humility must remain despite our strongly-held beliefs.

Granted, there is no view of things from nowhere; we all have our communities of understanding, our originating biases. I see most if not all of us in this room as "post" people, journeyers who truly believe and also are appropriately open to the possibility of some newness.

James: Thinking of the pulpit and proclaiming the good news in Christ, don't we have a very delicate tension here, Roger? We have something significant to share, and yet we must do so without demeaning other faith communities or overstating ourselves. Is that right?

Roger: It certainly is. Especially post-conservatives from the Wesleyan/Pietist traditions, like you, Barry, Clark, and me, divine revelation is thought to be real but more personal *transformation* than simple *information* (2007, 53). We remain free to question and even reconstruct any part of the Christian tradition in light of deeper and better understandings of biblical teaching.

I say this well aware of your presence in the room, Tom, and your appropriate concern that personal transformation not descend too deeply into subjectivism and that resisting revelation as mere information not eliminate the sturdy historical roots of the faith. After all, there is some information, just not libraries of it as some want.

Tom: I've studied your work, Roger, and am not concerned that you would allow such intolerable excesses.

Roger: Clark, you and Barry have explored all this very well in your book *The Scripture Principle*. And, Barry, you have made very clear in your *Approaching Theology* that, while reason, experience, and tradition contribute significantly to our understanding of the Bible, it still is the Bible that is the final authority (82-85). And it's the transforming Spirit of Christ who ministers to us as we read, allowing real understanding.

But it's more than just the Bible, basic as it is. We all live by stories that frame our perceived identities, and so much of the Christian story is unknown by most believers. There is a huge gap in our awareness between the New Testament times and our own day. During these centuries God has been leading the church into a fuller understanding and better application of the truth, our story of God with us in Jesus. In fact, that's what theology is, "faith seeking understanding of God's truth" (Preface, 1999). This is why I wrote *The Story of Christian Theology* and why my blog site is "a place for irenic exploration and conversation; it is not for insulting people or movements or inflaming them."

Tom: I come from a tradition sympathetic with many of your concerns, Roger, being a Methodist. I'm also anxious for the transforming work of the Spirit and, like you, about something else very basic, church history. The Great Tradition that framed the consensual Christian understandings of the Bible and the apostolic age must not subtly be set aside in the process of personal sanctification. This happens so easily in the face of modern fads of thought, conservative or radical. We certainly may progress in our understanding of the tradition, and we must. To stray far from the best of it typically leads to disaster. Your great 1999 book is a valuable tool to help us all.

Roger: I certainly have no interest in straying away, Tom, only being open to the ongoing work of the Spirit in our search for the fuller truth and its best contemporary expressions and applications. Clark and Barry, you have written insightfully of the "unfolding revelation" that allows a biblical text to have a "surplus of meaning" (2009, chap. 8). That is wisdom, while recognizing that must be handled with great care. We tramps for the truth must be careful where we walk without ever stopping to walk!

Clark: Barry and I readily agree. Evangelical theology must be biblical and contemporary. To repeat a title of one of your books, Roger, theology must be "Reformed and Always Reforming." This rejects modernity on the one hand and fundamentalism on the other. My position is a "progressive orthodoxy." Our vision of truth "changes as new light is discovered in God's Word by faithful, Spirit-led interpreters" (2007, 200). We must never forget that human slavery was once defended widely by "orthodox" believers as having solid biblical support. Likely, there still are strongly-held beliefs that stand in need of revision.

James: No question about it. We probed the slavery issue when James Cone was with us, and we explored discrimination against women when Rosemary Radford Ruether and Georgia Harkness were with us in different conversations. Now, Roger, how would you label yourself?

Roger: Labels are treacherous things. I've considered myself a "conservative" Christian all of my life, but this word sounds mindlessly defensive of the past and too committed to the status quo. I'm tramping for the fuller truth like the rest of you, but without losing the basic truths I have as the base to work from. We shouldn't be open to just anything. As Tom would quickly remind us, we must stay rooted in the orthodox tradition of the faith, but without being mindlessly anchored there and unwilling to get out of our comfort zones and risk vested interests for the sake of biblical fidelity and effective gospel mission.

Tom: No argument from me there, Roger. It's a perennial tension.

Louis: Well, gentlemen, as a Roman Catholic I'm supposed to teach as the church teaches and always has taught. Even so, there are my contemplative writings and occasional critiques of my own church's views on this or that. Maybe that makes me something of a Catholic progressive conservative, a little like you, Roger, an ex-pentecostal Baptist.

Your early Pentecostal background was in a tradition that often has insisted on "speaking in tongues" to be a Spirit-filled Christian, and such a Spirit-infilling experience has inspired many Protestant preachers to be absolutely sure of exactly what the Bible teaches about almost everything. Where have you wound up on such things?

Roger: Well, I did a little tongues speaking when a teenager and later concluded that this practice is clearly not insisted on by the Bible. As for biblical prophecy about end times, my early tradition spawned dramatic television preachers that I find embarrassing. They seem to have way too much inside information that supposedly comes straight from the Bible by way of immediate Spirit enlightenment. I see pre-millennialism as the best reading of the Bible on end times, for instance, but I don't have an axe to grind about this. Such things are hardly the heart of the matter. God in Jesus Christ through the Spirit is.

Tom: The consensual tradition of our faith backs up your hesitancy to grind axes, Roger. What we do know is that history is characterized by the revelation of meaning through events in a linear trajectory that leads to a final consummation. Along the way there are lots of unanswered questions as we pilgrims tramp along. I explain at length in my *Classic Christianity* that on the millennial business there is a lack of consensus on biblical interpretation, allowing differing doctrinal formulations, sequences, and explanations. We know, but only in part.

James: So true, Tom. We preach with confidence, but also with measured humility. This tension between boldness and caution causes me to recall again something that Georgia Harkness said to us in an earlier conversation:

> When we have finished our theologizing, we shall not understand all mysteries. We are but human pilgrims following the pathways of knowledge, and to the end of the earthly way we shall still "know in part." Yet our faith in Jesus Christ our Lord can give us the *assurance* of things hoped for, the *conviction* of things not seen. And is not that, after all, the object of the quest? (1955, 153)

As for myself, "I continue to value and depend upon a biblical perspective as I view life, experience its stages, confront its mysteries, order my ways, and make a mark in the fresh concrete of history" (2002-A, 448).

Elton: I fully agree, and would add only one thing. Reliance on the ancient authorities for the very meaning of Christianity is not being blindly anchored in some outdated yesterday. There is nothing more forward-looking than taking the risk of allowing ourselves to be addressed by the texts of the Bible and the best of well-tested tradition, especially if we think hard and well in the process.

Tom: Correct, and the simple fact is that the twelve books I wrote in the 1960s "were not all wrong, but flawed by the fervent desire to accommodate to modern worldviews.... In the season of Epiphany 1971 I had a curious dream in which I was in the New Haven cemetery and accidentally stumbled upon my own tombstone with this puzzling epitaph: 'He made no new contribution to theology.' I woke up refreshed and relieved" (2014, 145, 143).

We should be open, flexible, and intentionally relevant, but without losing the baby in the discarded bathwater. We must never lose our ancient footing. We are tramps who have truth to take with them as we explore our way ahead.

Barry: Well said, Elton and Tom. And, Malcolm and Roger, your experiences and thoughtful theological wisdom have been so helpful to our conversation today. You've been tramps at their best.

Jack: Symbols can reflect our deepest commitments. Examples come from the titles of our own biographies and autobiographies. Barry's is *A Pilgrim's Progress*. Clark, your story is in the book *Journey Toward Renewal*. The one carrying your story, James, is *Aspects of My Pilgrimage*. Tom, your published memoir is *A Change of Heart*. Elton, you wanted to capture your wonderful journey *While It Is Day*. Louis, symbolism is at its best in your *The Seven Storey Mountain*. Malcolm, your *Chronicles of Wasted Time* is fascinating and then your *Conversion* goes on to detail a spiritual journey rarely rivaled. I roamed far away and explain my coming home in *Surprised by Joy*.

Louis, you have journeyed in various ways with Roman Catholicism. Elton, as a young man you moved close to Unitarianism, but over the years became an outstanding spokesperson for a "rational evangelicalism." Like Malcolm and me, you moved more toward the mainstream of Christian orthodoxy that has been defined so well by Tom. Roger, you never were far from orthodoxy, but you have worked hard to treat it appropriately and relate it well to our present times.

Barry: I think one lesson is obvious. We all are travelers, brothers and sisters on a continuing faith journey. I think, Clark, of your fine book on God titled the *Most Moved Mover*. In one important sense, it seems that we all have learned that doing the work of Christian theology is a never-ending business of receiving, searching, and moving on. We don't really begin to arrive until we realize that it's been the loving and suffering God all the while having been moving toward us.

Let me refer again to one of Roger's book titles. We who are dedicated to the truth quest find ourselves in the ongoing process of being *Reformed and Always Reforming*. Great work, Roger.

An earlier guest of ours, James Cone, bolted into the theological scene in 1970 with his dramatic book *A Black Theology of Liberation*. He was bold and prophetic, and rightly so. And yet, in this book's fortieth-year edition, he admits that his was never intended as a final word. He was merely "trying to make a marginal note or correction in theology."

Maybe that's what most of us are (should be) doing most of the time. And there is some really good news. The God who first called us to the journey also walks by our sides, showing us the way.

So, as we close this wonderful set of conversations, and with obvious gratitude to you, Malcolm and Roger, for your presence here today, our hearts cry out, "Thanks be to God!"

Questions Related to Conversation #11

1. What is there about Malcolm that would make religious conservatives nervous, and might also serve him well in a pluralistic world like John Hick discussed in conversation #10?

2. What is there about Roger's book *Reformed and Always Reforming* that captures the challenges and joys of the Christian faith journey?

3. How do you react to Jack and Clark affirming roots but not anchors? Jack applauds leaving one's own isolated village of ideas, and Clark speaks positively of having changed his mind over the years. Is actually listening to others more pregnant with possibilities than filled with compromising dangers?

4. Are you more humbled than troubled by the fact that we see only one step at a time—when we want to see and understand everything right now?

5. Civilizations, philosophies, and theologians come and go. What is it that endures? What finally is the heart of the matter? Is it the God who is always seeking us in love?

6. Abraham is pictured in the Bible as a pioneer of faith, our model of how to journey into the unknown when called by God. Do you hear God's calling on your life? Will you journey with Jesus Christ and, like James, "make a mark in the fresh concrete of history"?

7. Are you inspired by the good news that the God who first called us to this faith journey also walks by our sides, showing us the way ahead, and finally the way home?

Works Cited

Allen, Steve. *Meeting of Minds* (Buffalo: Prometheus Books, vol. 1, 1989).
Barclay, William. *William Barclay: A Spiritual Autobiography* (Grand Rapids: Eerdmans Publishing, 1975).
Bloesch, Donald G. *The Struggle of Prayer* (Colorado Springs: Helmers & Howard, 1988).
_____. *A Theology of Word and Spirit: Authority and Method in Theology* (Downers Grove, Ill.: InterVaristy Press, 1992).
_____. *The Holy Spirit: Works & Gifts* (Downers Grove, Ill.: InterVarsity Press, 2000).
_____. *Spirituality Old & New* (Downers Grove, Ill.: InterVaristy Press, 2007).
Braaten, Carl E. *No Other Gospel!: Christianity among the World's Religions* (Minneapolis: Fortress Press, 1992).
Brown, Delwin. *What Does a Progressive Christian Believe?* (N.Y.: Seabury Books, 2008).
Brueggemann, Walter. *An Unsettling God* (Fortress Press, 2009).
Brunner, Emil. *The Word and the World* (Student Christian Movement Press, 1931).
Callen, Barry L. ed., *Sharing Heaven's Music: The Heart of Christian Preaching*, essays in honor of James Earl Massey (Nashville: Abingdon Press, 1995).
_____. *God As Loving Grace: The Biblically Revealed Nature and Work of God* (Nappanee, IN: Evangel Publishing House, 1996).
_____. *Clark H. Pinnock: Journey Toward Renewal* (Nappanee, IN: Evangel Publishing House, 2000).
_____. *Authentic Spirituality: Moving Beyond Mere Religion* (Lexington, KY: Emeth Press, rev. ed. 2006; originally Baker Academic, 2001).
_____. *Discerning the Divine: God Through Christian Eyes* (Louisville, KY: Westminster/John Knox, 2004).
_____. *Caught Between Truths: The Central Paradoxes of Christian Faith* (Lexington, KY: Emeth Press, 2007).
_____. *A Pilgrim's Progress: The Autobiography of Barry L. Callen* (Lexington, KY: Emeth Press, and Anderson, IN: Anderson University Press, 2008, rev. 2013).
_____. 2009-A. *The Church that God Intends*. Compiler and editor (Lexington, KY: Emeth Press, 2009).
_____. 2009-B. *In Deep Water: An Historical Novel of Violence and Virtue, Fear and Faith* (Lexington, KY: Emeth Press, 2009).
_____. 2009-C. "Heart of a Radical Reform: Christology and the Church of God

Movement (Anderson)," *Wesleyan Theological Journal* 44-2 (Fall 2009), 168-188.
_____. *Approaching Theology* (Lexington, KY: Emeth Press, 2015).
_____. *Bible Stories for Strong Stomachs* (Cascade Books, 2016).
Cobb, John B., Jr. *Process Theology as Political Theology* (Philadelphia: Westminster, 1982).
_____. *Can Christ Become Good News Again?* (St. Louis: Chalice Press, 1991).
_____. *Grace and Responsibility: A Wesleyan Theology for Today* (Nashville: Abingdon Press, 1995).
_____, with Clark H. Pinnock, eds., *Searching for an Adequate God* (Grand Rapids: William B. Eerdmans, 2000).
_____. *Jesus' Abba: The God Who Has Not Failed* (Fortress Press, 2015).
Cone, James H. *Black Theology and Black Power* (Harper, 1969; Orbis Books edition, 1997)
_____. *A Black Theology of Liberation* (40th anniversary digital edition, Orbis Books, 2010).
_____. "Some Brief Reflections on My Writing *Black Theology and Power*," in *Black Theology* (Nov. 2010,) 264-265.
_____. *God of the Oppressed* (Seabury Press, 1975; rev. ed. Orbis Books, 1997).
_____. *The Cross and the Lynching Tree* (Orbis Books, 2011).
Das, Lama Surya. *Awakening the Buddha Within: Tibetan Wisdom for the Western World* (New York: Broadway Books, 1997).
_____. *The Mind Is Mightier than the Sword* (New York: Doubleday, 2009).
Douglass, Frederick. *The Life and Times of Frederick Douglass* (New York: Pathway Press, 1941—reprint of the 1892 ed.).
Downing, David C. *The Most Reluctant Convert: C. S. Lewis' Journey to Faith* (Downers Grove, Ill.: InterVarsity Press, 2002).
Forrest, Jim. *Living with Wisdom: A Life of Thomas Merton* (Maryknoll, New York: Orbis Books, 1991).
Fosdick, Harry Emerson. *The Living of These Days* (N.Y.: Harper & Row, 1956). See below the biography of Fosdick by Robert Moats Miller.
Francis, Pope. The apostolic exhortation titled *The Joy of the Gospel*, 2013.
Grenz, Stanley J. *The Millennial Maze: Sorting Out Evangelical Options* (Downers Grove, ILL.: InterVarsity Press, 1992).
_____. *Theology for the Community of God* (Nashville: Broadman & Holman Publishers, 1994).
_____. *A Primer on Postmodernism* (Grand Rapids: Eerdmans, 1996).
_____. "Is Hell Forever?" in *Christianity Today* (October 5, 1998), 92.
_____. "Concerns of a Pietist with a Ph.D." in the *Wesleyan Theological Journal* (37:2, Fall, 2002), 58-76.
Harkness, Georgia. "The Ministry as a Vocation for Women," *The Christian Advocate*, publication of the Methodist Episcopal Church (April, 1924).
_____. *Foundations of Christian Knowledge* (Nashville: Abingdon Press, 1955).
_____. *Christian Ethics* (New York: Abingdon Press, 1957).
_____. *Beliefs That Count* (New York: Abingdon Press, 1961).
_____. *Mysticism: Its Meaning and Message* (Nashville: Abingdon Press, 1973).
_____. *Georgia Harkness: The Remaking of a Liberal Theologian*, ed. Rebekah Miles (Westminster John Knox, 2010).
Hick, John. *Faith and Knowledge* (1957; Ithaca, NY: Cornell University Press, 1966).
_____. *God Has Many Names* (Louisville: Westminster John Knox Press, 1980, 1982).
_____. *An Interpretation of Religion: Human Responses to the Transcendent*

(New Haven: Yale University Press, 1989; 2nd ed., 2004).
_____. *John Hick: An Autobiography* (Oxford: Oneworld, 2005).
Hunter, Ian. *Malcolm Muggeridge: A Life* (Nashville: Thomas Nelson Publishers, 1980).
Jones, E. Stanley. *A Song of Ascents: A Spiritual Autobiography* (Nashville: Abingdon Press, 1968).
Keller, Rosemary Skinner. *Georgia Harkness: For Such a Time As This* (Nashville: Abingdon Press, 1992).
Kostlevy, William, ed. *Historical Dictionary of the Holiness Movement*, 2nd ed. (Lanham, Maryland: The Scarecrow Press, 2009).
Lewis, C. S. *The Pilgrim's Regress: An Allegorical Apology for Christianity, Reason, and Romanticism* (Dent, UK, 1933).
_____. *Miracles* (N.Y.: Macmillan Co., 1947).
_____. *Surprised by Joy: The Shape of My Early Life* (N.Y.: Harcourt Brace Jovanovich, 1955).
_____. *The Four Loves* (N.Y.: Harcourt Brace, 1960).
_____. *Mere Christianity* (N.Y.: Macmillan Co, 1960).
_____. *The Case for Christianity* (Collier/Macmillan, 1989).
Lindsey, Hal. *The Late Great Planet Earth* (Grand Rapids: Zondervan, 1970).
_____. *There's a New World Coming* (Harvest House, 1973, rev. 1984).
Lausanne Covenant, International Congress on World Evangelization, July, 1974.
Maddox, Randy. *Responsible Grace: John Wesley's Practical Theology* (Nashville: Kingwood Books, Abingdon Press, 1994).
Massey, James Earl. *Spiritual Disciplines* (Grand Rapids: Francis Asbury Press, 1985).
_____. *Sundays in the Tuskegee Chapel: Selected Sermons* (Nashville: Abingdon Press, 2000).
_____. 2002-A. *Aspects of My Pilgrimage* (Anderson, IN: Anderson University Press, 2002).
_____. 2002-B. "Reconciliation: The Biblical Imperative," in *Wesleyan Theological Journal* (37:1, Spring, 2002), 7-24.
Merton, Thomas. *The Seven Storey Mountain* (New York: Harcourt Brace, 1948).
_____. *The Sign of Jonas* (N.Y.: Harcourt, 1953).
_____. *The Secular Journal of Thomas Merton* (New York: Farrar Straus & Cudahy, 1958).
_____. *Emblems of a Season of Fury* (New York: New Directions, 1961).
_____. *My Argument with the Gestapo* (New York: Doubleday, 1969).
_____. *New Seeds of Contemplation* (New Directions Books, 1961).
_____. *A Thomas Merton Reader*, ed. Thomas McDonnell (Garden City, N.Y.: Image Books, 1974).
_____. *Letters*, in William H. Shannon, ed., *The Hidden Ground of Love: The Letters of Thomas Merton on Religious Experience and Social Concerns* (NY: Farrar Straus & Giroux, 1985).
Miller, Robert Moats. *Harry Emerson Fosdick: Preacher, Pastor, Prophet* (N.Y.: Oxford University Press, 1985).
Moltmann, Jürgen. *A Theology of Hope* (London: SCM Press, 1967).
_____. *The Experiment Hope*. Trans. M. Douglas Meeks (Philadelphia: Fortress Press, 1975).
_____. *Theology Today*. Trans. John Bowden (Herder Verlag, 1988).
_____. *The Spirit of Life: A Universal Affirmation* (Minneapolis: Fortress Press, 1992).
_____. *The Coming of God: Christian Eschatology* (Minneapolis: Fortress Press, 1996).

_____. *A Broad Place: An Autobiography* (Minneapolis: Fortress Press, 2008).
Muggeridge, Malcolm. "Royal Soap Opera," *Saturday Evening Post* (Oct. 19, 1957).
_____. *Jesus Rediscovered* (1969; London: Hodder & Stoughton, 1995).
_____. *Chronicles of Wasted Time* (Vancouver: Regent College Publishing, 1972, 1973, 2006).
_____. *A Third Testament* (Boston: Little, Brown and Company, 1976).
_____. *Conversion: The Spiritual Journey of a Twentieth-Century Pilgrim* (Harper, 1988; Eugene Oregon: Wipf & Stock, 2005).
_____. *Confessions of a Twentieth-Century Pilgrim* (San Francisco: Harper & Row, 1988).
Nostra Aetate, "The Declaration of the Church to Non-Christian Religions," Pope Paul VI, 1965.
Nouwen, Henri. Introduction to the 1980 edition of Parker Palmer's *The Promise of Paradox* (Notre Dame, IN: Ave Maria Press).
_____. *The Wounded Healer* (Garden City, NY: Doubleday, 1972).
_____. *The Genesee Diary* (Garden City, NY: Doubleday, 1976).
_____. *In the Name of Jesus* (NY: Crossraod Pub., 1989).
_____. "All Is Grace," in *Weavings* 7:38-41 (Nov.-Dec., 1992).
_____. *Bread for the Journey: A Daybook of Wisdom and Faith* (San Francisco: HarperSanFrancisco, 1997).
Oden, Thomas C. *The Word of Life*: Systematic Theology, vol. 2 (HarperSanFrancisco, 1989).
_____. *Care of Souls in the Classic Tradition* (Fortress, 1984).
_____. "Then and Now," in *The Christian Century* (Dec. 12, 1990).
_____. "The Long Journey Home," in the *Journal of the Evangelical Theological Society* (March, 1991).
_____. *The Transforming Power of Grace* (Abingdon Press, 1993).
_____. *Requiem: A Lament in Three Movements* (Abingdon Press, 1995).
_____. General editor, *Ancient Christian Commentary on Scripture* (InterVarsity Press, digital edition, 2005).
_____. *How Africa Shaped the Christian Mind* (InterVarsity Press, 2007).
_____. *Classic Christianity: A Systematic Theology* (HarperOne, 2009).
_____. *In Search of Solitude: Living the Classic Christian Hours of Prayer* (Zondervan, 2010).
_____. *A Change of Heart: A Personal and Theological Memoir* (InterVarsity Press, 2014).
Olson, Roger E. *The Story of Christian Theology: Twenty Centuries of Tradition & Reform* (InterVarsity Press, 1999).
_____. *Reformed and Always Reforming* (Grand Rapids: Baker Academic, 2007).
_____. *How to Be Evangelical Without Being Conservative* (Zondervan, 2008).
_____. In *The Christian Century* (Dec. 15, 2009), 32-36.
Packer, J. I. "Still Surprised by Lewis," in *Christianity Today* (September 7, 1998, 54ff).
Palmer, Parker J. *The Promise of Paradox* (1980; San Francisco: Jossey-Bass, 2008).
Pennington, M. Basil. *A Retreat with Thomas Merton* (Warwick, N.Y.: Amity House, Inc., 1988).
Pinnock, Clark H. "An Evangelical Theology: Conservative and Contemporary," in *Christianity Today* (Jan. 5, 1979), 23-29.
_____, with Delwin Brown. *Theological Crossfire: An Evangelical/Liberal Dialogue* (Grand Rapids: Zondervan Publishing, 1990).
_____. *Flame of Love: A Theology of the Holy Spirit* (Downers Grove, Ill.: InterVarsity Press, 1996).

_____. *Most Moved Mover: A Theology of God's Openness* (Grand Rapids: Baker Academic, 2001).
_____, with Barry L. Callen. *The Scripture Principle* (Lexington, KY: Emeth Press, 2009 edition).
Rack, Henry D. *Reasonable Enthusiast: John Wesley and the Rise of Methodism* (Nashville: Abingdon Press, 1993).
Ruether, Rosemary Radford. *Sexism and God-Talk: Toward a Feminist Theology* (Boston: Beacon, 1983).
_____. *Gaia and God: An Ecofeminist Theology of Earth Healing* (San Francisco: Harper-Collins, 1994).
Snyder, Howard A. *Homosexuality and the Church* (Seedbed, 2014).
Sri, Edward. *Rediscovering the Heart of a Disciple*: Pope Francis and "The Joy of the Gospel" apostolic exhortation (Our Sunday Visitor, 2014).
Stafford, Gilbert W. *Theology for Disciples* (Anderson, IN: Warner Press, 1996).
Strong, Douglas M. *They Walked in the Spirit* (Louisville: Westminster John Knox Press, 1997).
Temple, William. *Nature, Man and God* (London: Macmillan & Co., 1934).
Trueblood, D. Elton. *The Essence of Spiritual Religion* (Harper & Row, 1936; paper reprint, 1975).
_____. *The Predicament of Modern Man* (Harper & Row, 1944).
_____. *Philosophy of Religion* (N.Y.: Harper & Row, 1957).
_____. *A Place To Stand* (N.Y.: Harper & Row, 1969).
_____. *The Company of the Committed* (N.Y.: Harper & Row, 1961).
_____. *The Validity of the Christian Mission* (N.Y.: Harper & Row, 1972).
_____. *While It Is Day: An Autobiography* (N.Y.: Harper & Row, 1974).
_____. *Quarterly Yoke Letter* (December, 1987; June, 1994).
_____. *A Life of Search* (Richmond, Ind.: Friends United Press, 1996).
Tuttle, Robert G., Jr. *Mysticism in the Wesleyan Tradition* (Grand Rapids: Francis Asbury Press, 1989).
Wainwright, Geoffrey, *Doxology: The Praise of God in Worship, Doctrine, and Life* (N.Y.: Oxford University Press, 1980).
_____. *Lesslie Newbigin: A Theological Life* (Oxford University Press, 2000).
Weaver, J. Denny. *Anabaptist Theology in the Face of Postmodernity* (Telford, Pa.: Pandora Press U.S., 2000).
Wilkens, Steve, and Don Thorsen, *Everything You Know about Evangelicals Is Wrong* (Grand Rapids: Baker Books, 2010).
Williamson, Clark M. *A Guest in the House of Israel: Post-Holocaust Church Theology* (Louisville: Westminster/John Knox Press, 1993).
_____. *Way of Blessing, Way of Life* (St. Louis: Chalice Press, 1999).
Yoder, John Howard, *The Original Revolution* (Scottdale, PA: Herald Press, 1971).